HARPER FORUM BOOKS

General Editor Martin E. Marty

HARPER FORUM BOOKS
Martin E. Marty, *General Editor*

Literature and Religion

edited by

Giles B. Gunn

1817

HARPER & ROW, PUBLISHERS

New York, Evanston, San Francisco, London

FIRST UNITED STATES EDITION

LIBRARY OF CONGRESS CATALOG CARD NUMBER: 71-109078

CONTENTS

HARPER FORUM BOOKS

OFTEN dismissed with a shrug or accepted with thoughtless piety in the past, religion today belongs in the forum of study and discussion. In our society, this is particularly evident in both public and private colleges and universities. Scholars are exploring the claims of theology, the religious roots of culture, and the relation between beliefs and the various areas or disciplines of life. Students have not until now had a series of books which could serve as reliable resources for class or private study in a time when inquiry into religion is undertaken with new freedom and a sense of urgency. *Harper Forum Books* are intended for these purposes. Eminent scholars have selected and introduced the readings. Respectful of the spirit of religion as they are, they do not shun controversy. With these books a new generation can confront religion through exposure to significant minds in theology and related humanistic fields.

MARTIN E. MARTY, GENERAL EDITOR
The Divinity School
The University of Chicago

The reader will notice that the authors represented in this volume sometimes vary in their spellings and systems of reference. This is because the extracts are taken from previously published works, and we have not attempted to impose a consistency which could conceivably be distasteful to an individual author or publisher.

PREFACE

As with the other volumes in this series, the purpose of this collection of essays is to further discussion, not close it. Its aim is to raise questions, clarify problems, amplify issues, and extend interest in this subject. Hence it will have achieved its purpose if readers come away from this collection of essays with a fresh sense of the possible variety of approaches to and aspects of this subject and a deepened awareness of its significance both for our understanding of literature and for our understanding of religion.

In the last several decades there has been an unusual amount of attention devoted to the subject of literature and religion. Those who have exhibited an interest in this subject have ranged all the way from highly specialized scholars of language, literature, and religion to cultivated preachers with a taste for the classics. Literary critics seek to define the religious meaning or significance of particular works, writers, or literary movements. Theologians of culture attempt to elaborate the grounds of a religious poetic. Historians of culture and religion study traditions of literature and the other arts for clues to the inner moral and spiritual propulsions of an entire age or epoch.

With interest in this subject generated from so many different quarters and with such a variety of purposes in view, it is hardly surprising that the actual critical and scholarly work in this whole area of inquiry has been very uneven in quality as well as character. Some of it has been quite simply amateurish or self-serving, of greater significance for what it belies of the mixed motives of those who undertake it than for whatever illumination it might shed upon the subject itself. Yet a significant if smaller portion of scholarship in this area not only deserves comparison with but actually constitutes some of the very best critical and theological work of our own time; and it is this significant portion of it that I have sought to represent as fully as possible in this volume.

Any editor of a volume of this kind is conscious of his inevitable omissions. Even if he limits himself to critical and scholarly work of the very first rank, there is still no way of including all of it, or even a completely satisfactory representation of it, in a volume of this size – unless, of course, he resorts only to small pieces of an argument or mere fragments of a point of view. I have rejected this latter alternative on the grounds that it would be more likely to confuse rather than to clarify. Instead I have tried to include the whole, or as much of the whole as was feasible, of any article or essay I have selected. The result is a volume which, if not fully representative, is at least highly indicative of much of the more important and illuminating scholarship in this whole area of critical and theological interest.

I have, however, attempted to compensate for certain omissions by providing a general introduction to *Literature and Religion* which is less an introduction to the volume *per se* than to the entire subject. Further, I have tried to resist the temptation of permitting my own personal view of the subject as a whole to determine fully either my specific selections or my organization of the anthology. While my general introduction to *Literature and Religion* is organized around the question of how, from a theoretical perspective, critics and theologians typically conceive of the relationship between literature and religion, the anthology itself is organized around the somewhat different question as to what, from a more practical point of view, critics and theologians actually do once they have conceived such a relationship.

From my own observation, I think it would be fair to say that critics and scholars tend at the very minimum to do one of three things as they study the inter-relations between literature and religion: either they seek to account for those relations in conceptual terms; or they seek to explore them in the concrete materials in which they occur; or they try to assess the effects literature and religion, when taken together, seem to have upon one another both in the abstract and in the concrete. Hence Part I includes several essays which attempt in a fairly theoretical fashion to isolate and define some of the more important and obvious points of contact, convergence, or coincidence between particular forms of literary expression and religious experience. Part II includes another group of essays which elaborate in a more practical manner the various ways in which religious beliefs or impulses have shaped or been shaped by literary and cultural experience in selected works, writers, traditions, and periods from antiquity to the present. Part III is devoted to a still different group of essays which probe the ways in which literary insight enhances moral and religious understanding, and vice versa, when both literature and religion are seen through a variety of critical and theological lenses all of which, none the less, presuppose their deep and intimate interconnection.

Thus it should be apparent that the three sections or parts of the anthology represent more of a natural division of labor than of any *a priori* difference in method or point of view. Such differences there are, of course, throughout the anthology, but they are to be found within sections as well as between them. In actual practice, many of the critics or theologians included here have, at one time or another in their careers, addressed themselves to each of the topics or issues expressed by the sectional division of the anthology. Thus while their essays exemplify representative modes of approach to each of these issues, they are not meant to be in all ways fully representative of their author. In each case my principle of selection has been the indicative and exemplary character of the treatment rather than the man. Yet I would hasten to add that all of the critics and scholars included here are in some sense representative figures, and, further, that each essay illustrates an important and characteristic way of exploring the larger subject indicated by the title of this volume.

For help in the preparation of this volume, I am indebted to my typist, Mrs. Toshi Takahashi, and my student assistant, Mr. Peter Vasile. I am also grateful for the support and advice of Professors Nathan A. Scott, Jr., Anthony C. Yu, Jonathan Z. Smith, Martin E. Marty, and the late Henry Rago. But my deepest debt of gratitude is reserved for my wife, Janet, who in this, as in all things, was and is my chief collaborator.

GILES B. GUNN

I

INTRODUCTION: LITERATURE AND ITS RELATION TO RELIGION

Giles B. Gunn

> The poem refreshes life so that we share,
> For a moment, the first idea . . . It satisfies
> Belief in an immaculate beginning
>
> And sends us, winged by an unconscious will,
> To an immaculate end. We move between these points:
> From that ever-early candor to its late plural
>
> And the candor of them is the strong exhilaration
> Of what we feel from what we think, of thought
> Beating in the heart, as if blood newly came,
>
> An elixir, an excitation, a pure power.
> The poem, through candor, brings back a power again
> That gives a candid kind to everything.
>
> Wallace Stevens

It has now become something of a commonplace to observe that the study of literature and, with it, the study of the kind of experience literature is designed both to reveal and create has undergone considerable revision in recent years. Where once not too many years ago literary critics tended to forgo all attempts at relating individual works of literature to anything beyond their own verbal matrix, now an increasing number of scholars and critics seem bent upon exploring the relations literature possesses to everything from sociology to music, from myth and history to psychology and religion.[1] Whether or not this growth of interest in the extra- and intra-mural relations of literary study signifies a thoroughgoing trans-formation of our conception of the nature and purpose of literary art, it surely points to the greater demands we have come to place upon our reading. In the age of Belsen and Buchenwald, which presents us with the spectacle of highly cultivated men and women who could read their Goethe and their Hölderlin at night and then go to work in the death camps the next morning, it will no longer suffice to read works of literature – as until recently has been our habit – solely for the pleasure of discovering the perfection of their form. As George Steiner has so convincingly argued, the dutiful Germans of the 1940s – and, one might add, their American counter-parts in the 1970s – may be taken as symptomatic of a new develop-ment in our culture: the appearance of great masses of people who have simply not been humanized by their education.[2] And it may not be altogether accidental that the emergence of these new bar-barians of the baccalaureate coincides, at least in part, with the development of a literary theory in the modern period which had had the effect, though by no means the intention, of establishing, as one of its critics has suggested, "an apparently impassable chasm between the facts of our existence in contemporary society and the values of art."[3]

This is of course in no way to blame the early advocates of modern critical theory for the fact that our society is now flooded with countless numbers of "educated" people whose reading, far from awakening and quickening their sensibilities, has only deadened them by inuring them to the atrocities which they have learned to accept, even on occasion to commit, as a part of everyday reality. The major intent of the first proponents of the New Criticism was to rescue aesthetic value from being submerged in a welter of historical, etymological, political, social, and economic fact and thus, by redefining literature in terms of aims and principles intrinsic to its own mode of being, to re-establish literature in its rightful place within human experience. Their work was undone only by later disciples who carried contextualist assumptions too far by altogether divorcing literary values from the social and cultural matrix from which they emerge and to which they are inextricably related. As a result, critics became less interested in the purposes than in the properties of literature, and criticism in turn narrowed the focus of its responsibility by concentrating less upon any particular work's total design than upon a careful explication of the structural purpose and internal design of any one of its individual parts.

This gradual diminution of the critical enterprise was not lost upon those who were prepared in whatever fashion to take an interest in the relations between literary expression and religious commitment.[4] In fact, I think it is fair to say that the new interdisciplinary interest in religion and literature, at least in its contemporary post-war form, has arisen chiefly as a result of this contraction of the critical endeavor with its concomitant tendency to separate "the values of art" from "the facts of our existence in contemporary society." Critics and scholars of whatever confessional persuasion or philosophic commitment who have worked to develop the relations between literature and religion have usually been motivated to do so out of some deeply felt personal conviction about the organic connection between literature and culture, art and belief. Whether they have sought to demonstrate how certain writers are able to intensify their rendering of the human story to the point where, as R. W. B. Lewis suggests in reference to Henry James, it gives off "intimations of the sacred,"[5] or instead have proposed, as Perry Miller has done in connection with Emerson and Thoreau, that at least some thinkers make what can only be called "a religious demonstration" by putting "their cause in the language of philosophy and literature rather than theology,"[6] most of these same critics have assumed that neither the specific work of literature nor the total corpus of an individual writer can be divorced from the actual culture from which it springs or to which, in some complex sense, it is addressed.

Even a rapid scanning of some of the work which has been done in this area will quickly disclose the broad range of critical theory and method which has characterized it. The spectrum seems to run all the way from those who seek to elucidate the manner in which literature can be instructed by doctrine or doctrine "fleshed out" in literature to those who conceive of literature, as Baudelaire says somewhere, as "a metaphysics made sensible to the heart and expressing itself in images." Between these two alternatives, however, there are a variety of positions which oblige one neither to construe the relationship between literature and religion as a forced marriage between incompatibles nor to view literature itself either as a substitute for religion or as a propaedeutic for faith.

Some critics and scholars assume that literature still holds the mirror up to nature by serving as an index to or assessment of our modern cultural and religious distress. Others believe that in the perfection of its formal organization and because of the greater intensity and purity of self-revelation which this allows, literature offers a kind of golden alternative to our "gong-tormented" world of brass which can provide a religious stay against the confusion of values and commitments which otherwise determine our experience. Still others maintain that every successful individual work of literature, as an instance of the artist's sacrifice of himself and his own intentions to the objective requirements of his craft, presents us with the paradigmatic religious situation, a virtual re-enactment of the Crucifixion in which the artist empties himself for the sake of his materials so that their meanings may live. Yet another group of critics work on the contrary assumption: instead of emptying himself of the very last vestige of his personality, his inwardness, the true artist, they argue, serves a religious function precisely to the extent that he carries the expression of his own personality, his own *humanitas*, to its uttermost extreme, since truth of a religious order is only disclosed to man under the shadow of ultimacy. A variation on this same theme is played by still another group of critics who contend that the great writer, through his capacity to penetrate beneath the superficial appearances of his age to its deepest, unspent sources of life, is a spokesman for Being itself. And by giving formal expression to life's deep-running currents, he thus helps in his work to conserve what has survived from the past and to release what may shape the present and the future.

Nevertheless, in spite of the wide latitude of theory and practice which these disparate examples disclose, it is possible to reduce the seemingly endless variety of ways critics have discussed the relations between literature and religion to several basic types.[7] No one of these types exists independently of any of the rest; each of them shades off into one or more of its neighbors just because the critics who exemplify them conceive of and then set about developing the relationship between literature and religion in more than a single manner. But the artificiality of such a typology does not gainsay the service it can perform in helping us to clarify what is otherwise a hopeless Babel of approaches, assumptions, and points of view.

My ultimate object, however, is not merely to adumbrate the several types of critical theory which have influenced the work which has already been done in this whole interdisciplinary area; it is rather to construct, even in barest outline, a kind of composite model or type of my own which attempts to utilize the major strengths and possibilities of the other types while avoiding some of their obvious limitations. This requires first of all, however, a backward glance at the history of critical theory itself, because the very possibility of organizing current discussion of this subject along typological lines depends upon an initial investigation of the models which the history of literary criticism has already provided for it.

I

The art of literary criticism in the West is an ancient one, probably as old as the art of literature itself, and the theories of literature which have developed as a result of its practice are legion. To a casual student of the history of criticism, nothing may be so obvious as their variety and abundance. Yet there is a sense in which, as M. H. Abrams has demonstrated, every theory of literature in the history of criticism which has sought comprehensiveness has had to take some account of at least four elements basic to the total situation of any work of art: the artist who creates the work, the work itself, the world the work creates and reveals, and the audience the work affects.[8] While none of the important theories of literature in the history of criticism has emphasized one of these elements at the expense of excluding all the others, every major theory has tended to interpret one element in the total situation of the work as the key to an understanding of the significance and status of the other three. Thus Professor Abrams has been able to distinguish four predominant kinds of critical theory in the history of criticism, each particular theory being a function of the specific element toward which the theory is basically, even if not exclusively, oriented.

The oldest and probably the most influential literary theory in the history of criticism is the theory of mimesis, which has been the basic theoretical orientation for critics from Plato and Aristotle to Dr. Johnson and beyond, and has also enjoyed a modest renaissance in our own time.[9] Its principal concern has been with the world revealed by the work, and its key word is *imitation*. Though Plato was its first major theorist, Aristotle has undoubtedly been its most influential because of the way he implicitly challenged the strictures which Plato placed upon it.

Those strictures left Aristotle, if he was to defend a mimetic theory at all, with the task of demonstrating how literature is less the imitation of what is merely an appearance or illusion of reality than an imitation of what is essential or basic about reality itself. What Aristotle was at pains to show was how literature, and particularly tragedy, could be said to complete and fulfil nature, rather than merely imitate or copy it, by presenting through its formal organization the completed imitation of an action which in nature or experience is never so unified or fully realized. Aristotle's mode of procedure was to show how art appeals not, as Plato had argued, to the more inferior human faculties – to the emotions and passions instead of the intellect or soul – but rather to the natural human instinct to imitate, and that, moreover, art arouses and excites the passions, instead of merely disciplining and controlling them, only so that it may finally allay them. This was the intention of his definition of tragedy as

an imitation of an action that is serious, complete, and of a certain magnitude; in language embellished with each kind of artistic ornament, the several kinds being found in separate parts of the play; in the form of action, not of narrative; through pity and fear affecting the proper purgation of these emotions.[10]

Significantly, Aristotle understood the excitation and eventual catharsis of the emotions to be a direct result of the object imitated and the manner and means of its imitation, and thus integral to the nature and function of the work itself. Hence the aim of criticism was not restricted to an elaboration of the nature of the imitated object (or, in other terms, to the world revealed in and through the work), but was rather conceived to include an elucidation of the principle by which the entire work, understood as the imitation of a particular kind of action, was organized to effect the proper response.

But there was a danger inherent in Aristotle's theory of art as mimesis should any society or individual prescribe the affective significance of art out of an inordinate interest in the needs and requirements of a particular audience. This necessity arose during the Renaissance, partly as a result of the influence of the study of rhetoric with its preoccupation with the way in which audiences can be most deeply moved, and gave rise to the second major orientation in critical theory, what Abrams calls the pragmatic theory of literature. Sir Philip Sidney was probably its most typical, though not necessarily its most important, exponent, and *instruction* was its most representative word.

Sidney wrote his *Defense of Poesie* in answer to Puritan charges that poetry was immoral and provocative. He countered these charges in at least three ways: first, by reminding his audience of the long and civilizing influence of poetry in the history of culture; second, by arguing that poetry imitates the real less than it invents and then represents the possible; and third, by insisting that the purpose of poetry is not to please the emotions but to instruct the mind, or if to please at all, then merely in order finally to persuade. Poetry, and by implication all art, was thus understood by Sidney to serve an explicitly healthy purpose by pleasing in order to instruct. The purpose of poetry's instruction was to lead men to virtue by exhorting them to contemplate and then to imitate a different but a better world than our own, a world where virtue always prospers and vice always perishes. Thus Sidney could conclude that the poet is superior to the historian in that, unlike the latter, he is less concerned with what actually does happen in life than with what ideally should happen instead.

The importance of Sidney's theory of literature can in some sense be measured, according to Professor Abrams, by the extent to which it represents all those critical theories from Horace to the Enlightenment which have considered literature chiefly as a means to an end, and which have therefore tended to evaluate individual works of literature in terms of their achievement of that end. For most theorists of the pragmatic orientation, literature's ability to serve moral ends has always been its chief aim, its ability to serve pleasurable ends merely an ancillary aim. But from Dryden through the eighteenth century, the balance began to swing the other way: poetry imitated nature in order to instruct, but instructed primarily in order to please.

Yet inherent in the most important tendency of this orientation – the inclination to subordinate all other poetic matters to the spiritual and moral requirements of a particular audience – were the seeds of its own dissolution. For if the real purpose of poetics was to discover the means whereby certain kinds of significance might be effectively impressed upon a particular kind of audience, the most important subject of inquiry for poetics could easily become the particular training, resources, and personal qualifications required by the poet or artist to produce the desired effect. Such a transition actually took place toward the end of the eighteenth century when an interest in the audience gave way to an interest in the poet, turning the expression of his own needs and abilities not only into the predominant cause of poetry but also into its final aim and ultimate task. The result of this major shift in emphasis, according to Abrams, was the emergence of the third critical orientation in the history of literary theory – the Romantic theory of literature. Though Wordsworth was its first exponent in the nineteenth century, Coleridge was undoubtedly its most important, and *expression* was its most representative word.

Though Coleridge differed from Wordsworth and many of the other critics of the nineteenth century in believing that literature, particularly poetry, is at once inspired and contrived, at once the spontaneous expression of the assimilating power of the creative imagination and the result of a deliberate adoption of means to ends, he nonetheless revealed himself very much a man of his own age when he transformed the question of the nature of poetry into a question of the nature of the poet. Coleridge gave voice to the most characteristic assumption of all expressive theories of art when he remarked that "what is poetry? is so nearly the same question with, what is a poet? that the answer to the one is involved in the solution of the other."[11]

Coleridge defined the poet in his ideal perfection as the creature who "brings the whole soul of man into activity" by diffusing "a tone and spirit of unity, that blends, and (as it were) fuses, each into each, by that synthetic and magical power, to which we have exclusively appropriated the name of imagination. This power . . . reveals itself in the balance and reconciliation of opposite or discordant qualities."[12] In this definition Coleridge came perilously close to reducing the poet to little more than a vehicle for the expression of the creative imagination which then creates poetry by a reconciliation of opposite or discordant qualities; but his intention was the very opposite. By claiming for the poet the ability to utilize the creative imagination, Coleridge hoped to demonstrate that the poet, in effecting a reconciliation of opposite or discordant qualities, in fact imitates the ongoing work of creation itself. For Coleridge conceived that the whole universe, both in what he called its "eternal act of creation in the infinite I AM"[13] and in its continuous repetition of that act in the process of synthesizing and recreation by individual minds, consists in the creative resolution of conflict and disparity.[14] Hence the poet, in continuing that act in the creation of his poetry, was simply participating in the most characteristic activity of life itself, an activity which was then mirrored and expressed in his poems.

The great liability of Coleridge's theory was its exhalted conception of the poet, and hence of poetry itself, which, in a later, more skeptical age, might come to seem overly optimistic, if not downright blasphemous. Indeed, this is exactly what happened at the beginning of the twentieth century when T. E. Hulme set off the modern critical reaction to nineteenth century expressive theory by launching his attack against this side of Coleridge's thought, charging that it elevated the poet to the stature of a God with the power to create *ex nihilo*.[15] To counteract this tendency, Hulme called once again for the very kind of poetry which Coleridge had tried to overthrow, a poetry of fancy instead of imagination, and thus helped to establish the fourth theoretical orientation cited by Abrams, what we may call the modern or semantic theory of literature.

The major point of departure for modern theories of literature is neither the poet, nor his audience, nor even the world he reveals or creates, but rather the specific work of the poet considered for the most part in its own right. The major concern of this critical theory, which follows both Coleridge and T. S. Eliot at this point, is to consider works of literature as self-sufficient entities whose particular mode of being can only be understood in terms of the parts internal to them, and the most representative word of this orientation is *objectivity*.

Modern critics have thus tended to be of one mind in seeking to define the nature and function of literature, primarily poetry, in terms that are broadly semantic.[16] Their chief interest has resided in language's capacity to generate the images and symbols by which literature is composed, and particularly in the relations between words in all their contextual specificity and the realities which they signify, indeed create, in experience by virtue of the poet's special use of them. Their assumption has been that the poet, given his capacity to use language in fresh and unusual ways, is able to express certain kinds of experience in a manner which no other medium can duplicate. Hence the business of the literary theorist of this orientation has been to define as precisely as possible the particular nature and structure of the poet's language so that his readers will not look for meanings poetry is unable to express or fail to comprehend the special kinds of meaning only poetry can disclose.

This is not to suggest, however, that by virtue of sharing certain basic assumptions, modern critics have written but one kind of criticism. A similar respect for the essentially semantic nature of literature has not prevented Edmund Wilson from following Sainte-Beuve in producing a criticism which is at once biographical and sociological; or Northrop Frye from using Frazer and Jung to produce a criticism that is basically mythic and archetypal; or, finally, Yvor Winters from turning back to Arnold to produce a criticism which is both critical and moral.

Yet, despite the wide variety of method and insight which any close reading of modern semantic criticism yields, R. S. Crane has been able to discern two predominant points of view which characterize all those critics who share the modern predisposition to view literature as a special kind of language written in words. The first tendency, he suggests, is shared by critics and theorists like I. A. Richards, William Empson, Wilson Knight, John Crowe Ransom, R. P. Blackmur, Allen Tate, Cleanth Brooks, and their many imitators who view literature primarily as language in the ordinary sense of a statement in words. Their particular problem has thus been the negative one of distinguishing between the language of literature and the language of other kinds of discourse, so that they may vindicate their claim that literature expresses certain things which are inexpressible in any other language. Their typical method of procedure has been to follow Coleridge by contrasting the language of poetry with the language of some other, more familiar mode of discourse, usually scientific discourse, in order to define by comparison the distinctive attributes, powers, and possibilities of the language of poetry. Because they have emphasized the various but special ways in which poetry communicates its meaning, they have characteristically conceived of poetry as a special kind of meaningful expression.

The second tendency in modern criticism, according to Crane, is shared by such different critics and theorists as Kenneth Burke, Maud Bodkin, Edmund Wilson, Lionel Trilling, Richard Chase, Francis Fergusson, and Northrop Frye who, instead of concentrating on the particular way in which poetry communicates its meaning, have emphasized the particular kind of meaning poetry communicates. Thus they have tended to conceive of poetry not as a special kind of meaningful expression but rather as the expression of a special kind of meaning. Their most outstanding characteristic has been the reductive nature of their criticism, their inclination to interpret poetry in terms of something assumed to be far more basic and essential in human experience than poetry itself. Hence they have generally been of one mind in thinking of poetry as a certain kind of symbolic language which, instead of being more unique and eccentric than any other, is more natural and universal than any other.[17]

II

My more particular concern, however, is with the way in which each of these orientations, when understood in its essentials, can suggest the possibilities and limitations of various typical approaches to the relationship between literature and religion. If, then, one asks what implications the modern objective orientation possesses for imagining such a relationship, one must begin by observing that the commitment to language and language's capacity for creating new meaning, which is presupposed in this orientation, usually carries with it the assumption that man is a symbol-making animal whose ability to form images and metaphors expressive of the reality he at once rediscovers or recreates through his intensive use of them is generally regarded as, at the very least, one of the most significant elements of his humanity and, at the very most, a sign of his divine inheritance. Several possible consequences naturally follow from this assumption. For those theologically-inclined literary critics who view literature as a special kind of meaningful expression, poetry – and by implication all literature – acquires its religious character either, for example, because it represents in its most intense metaphorical embrace the closest approximation of which man himself is capable of that unification of opposites which is only perfectly envisioned in the Christian doctrine of the Incarnation;[18] or because it expresses through a radically contextual language which is iconic, plurisignative, soft of focus, and paradoxical an intimation of the archetypes or universals which are resident within the concretely particular;[19] or because, in its essential character as a word to be spoken and heard as well as formed, literature represents the attempt to communicate the "intensification of an interior" and thus serves as the invitation of an "I" to enter into dialogue with a "Thou."[20] For those critics and scholars who view literature instead as the expression of a special kind of meaning, literature acquires its religious meaning and significance either because, like all other forms of symbolic expression, it is ultimately hierophantic, manifesting in its images and metaphors nothing less than the bond between man and the sacred;[21] or because it employs images, archetypes, and myths which derive from religious traditions and which, at least in certain circumstances, continue to exert a religious hold over the imagination which is compelled to use them;[22] or, finally, because literature represents an extension and completion in language of a response to reality which, however unconventional in form when measured by the standards of orthodoxy, is none the less essentially religious in character.[23]

The difficulty this orientation can present as a model for the relationship between literature and religion is that, whether one focuses upon the particular kind of meaning literature communicates or instead upon the specific way in which literature communicates its meaning, one is still left with the problem of elaborating a theory of literature which, on the one hand, demonstrates how religious elements somehow enter into or at least help determine its character as a literary object without, on the other, so closely identifying those elements with the literary aspects of the work that they simply cease to deserve the designation "religious" at all. More concretely, how does one discuss the religious elements, motifs, or characteristics of any given work of literature without either turning literature into a surrogate for philosophy or theology on the one hand, or reducing religion merely to any and every work's dimension of seriousness or depth on the other?

This has been a special problem for critics of this orientation because of their wholly salutary concern to retain for literature those qualities and virtues which set it apart from other forms of verbal expression. Hence in their zeal to preserve the integrity of

art, some have found a kind of refuge from these problems by turning their attention from a consideration of the religious elements
within particular works of literature to a consideration of the
potentially religious character of the creative process as such. Here
T. S. Eliot – with Henry James and Flaubert in the not-too-distant
background – often serves as a kind of model with his implicitly
religious theory of the martyrdom of the poet to his poem. In order
for the poem – or any work of literature – to achieve its true character as an autonomous, objective entity, so the interpretation goes,
the poet must sacrifice his personal desires and intentions to the
formal requirements of his art. The poet as an individuated self
dies so that his poem as a concrete, impersonal object may live, the
very gesture of poetic utterance thus becoming the representative
religious act. The difficulty here is that if one locates the religious
dimension of particular works in the process of their making, of
their creation, instead of in the nature or function of the thing made,
one can easily lose sight of the fact that literature not only represents
the collaboration of the poet as craftsman with the materials of his
craft, but also the union of his art, in all its ramifications, with his
matured vision of experience. What the artist wishes to say, however
much it may be conditioned by his manner of saying it, together
with the purpose of his saying it, is overshadowed by the miraculous
possibility of his saying anything at all.

This appears to be less of a problem for those critics and
scholars who rely more heavily upon the Romantic model of literary
theory with its attendant interest in the expressive character of art.
Whether such critics follow Wordsworth, and the eighteenth century
generally, in conceiving of literature as a way of exploring and
expressing what is natural or essential in human nature and experience,[24] or instead follow Coleridge in grounding the nature and
function of literature in what is believed to be fundamental and
characteristic about the nature of reality itself,[25] they tend to demonstrate less of an interest in the thing made, or even in the process of
its making, and more in the character and point of view of its maker.
Literature from this perspective is thus understood to be expressive
of vision – the artist's vision – which is itself very often conceived
to be the result of the interaction between the artist's own personality
and the stress and pressure of his times. Hence theological criticism
based upon the Romantic model tends to open out from the indivi-

dual work to the embodied vision which informs it, and from the embodied vision itself to all of the influences – cultural, historical, religious, and theological as well as personal – which have worked to affect and enrich it.

But again there can be problems if the critic moves too hastily through the densely realized particulars of the work itself to the vision which informs it, or beyond to the *Zeitgeist* it may reflect. An interest in the artist's represented vision can easily lead the impatient reader to an over-hasty identification of the artist's own point of view with that of any one of his character's or even his narrator's, when instead it is more likely to exist in the complex structure of meaning which makes sense of all the work's conflicting points of view in their manifold relationships. And, similarly, an excessive preoccupation with the cultural matrix from which particular poems, plays, and novels emerge and to which they implicitly appeal can lead to the reductive tendency to view literature merely as an index to the age, when again it is more likely that every work of any historical significance not only reflects its age but also helps to produce and shape it.

It is precisely this last insight which informs the best work of those critics and theologians who rely upon the pragmatic orientation in literary theory. Neither predisposed to view works of literature merely as the result of a certain technical process, nor as the expression of a particular perspective, nor even as the creation of a special kind of object, critics working from this orientation tend to interpret works of literature in terms of their aims, goals, or purposes, whether expressed or implied, and thus are inclined to locate their religious meaning or significance in the particular functions they are designed to serve or assumed to perform in human experience. Most pragmatic critics follow Sidney in believing that literature presents an actual world less than it re-presents a possible one, and that its primary function is thus not simply to please or even to inform but somehow to instruct and by instructing to transform. Yet in spite of certain assumptions common to them all, the actual practice of critics of this orientation admits of a wide margin of variance.

On the one side are those more theologically self-conscious critics who are inclined to invest literature, at least in certain of its forms, with the capacity to reify, or at any rate to clarify, the intent, import or effect of particular religious beliefs or theological doctrines.

Hence certain forms of literary expression, some argue, may, even unknowingly, serve a Christological function by demonstrating in their exacting explorations of the concrete and the particular how, as in any radically Incarnational theology, the actual and the finite can be trusted as a way into the infinite, into God Himself.[26] Other forms of literature, still other critics argue, testify to the Trinitarian character of human experience when the artist, in serving his potentially sacred mission to rekindle our love of the created world, in turn creates realities incarnate with his own inspiration.[27] Again, still other critics, following the later Heidegger, try to maintain that literature, as the art of unconcealment and unveiling, is not so concerned with what is theologically distinctive and peculiar about Being as with what is religiously *a priori* and ultimately mysterious when Being itself is experienced in its full immediacy less as a symbol, structure, or concept than simply as Presence.[28]

On the other side are those more purely academic critics who for any number of reasons believe that literature does, or at least can, serve a function analogous to, if not identical with, religion in certain of its aspects. Thus certain forms of literature, particularly tragic literature, perform the ancient mithridatic function, according to one interpretation, by exposing the worst of our evils and the darkest of our terrors and thus releasing us from our bondage to them.[29] According to another, literature, as the record of "communalized experience,"[30] not only reflects community but actually helps to create it by putting its society's most profound sense of self to its most rigorous tests, thus adumbrating the terms and conditions for its survival.[31] In yet a third, literature is viewed as providing "the vindication of the worth and value of the world, of life and of human experience. At heart all poetry is praise and celebration."[32]

The temptation to ascribe a quasi-sacred or religious office to certain kinds of literary expression, however, is not limited to a select number of critics in the modern period. In a time when all forms of traditionalism are on the wane, a great many critics with no particular ties to religion have found themselves compelled to think of literature in terms similar to those so eloquently rendered by Wallace Stevens in "Of Modern Poetry" where he gave his famous definition of "The poem of the mind in the act of finding/What will suffice." Poetry was not always invested with this awesome responsibility. As Stevens continues,

It had not always had
To find: the scene was set, it repeated what
Was in the script.
                    Then the theatre was changed
To something else. Its past was a souvenir.[33]

As a result, critics, like writers themselves, have come to put heavier demands upon literature, investing it with a kind of ultimate significance in the economy of human affairs. Thus for I. A. Richards "Poetry is the supreme use of language, man's chief coordinating instrument, in the service of the most integral purposes of life";[34] for Philip Wheelwright "The ground-bass of poetic truth is the truth, contextual but real, of man's possible redemption through the fullest imaginative response";[35] for Eliseo Vivas "The poet brings forth values with which history is in the pain of labor";[36] for R. P. Blackmur "poetry is the *nous poetikos*, that deep habit of mind, deeper than any sea of hope, calmer in its long swell than any mirror of despair, which imitates in forms and images dear to herself the life she has lived, the life she dreads to live, and the life she aspires to live."[37]

The faith is deep and the hope is high for the kind of fulfilment which literature alone can provide in these statements. Poetry is described as an instrument of redemption in one statement, as a creator of value in another. Whether it simply serves the most integral purposes of life, as for Richards, or very nearly becomes the most integral purpose of life, as for Blackmur, poetry seems to be able to do in these statements what only something akin to religious belief would have been expected to do in an earlier, more traditional period.

Observations such as these have led Richard Foster to conclude that for many of the American New Critics poetry has achieved the status of a form of metaphysics or revelation.[38] Professor Foster has supported this contention by demonstrating a shift of emphasis in the work of four modern American critics (Richards, Vivas, Blackmur, and Tate) from the idea of poetry conceived as form to the idea of poetry conceived as meaning, "from a formal-aesthetical to a moral-spiritual view of the nature and function of art."[39] Professor Foster has deemed it a significant shift of emphasis "because it shows the critics as typically 'modern' men of letters in uncertain quest of value and meaning in a world which looks to them like a chaos or a wate land."[40] And thus he has referred to them as "pilgrims in search of truth" in order to underscore "the essentially spiritual or religious motif of their seeking. . . ."[41]

As a gloss on Professor Foster's argument, we might say that, having suffered the full onslaught of modern experience by their own close inspection and evaluation of modern literature, these critics, and many others like them, have attempted to produce a literary theory which establishes poetry as a source or instrument of the religious values which they have discovered to be so radically threatened by recent history. Hence they have turned poetry into what is virtually a substitute for religion and have thus exhibited the extent of their debt to that side of Coleridge's criticism which originally inspired their reaction against Romantic, expressive theories of literature in the first place.

Yet it is hardly necessary to go all the way back to Coleridge to explain the religious impulse behind so much modern criticism. Much nearer in time and spirit to our own situation is Matthew Arnold, one of the first great critics to experience the threat of modern science and the consequent loss of the power to believe in the face of its numerous implications. It was Arnold who first set the precedent for subsequent criticism by reacting positively to the crisis of belief produced by modern science, in claiming for poetry the possibility of providing a stay against the confusion of values, meanings, and convictions generated by this encounter. The opening paragraph of "The Study of Poetry" still rings with his fervor:

> The future of poetry is immense, because in poetry, where it is worthy of its high destinies, our race, as time goes on, will find an ever surer and surer stay. There is not a creed which is not shaken, not an accredited dogma which is not shown to be questionable, not a received tradition which does not threaten to dissolve. Our religion has materialized itself in the fact, in the supposed fact; it has attached its emotion to the fact, and now the fact is failing it. But for poetry the idea is everything; the rest is a world of illusion, of divine illusion. Poetry attaches its emotion to the idea; the idea *is* the fact. The strongest part of our religion *today* is its unconscious poetry.[42]

It is no doubt a simple matter to puncture Arnold's great optimism regarding the future of poetry. We have witnessed too much barbarity, destruction, and inhumanity in this century ever to be able to find in a poetry which so easily disposes of facts for the sake of ideas "What will suffice." Moreover, only relatively few people have actually found in poetry a substitute for "what now passes with us for religion and philosophy. . . ."[43] Instead, those who have successfully supplanted ideas and emotions only with facts, and facts thus devoid of all intellectual and moral significance, have dispensed with poetry for the same reason that they have also dispensed with religion or philosophy: because, unlike Arnold, they have had no need to turn to poetry or to anything else "to interpret life for us, to console us, to sustain us."[44] Yet this observation does not gainsay the relevance of Arnold's example: for those modern critics who have followed him in defining poetry, usually in distinction to science, as a source of value and meaning scientific relativity cannot threaten, have also shared the religious or spiritual impulse propelling Arnold's fervid, if not Romantic, humanism. And, like him as well, they have in the process run the risk of turning literature into something else.

Indeed, this is the great temptation for all critics who employ the pragmatic orientation in literary theory. Inclined to subordinate the design of any particular poem, novel or play to its design upon its audience, to view the writer in terms of his capacities to produce the requisite response, and to ground the norms or canons of literary judgment and evaluation in terms of the needs or desires of a particular public, theological criticism following Renaissance models tends to reduce the meaning of works of literature to their supposed or intended effects and to view them simply as the means to a particular end.[45] And when one conceives of literature not as an object organized in terms of principles and aims intrinsic to its own mode of being but rather as the means to an end independently deduced for it, no matter how humanly significant or theologically meaningful that end or purpose may be, then one's critical discriminations will simply be limited by the suitability of the aim or purpose so envisaged for it. At worst literature is turned into a form of propaganda or reduced to an object lesson. At best literature often achieves a central religious or theological role in the economy of human affairs only at the expense of sacrificing whatever is internal to its own nature which would thereby differentiate it from, say, revelation on the one hand or some form of therapy on the other.

Yet it would be a serious mistake to assess the significance of this orientation as a model for the relation between religion and literature merely on the basis of certain limitations sometimes typical of it. The conception of literature as an instrument of instruction and human enrichment has characterized much of the most intelligent and surely the most valuable literary criticism from Dr Johnson to the present; and it still remains the underlying assumption for all those critics and scholars, both within the theological circle and without, who have attempted to specify what great works of literature have to teach us and, in teaching us, to contribute to man's being as a moral and spiritual animal.

This brings us to the fourth and final orientation under consideration, that provided by the mimetic theory of literature. As the oldest critical theory in the history of criticism, mimesis has also been the most consistently misused. To many students of criticism, mimetic theory suggests the notion that literature merely imitates or reflects life, thus providing us with an only slightly distorted – or better, refracted – mirror-image of the world around us. Literature, according to this understanding, thus acquires its religious or theological character from the nature of the event, object or feeling which it imitates. Hence the prevalent belief that literature, indeed all art, is most deeply religious or genuinely theological when it imitates or is "about" such specific religious subjects as God, sin, prayer, atonement, beatitude, and the like.

I. A. Richards gave the lie to such crude distortions of mimetic theory when he once remarked the works of literature are not about – that is, do not mean – anything at all, if by "being about" or "meaning" we intend to suggest that statements made in the work can be taken as propositions about the real world of everyday experience. Whether such statements concern man or God, sin or salvation, holy wonder or holy dread, they acquire what meaning they possess, mimetic theory contends, only in terms of the presiding principle which orders the whole work toward some particular end. Hence the notion of imitation refers not to the recognizable objects, events, or feelings from ordinary experience which the work inevitably presents to us, but rather to the executive principle by which they are thrust into new and significantly different relationships and then expressed. The emphasis is not upon the way everyday occurrences are seen and interpreted but rather upon the way they are re-seen and reinterpreted in terms of the highly selective and very limited context in which the work presents them to us.

From this perspective, one seeks to correlate literature with religion neither by relating the world view rendered in the one with the world view characteristic of the other nor by comparing similar expressions of intent or patterns of implication. One looks for the distinctively religious significance or theological meaning of particular works of literature in terms of the inner movement and dramatic structure of the works themselves. Thus Christian tragedy is not to be distinguished from tragedies of other kinds either primarily in terms of its aims or of its ideas or even of its techniques (though all of these are important), but rather in terms of its action.[46] In like fashion, it is possible to differentiate meditative poetry from other kinds of religious verse not by its theology nor by its style, but rather by its characteristic dramatic strategy.[47]

Yet it is apparent that a criticism which focuses too exclusively upon the inner dynamics of any work of literature, upon the way one part unites with others to describe a certain meaningful trajectory of events and their significance, has its limitations. The tendency the mimetic orientation shares with all other formal theories of literature, the tendency to define each work in terms of laws of its own origin, can, unless employed with great tact and sensitivity, isolate the work from the general religious and cultural situation it may be said to disclose or illumine. As a consequence, it may also sever the work from those larger social, moral, and spiritual values whose inevitable implication in great literary texts constitutes one of the reasons we find it necessary to read at all. Finally, in laying such heavy stress upon each work's particular design, the mimetic orientation can lead to a neglect of every work's special design upon us, and thus fail to account for what every significant work of literature has to teach us.

It cannot be overstressed, however, that the limitations frequently typical of various orientations are in no sense always typical of those who rely upon them. For very few critics are thoroughly consistent, and no one orientation is exclusive of the other three. The several orientations thus far discussed simply describe significant, but by no means absolute, shifts of emphasis in the history of critical theory, and thereby provide a useful heuristic device for distinguishing and evaluating some of the ways in which a variety of critics and theologians have pursued the relationship between religion and literature. Further, they suggest that no single theory or method will suffice to comprehend the full range of experience and illumination which has resulted from the encounter of literature with religion and religion with literature. In developing a viable critical conception of the relationship between these two modes of awareness and expression, our best hope, it seems to me, lies in the direction of a principled eclecticism in all questions of theory and method. That is, we need with the moderns to respect the formal, objective character of literary expression without overlooking the fact that, as the Romantics insisted, literature does in fact express something compelling our response; and we need to take with full seriousness the normative significance such expressions can have for us, as the pragmatic critics do, without forgetting that, as the neo-Aristotelians have reminded us, works of the imagination acquire such significance precisely because of the matter, medium, and manner in which they are expressed.

Once this is granted, several further observations follow. Whether one is examining St Thomas Aquinas' importance to the cosmology of *The Divine Comedy*, or the significance of St Augustine's theory of mind for Donne's "Batter my heart, three person'd God," or the relationship between Jonathan Edwards' democratic view of Being and Melville's understanding of creation in *Moby Dick*, it is obvious that all such study requires an abandonment of the doctrinaire and the parochial both in theology and in literary theory. For the primary, if elemental, lesson such study yields is that both literature and religion, when brought into contact in such texts, have a way of transforming one another. Whether T. S. Eliot submits a fairly orthodox theology of the Incarnation to the musical form of the *Four Quartets,* or Theodore Roethke carries a language experiment on natural processes to the point of meditation and revelation in the greenhouse poems, one is witness to what Professor Henry Rago has called "a wholly new making of experience into language, and of language into experience,"[48] and "the principle each time is some new identification of the authentic"[49] which does something in turn both to the language and to the experience.[50] It is this, surely, which anyone encounters in reading of Priam's secret night meeting with Achilles in Book XXIV of the *Iliad*, or in coming upon Cleopatra's sudden, striking comparison of herself to the common maid who milks "And does the meanest chares" in Act IV of *Antony and Cleopatra*, or in following Ishmael's miraculous discovery of the mute center of calm and joy "amid the tornadoed Atlantic of my being" which he finds for the first time as he looks into the deep clear pool at the center of the whirling maelstrom in "The Grand Armada" and watches the young and new-born whales revelling in "dalliance and delight." The names we so glibly attach to such revelatory experiences suddenly grate upon the ear. Certain actions which all at once seem inevitable and necessary fill familiar beliefs and former ideas to the bursting point with new and unforeseen meaning. Life suddenly releases some of its unspent force, and conventional expectations and interpretations are toppled by the flood of new insight and illumination.

Moments such as these, which transpire in every great work of the imagination, thus suggest that our understanding of religious belief, as it is encountered in literary texts, simply cannot be reduced to a set of dogmatic propositions. Nor can we afford to permit the ffieaning and scope of religious experience to be imprisoned in some rigid definition. As literature under the influence of religious propulsions is always tending to regress to its primitive character as a form of action, a kind of gesture, a mode of re-awakening and renewal, so religion, when forced to submit to the pressures and expansions of imaginative release, tends to recover something of its primordial form in "images and signs; events and visions; parables and hard sayings; a Life."[51]

In stressing the need for flexibility and openness, whether in theological definition or critical theory, I am of course setting myself in firmest opposition both to those who would subsume our experience of literature under some doctrinal umbrella and to those who would, on the contrary, insist that literary experience bears no affinities, much less identities, with other kinds of experience. While the first turn literature to some ideological or apologetic use which is rarely if ever appropriate to it, the second seriously truncate and distort our actual experience of literature by striving to maintain the illusion of its purity. Yet it is as fallacious to assume, say, that a contextualist position in criticism inevitably enforces a distinction between the mind which reads and the man who thinks and feels as it is to suppose that a committed believer is compelled to make his reading corroborate precisely the way he feels and thinks. Hence a genuine awareness and appreciation of the particular complexities which inhere in every inter-relationship between literature and religion should have a beneficial, retroactive effect upon the disciplines in and through which it has been, up until now, customary to study them: by enabling us to see what precisely as disciplines both theology and criticism, when taken together, tend to leave out of account.

From this it should be apparent that at the conceptual level our need is neither for greater precision of definition nor for a more rigorous and systematic methodology if either of these would have the effect of restricting our access to the multitude of ways literature and religion have and do become intertangled in specific works, careers, periods, or genres; or, beyond that, if they would lead us to suppose either that there is but one kind of religious meaning or significance which all works possess, or that such religious meaning or significance as any work may possess is always to be located in the same place and under the same condition. While rigor and clarity of thought are always to be regarded as virtues, such clarity and rigor as we can attain should be used not to constrict our modes of access but rather to expand it both to what works of literature *can mean* religiously and to how they *can be meaningful* from a religious perspective. What is needed at this point, then, is not greater narrowness but greater catholicity – flexible definition of the literary object which will utilize the essential insights of all four theoretical orientations and yet permit the widest variety of approach to the question of any particular work's religious nature, meaning, or significance.

III

It is my conviction that we can move some way toward that ideal model of the literary artifact, and at the same time overcome many, if not most, of the exclusive and limiting tendencies of the several orientations, thus bringing them into closer relation and collaboration, if we complement our several senses of the imitative, the pragmatic, the expressive, and the semantic character of literature with an appreciation of its hypothetical character as well. For, as Dorothy Van Ghent and Northrop Frye have recently reminded us, literature is nothing if not conjectural or hypothetical. Every work of literature argues implicitly, whether it is a poem, novel, or play, "If you will grant me my initial premise or set of conditions, then such and such would, or at least could, follow from them." What the work of literature takes from life, from what is actual, to paraphrase Miss Van Ghent, are the conditions for its hypothesis, the terms and substance of its original premise. It starts from the empirical data that we all generally recognize as given in experience. But then it selects, organizes, and motivates those conditions "in a way that suggests a purely creative issue – a series of hypothetical events not 'given' at all but cogent as cause and effect from the initial selection."[52]

Roy Harvey Pearce has provided further elaboration of this process by suggesting that the work so conceived is thus literally not "true":

. . . it consists instead of a series of hypothetical situations, imaged and motivated in such a way that, within their confines, we can accept as necessary the actions and responses into which the situations – and the imagined human beings in them – are made to issue. What primarily interests us in "created" situations of this sort is, of course, not their inevitable relevance to factuality, but their possibility: their resonance with our deepest sense of ourselves.[53]

Pearce is here closest to the pragmatic orientation in critical theory when he asserts that it is neither our instinctive delight in imitations, nor our interest in personality, nor even our pleasure in discovering and unravelling complex linguistic patterns, which enables literature to hold our strictest attention, but rather our "interest in possibility" which then permits us to "willingly suspend our ordinary disbelief in such imagined situations and accordingly assent to them as fully as an artist can compel us to."[54] The point is that our assent is what Pearce calls an "as-if assent,"[55] and it is not directed to a verifiable proposition but rather to an imaginative conjecture.

Yet the artist would not gain our assent to follow him as far into the realm of the possible or the potential as he can take us if he did not possess to an extraordinary degree both a heightened "awareness to such possibility" and the "ability to express that possibility in language and all the formal, constructivist means which language bears within itself."[56] Moreover, his capacity to see in the realities we all know hidden possibilities and potentialities we never dreamed of would not remain convincing to us if it were not based upon his and our knowledge of what apparently or most probably is. The sequence or structure of possibility, which at its most abstract defines the form of his work,[57] must ultimately seem, if not altogether natural and inevitable, at least plausible and compelling to "our deepest sense of ourselves."

That it can and usually does seem so stems from the fact that every writer draws from the common fund of human experience which has been bequeathed to us by history, society, and, as it were, blood. But his procedure is to select from that common fund some single assumption or interrelated series of assumptions about the way things are, or can be, or should be, and then order his entire work in terms of it. His purpose, however, is never merely analytical but always critical and evaluative. In choosing from the vast store of human experience some simple or complex notion about life, or one of its particular aspects, a notion which can then function for the duration of the work as life's ultimate truth, the artist is finally interested in both the possibilities and the limitations of life when it is viewed in terms of this particular principle of ultimacy.

These observations should make clear that while literature, in this understanding of it, is closer to one of our four orientations than to the other three, it is not exclusive of any of them. With the imitationists it assumes that every work of literature is unified neither by the world it reflects, nor by the vision it expresses, nor by the end which it serves, but only, finally, by the presiding principle or cause which gives its various parts their ordered and meaningful coherence. With the pragmatists it asserts that, in creating a possible world instead of an actual one, literature is nothing if not critical and ultimately revolutionary since, as John Dewey once remarked, "it is by a sense of possibilities opening before us that we become aware of constrictions which hem us in and of burdens that oppress."[58] With the expressionists it agrees that every work of literature springs from and appeals to our common sense of *humanitas*, thus attesting what is essential to or ultimately characteristic about life itself; and yet that because it is a unique, personal achievement, every work of literature also represents the creation of something new and absolutely individual which life otherwise would not possess. And, finally, with the moderns it acknowledges that nothing in literature can be rendered but in words which, as they are selected, ordered, and bent to fit the purpose of the work itself, remain the most creative as well as definitive constitutive element in every poem, novel, or play.

From this perspective literature is neither totally immersed in the world of everyday experience nor completely divorced from it. Ontologically it belongs to the realm of hypothesis and not of actual fact. But there is, as Stevens' poem suggests, a beautiful circuit of belief and desire between them:

> We move between these points:
> From that every-early candor to its late plural
>
> And the candor of them is the strong exhilaration
> Of what we feel from what we think, of thought
> Beating in the heart, as if blood newly came,
>
> An elixir, an excitation, a pure power.
> The poem, through candor, brings back a power again
> That gives a candid kind to everything.[59]

The tendency of all great literature, then, is to take the known, the empirically given in experience, and, as Dorothy Van Ghent has remarked in specific reference to the novel, "push it into the dimension of the unknown,"[60] into the dimension of the merely potential. From this it inevitably follows that literature's value and significance for us "lies less in confirming and interpreting the known" than in compelling us to suppose, indeed at least for a time to believe, *"that something else might be the case."*[61] Hence our purpose in the study of literature cannot, in any conventional sense, be to extend our knowledge of ourselves. "It is rather," as J. V. Cunningham has so trenchantly reminded us, in echoing Stevens, "to enable us to think and feel otherwise than as we do. It is to erect a larger context of experience within which we may define and understand our own by attending to the disparity between it and the experience of others."[62]

Observations such as these, while protecting the integrity of art without severing it from its connections either with the artist or with the traditions and experiences upon which he draws and the society to which he addresses himself, leave quite open the variety of approaches which may be possible or appropriate to an investigation of the religious nature, meaning, or significance of particular texts. Yet they raise further questions about whether there is not something intrinsically religious about this conception of literature itself. It is my conviction that there are at least several ways in which this theory or model not only invites a religious interpretation of literature but actually presupposes it if we are to do complete justice, as perhaps we never actually can, both to the work itself and to our response to it; yet I would hasten to add that this does not exclude the possibility of other ways of approaching the religiousness of any given work, nor does it assume that by possessing certain religious components every work is therefore *sui generis* religious. All I would maintain is that the existence of these components more than justifies, in fact requires, that we take the possibility of any given work's religious or theological meaning every bit as seriously as we now so easily view a work's potential psychological, political, or social meaning, and this quite apart from the critic's own religious persuasion.

First, every work of literature, as a hypothetical creation, presupposes for its very existence a belief in what Pearce calls, borrowing a phrase from Americo Castro, a "commitment to vital possibility."[63] Without such a commitment the writer could not envisage the element of potentiality in our experience of the actual nor the reader give even tacit assent to it. A "commitment to vital possibility" thus represents that half-conscious, half-unconscious faith in all that lies beyond the range of our immediate perception, that points to what the American theologian Bernard Meland has designated, following William James and Josiah Royce, as the element of the "More" in human experience, that element which constitutes at once the substance of our hope and the ground of the imagination itself – indeed, without which we could not imagine at all. Northrop Frye has given this faith, this commitment, unusually forceful expression by stating that "the work of the imagination presents us with a vision, not of the personal greatness of the poet, but of something personal and far greater: the vision of a decisive act of spiritual freedom, the vision of the recreation of man."[64]

Second, the question of religion is also involved in our inability to give our full assent to the hypothetical situations literature imagines for us unless the conditions upon which they are based and the potential outcomes in which they are made to issue are in fact commensurate with "our deepest sense of ourselves." That inherent "sense of ourselves" determines the range of possibilities we are willing to entertain and thus constitutes an essential component of our response to every work of literature. This is but to reaffirm that, even as readers, we are men and not machines, human beings and not disinterested robots; we simply cannot be made to suspend our ordinary disbelief in the imagined situations literature presents to us, or to give even temporary assent to the hidden poten-

tialities those situations then disclose to us, unless each work of
literature, by virtue of all the formal devices through which it
maintains its hold upon our attention, is able to convince us that
"such and such" at least might have been the case if life possessed
the coherence and clarity which in everyday experience it never
does. Beyond this, however, that "sense of ourselves" is at the root
formed, conditioned, and nourished by what we take, however
mysteriously or darkly, to be ultimately real and unalterable. It is
informed by and informing of whatever for us finally matters. Thus
in responding to every work of literature, we are – if we are bringing
the whole of ourselves to that response – responding with whatever
for us is the religious center of our being.

Yet, by the same token, our response to literature, while unavoid-
ably dependent upon "our deepest sense of ourselves," is not absolutely determined by that sense. Indeed, it is precisely that sense
which literature, in suggesting "that something else might be the
case," seeks to extend, to complicate, and ultimately to transform.
Which is only to say that at bottom literature seeks to convert by
extending the range of our imaginative capacity and hence "our
knowledge and governance of human possibility."[65]

Third, and finally, there is in our experience of every work of
literature something analogous to – I do not say identical with – the
religious experience of reality as ultimate, where, as Joachim Wach
once remarked, "we react not to any single or finite phenomenon,
material or otherwise, but to what we realize as undergirding and
conditioning all that constitutes our world of experiences."[66] This
is precisely what happens in each literary text. Every work of
imaginative literature is based upon some deeply felt, if not fully
or even partially conscious, assumption about what can, or just
possibly does, constitute the ground of experience itself. This
primal intuition then becomes the organizing principle for the
hypothetical structure which the work turns out to be. And because
this intuition or assumption thus undergirds and conditions all that
transpires within the world of the work, it in turn becomes the
interpretive key which will unlock the work's special logic, its
peculiar causality, and thus lay bare the axis upon which the world
of the work turns. Call it what you will – the informing or presiding
assumption, the shaping cause, the concrete universal, the embodied
vision, or the metaphysic – every meaningfully coherent work of

literature has such an executive principle, and it functions analogously to the notion of ultimacy in religious experience.[67]

The signal difference between literature and religion, however, is that in literature our assent to the consequences of such ultimate intuitions and assumptions is, as I have already mentioned, an "as-if assent" to what Pearce calls a conditional [possibly] contrary-to-fact statement."[68] Readers believe primarily in order to understand, whereas believers also understand in order the more vigorously and self-consciously to believe. Yet the great works of literature are hardly without their effect upon our beliefs. As dramatizations of what it would or could be like to experience life, or some selected aspect of it, ordered in terms of some specific principle of ultimacy, their function is to show us how various notions of what is or can be ultimate in our experience of life accordingly vary the possible or potential constitutive elements of our experience. And in so doing they require us "to take into our purview, as a vital human possibility, all the historically definable forms of life in which that possibility is made operative."[69] In elucidating how the facts might have been otherwise, they compel us to imagine the innerness and otherness of different ways of being and thinking and feeling than our own. Yet great works of the imagination would have little real effect upon the structure of our beliefs, little impact upon the shape of our affections, if their designs upon us were not imbedded in all the concrete particulars of lived experience, in terms of what Yeats called "the fury and mire of human veins." We are disturbed and moved and even altered by what we read because the possibilities and potentialities which arise from such ultimate commitments are measured in terms of the price they exact from those who must test and suffer them on the pulses – characters in whose aspiration and travail is revealed something of our own at least dimly perceived human image.

There is little cause to suppose that literature so conceived can make us any more or less religious, but then there is even less support for the view that it would be a good thing if it did. There is some evidence, however, that literature can, by quickening our sense of possibility and complicating our imagination of good and ill, at least help to make us a little more human. And that is probably more than we deserve and considerably more than we could otherwise hope for.

NOTES

1. See *Relations of Literary Study: Essays on Interdisciplinary Contributions*, ed. James Thorpe (New York: Modern Language Association of America, 1967).

2. *Language and Silence: Essays on Language, Literature and the Inhuman* (New York: Atheneum, 1967).

3. Henry Nash Smith, "Can American Studies Develop A Method?" *American Quarterly*, IX, Pt. 2 (Summer, 1957), p. 203.

4. For a representative sampling, see the Bibliography in *The New Orpheus: Essays Toward a Christian Poetic*, ed. Nathan A. Scott, Jr. (New York: Sheed and Ward, 1964), pp. 420–31.

5. *Trials of the Word: Essays in American Literature and the Humanistic Tradition* (New Haven and London: Yale University Press, 1965), p. 110.

6. *The Transcendentalists: An Anthology* (Cambridge: Harvard University Press, 1960), pp. 8–9.

7. For alternative analyses of the various approaches critics have taken to the study of religion and literature, see Sallie TeSelle, *Literature and the Christian Life* (New Haven and London: Yale University Press, 1966), pp. 7–59; and J. Hillis Miller, "Literature and Religion" in *Relations of Literary Study: Essays on Interdisciplinary Contributions*, pp. 111–26.

8. See *The Mirror and the Lamp: Romantic Theory and Critical Tradition* (New York: The Norton Library, W. W. Norton and Co., 1958), pp. 3–29.

9. See R. S. Crane *et al.*, *Critics and Criticism, Ancient and Modern* (Chicago: University of Chicago Press, 1952).

10. *The Poetics*, trans. S. H. Butcher, *Aristotle's Theory of Poetry and Fine Art* (London: Macmillan and Co., 1895), pp. 21–23.

11. *Biographia Literaria* (London, 1817), reproduced in *Criticism: The Major Texts*, ed. Walter Jackson Bate (New York: Harcourt, Brace & World, 1952), p. 379.

12. *Ibid.*

13. *Ibid.*, p. 387.

14. See Abrams, *The Mirror and the Lamp*, p. 119.

15. See Murray Krieger, *The New Apologists for Poetry* (Minneapolis: University of Minnesota Press, 1956), pp. 33 ff.

16. For this description of the general characteristics of modern semantic criticism, I am chiefly indebted to R. S. Crane, *The Language of Criticism and the Structures of Poetry* (Toronto: University of Toronto Press, 1953), pp. 80–115.

17. Crane's distinction between the two major tendencies in modern semantic criticism is reiterated in different terms by Lee T. Lemon, in his *The Partial Critics* (New York: Oxford University Press, 1965). Lemon reduces the numerous examples of modern critical theory to formalistic theories which conceive of literature, in Crane's terms, as a special kind of meaningful expression and mimetic theories which conceive of literature as the expression of a special kind of meaning. Lemon's categories have the advantage of greater specificity because he has broken down each classification, suggesting three variations of formalistic theory (closed form theories, open form theories, and symbolic form theories)

and six variations of mimetic theory (personality and experience theories, edification theories, social theories, tradition theories, psychological theories, and perception theories). Lemon is careful to insist that any given critic may be classified under any one of several of these categories. His purpose, however, is not so much to classify critics but, as any typology should, to help systemize critical discussion, and his method works admirably.

18. See William K. Wimstatt, Jr. and Cleanth Brooks, *Literary Criticism. A Short History* (New York: Alfred A. Knopf, 1962), pp. 724 ff.

19. See Philip Wheelwright, *The Burning Fountain: A Study in the Language of Symbolism,* new and rev. ed. (Bloomington and London: Indiana University Press, 1968).

20. See Walter J. Ong, S.J., "A Dialectic of Aural and Objective Correlatives," *The Barbarian Within* (New York: The Macmillan Company, 1962), pp. 26–40.

21. See Paul Ricoeur, *The Symbolism of Evil* (New York: Harper and Row, 1967).

22. See R. W. B. Lewis, *The American Adam: Innocence, Tragedy and Tradition in the Nineteenth Century* (Chicago: University of Chicago Press, 1955).

23. See, for example, Vincent Buckley, *Poetry and the Sacred* (London: Chatto and Windus, 1968); J. Hillis Miller, *Poets of Reality* (Cambridge: The Belknap Press of Harvard University Press, 1965); and R. W. B. Lewis, *Trials of the Word: Essays in American Literature and the Humanistic Tradition* (New Haven and London: Yale University Press, 1965).

24. See Amos N. Wilder, *Theology and Modern Literature* (Cambridge: Harvard University Press, 1958).

25. See Nathan A. Scott, Jr., *The Broken Center: Studies in the Theological Horizon of Modern Literature* (New Haven and London: Yale University Press, 1966), and *Negative Capability: Studies in the New Literature and the Religious Situation* (New Haven and London: Yale University Press, 1969); and William F. Lynch, S.J., *Christ and Apollo: The Dimensions of the Literary Imagination* (New York: Sheed and Ward, 1960).

26. William F. Lynch, S.J., "Theology and the Imagination," *Thought,* XXIX (Spring, 1954), pp. 61–86.

27. Denis de Rougemont, "Religion and the Mission of the Artist," *Spiritual Problems in Contemporary Literature,* ed. Stanley Romaine Hopper (New York: Harper Torchbooks, 1957), pp. 173–86.

28. Stanley Romaine Hopper, "Introduction," *Interpretation: The Poetry of Meaning,* ed. Stanley Romaine Hopper and David L. Miller (New York: Harcourt, Brace & World, Inc., 1967), pp. ix–xxii.

29. F. O. Matthiessen, *The Achievement of T. S. Eliot: An Essay on the Nature of Poetry* (New York: Oxford University Press, 1935); and Lionel Trilling, "Freud and Literature," *The Liberal Imagination: Essays on Literature and Society* (Garden City, N.Y.: Doubleday Anchor Books, 1957), pp. 32–54.

30. The phrase is Howard Mumford Jones', which he uses to describe the theory of literature Bacon adumbrated in the *De Augmentis Scientiarum,* in *The Theory of American Literature,* rev. ed. (Ithaca: Cornell University Press, 1965), p. 14.

31. See Roy Harvey Pearce, *The Continuity of American Poetry* (Princeton: Princeton University Press, 1961).

32. Erich Heller, *The Disinherited Mind: Essays in Modern German Literature and Thought* (New York: Farrar, Straus and Cudahy, 1957), p. 268.

33. *The Collected Poems of Wallace Stevens* (New York: Alfred A. Knopf, 1964), p. 239.

34. *Coleridge on Imagination* (Bloomington: Indiana University Press, 1960), p. 230.

35. *The Burning Fountain: A Study in the Language of Symbolism*, p. 205.

36. *Creation and Discovery* (New York: The Noonday Press, 1955), p. 87.

37. "Between the Numen and the Moha," *The Lion and the Honeycomb* (New York: Harcourt, Brace and Co., 1954), p. 297.

38. *The New Romantics* (Bloomington: Indiana University Press, 1962), p. 32.

39. *Ibid.*, p. 42.

40. *Ibid.*

41. *Ibid.*

42. *Essays in Criticism*, Second Series (London: Macmillan and Co., 1891), pp. 1–2.

43. *Ibid.*, p. 3.

44. *Ibid.*, p. 2.

45. See Abrams, *The Mirror and the Lamp*, p. 15.

46. See Preston T. Roberts, Jr., "A Christian Theory of Dramatic Tragedy," *Journal of Religion*, XXXI (January, 1951), pp. 1–20.

47. See Louis L. Martz, "Introduction" to *The Meditative Poem: An Anthology of Seventeenth-Century Verse*, ed. Louis L. Martz (Garden City, N.Y.: Doubleday Anchor Books, 1963), pp. xvii–xxxi.

48. Henry Rago, "Faith and the Literary Imagination – The Vocation of Poetry," *Adversity and Grace: Studies in Recent American Literature*, ed. Nathan A. Scott, Jr. (Chicago: University of Chicago Press, 1968), p. 240.

49. *Ibid.*, p. 248.

50. cf. R. W. B. Lewis, *Trials of the Word*, p. 110.

51. Rago, p. 241.

52. Dorothy Van Ghent, *The English Novel: Form and Function* (New York: Harper Torchbooks, 1961), p. 3. Miss Van Ghent's references are to fiction, but we may as easily apply her remarks to poetry and drama as well.

53. "Historicism Once More," *The Kenyon Review*, XX (Autumn, 1958), p. 566.

54. *Ibid.*

55. *Ibid.*

56. *Ibid.*

57. For this insight, and several others which follow, I am indebted to Dorothy Van Ghent, *The English Novel*. See particularly pp. 3–7.

58. *Art as Experience* (New York: Minton, Balch and Company, 1934), p. 346.

59. *The Collected Poems of Wallace Stevens*, p. 382.

60. *The English Novel*, p. 3.

61. *Ibid.*, pp. 3–4.

62. *Tradition and Poetic Structure* (Denver: Alan Swallow, 1960), p. 141.

63. "Historicism Once More," p. 567.

64. *Anatomy of Criticism* (Princeton: Princeton University Press, 1957), p. 94.

65. George Steiner, *Language and Silence: Essays on Language, Literature and the Inhuman* (New York: Atheneum, 1967), p. 6.

66. *Types of Religious Experience Christian and Non-Christian* (Chicago: University of Chicago Press, 1951), p. 32.

67. I am indebted to an unpublished paper by Professor Edward Wasiolek for some of the insights which provoked the notion discussed in this paragraph.

68. "Historicism Once More," p. 567.

69. *Ibid.*

PART ONE: APPROACHES TO LITERATURE AND RELIGION

2

THE USES OF A THEOLOGICAL CRITICISM

Amos N. Wilder

Amos N. Wilder is Hollis Professor of Divinity Emeritus *of the Harvard Divinity School. Among his many books are* Eschatology and Ethics in the Teaching of Jesus (1939), The Spiritual Aspects of the New Poetry (1949), Modern Poetry and the Christian Tradition (1952), New Testament Faith for Today (1955), Theology and Modern Literature (1958), *and* The Language of the Gospel: Early Christian Rhetoric (1964). *This essay was first published in* Soundings: An Interdisciplinary Journal (*Vol. LII, No. 1, Spring* 1969). *Reprinted by permission of the author and* Soundings.

This essay seeks to clarify that special approach to literary assessment often designated as a "theological criticism" or even a "Christian criticism." Though there is properly only one kind of criticism, only one cumulative discipline of criticism, yet contributions to it can be and have been made from various perspectives. It is to be recognized from the start that dogmatic shortcuts are impermissible, but this veto should apply to any and all imperialistic strategies from any quarter. Any serious artistic assessment, whether that of an individual or of a particular school of criticism, has its acknowledged or latent presuppositions, and all such can further the common task.

Discriminations in the arts, oriented to the Christian tradition, may indeed involve a clash of criteria and judgments as in all vigorous wrestling with our humanistic legacies or with contemporary works. But such discriminations need not be dogmatic any more than those arising from other long-espoused and passionately maintained traditions in culture which appeal to their own various archetypes and classics and summarizing formulas.

In what follows, therefore, it should be understood that I reject the idea of a specifically Christian criticism whether in terms of the experience of the believer or of theological categories. The analogy of a Marxist criticism may be useful. This can only mean the contribution that a Marxist can bring to the common undertaking. So it is with what for shorthand purposes can be spoken of as a "Christian" criticism. When I use the expression it is to be understood in this sense.

I

Some preliminary considerations can be offered in favor or in explanation of that rather extensive activity referred to as theological criticism which has developed in England and America now for several decades. There surely can be no objection to the concern in some theological faculties since the thirties to alert the churches to the significance of modern letters. Nor can objection be made to the efforts of the theologian-critic to repossess his religious tradition and to renew its language through an engagement with the contemporary arts and sensibility. Nothing but good, moreover, could come from his critique of the blighting effects of the inherited patterns of asceticism in certain religious traditions, nor from his critique of the bad taste associated with a more recent religious aestheticism. In all such areas qualified churchmen have sought first of all to carry over into the consciousness of the religious institutions and into the religious arts the standards of excellence and of artistic integrity defined by the most perceptive critical ⟨ ⟩les of the time.

More debatable has been the increasingly sophisticated participation of the theologian in the forums of general criticism. Since such activity has at first been associated with theological faculties and with commissions, lectureships and conferences under religious auspices, and its publication with religious journals and the religious departments of the various presses, it could be construed as mainly apologetic and partisan, even when participated in by leading secular critics. In England F. R. Leavis voiced a vigorous indictment of the phenomenon known as "Christian discrimination" identified with the title of a book by the Anglican critic, Brother George Every. It would be interesting to analyze the totally different context of these issues in France, where theological polemic has had so prominent a place in general criticism. In the United States in any case we have not had to reckon with a self-proclaimed Catholic or confessional group of writers and critics of the order of Mauriac, Bernanos, and Claudel. Eliot's literary criticism largely transcended any such dogmatic partisanship, and W. H. Auden has gone out of his way in his critical writings to set a Kierkegaardian gulf between all aesthetic activity and the existential dimension of faith.

But the situation is changing today and the role of the theologian in criticism appears in a new light. We see an increasing number of religious scholars who are also trained in literary studies. Their base of operations is often now in the college and university rather than in the seminary, and in departments in the humanities rather than in those of religion. Meanwhile teachers in departments of language and literature, especially in dealing with our modern classics, often find themselves involved in issues which even under strictly literary assessment require religious and theological expertise and empathy.

Still more fundamentally we observe that the very conditions of contemporary culture tend to relativize critical orthodoxies, to require interdisciplinary resources, and to open the interpretation of the arts of language to a total anthropological and linguistic approach. Literary criticism has had to take account of new explorations of the whole phenomenon of language, not only in the global sense of comparative literature and the history of genres, and not only in the social-psychological dimension of the study of myth and symbol, but more fundamentally in all that has to do with the correlation of language and reality. Western humanism and its canons are compromised by a new experience and our critical repertoire must be widened. But this richer and more baffling context of the arts at many points involves the category of religion, so inseparably linked with those older vicissitudes of language and consciousness which have now again in strange ways become contemporary for us.

The epochal character of the cultural transformation now in process has brought with it a crisis in language and in the arts, reflected in the revolution and dissolution of literary forms, in a combination of both iconoclastic impulse and ontological power, and even in the surfacing of archaic structures and motifs. The interrelation of the disorders in society and the arts places the critic in a difficult position. It is not easy to safeguard the proper autonomy of his discipline when his literary texts are so closely related to the anomie of the age. Recently this embarrassment has even led to shrill forms of moralistic revulsion against current critical schools and to diatribes against the Academy generally. One may sympathize at many points with any such exposure of the complicity of the artist or critic today with contemporary nihilism, but any critique of criticism at this fateful level requires grounded humanistic sanctions. At this point the relevance of the religious sources of culture cannot well be denied.

II

Modern letters and the modern arts as a whole testify to the changing experience of mankind, at least in the West. A concern with this change is one legitimate approach to literature since language and reality are so closely related. The vicissitudes of the word open up to us today as in all periods basic issues with respect to past and present, tradition and revolt, meaning and vitality. What we are going through can be seen as a crucible of language, a crucible of images, a testing and transformation of signs and symbols, a revolution of sensibility. This situation is one which engages all our disciplines, all our traditions, all our vocations in mutual illumination.

The modern reality here testified is a new thing, but it is related to the realities of the past. It is in process and it has many facets. It is transient and relative, and only one window on any true or final reality. Therefore while the first task is that of knowing it and examining its witnesses, we cannot stop with that. We must assess it, defend it, criticize it, and seek as participants to shape it. So far as such discrimination relates to the arts, especially the arts of language, this means an aesthetic criticism, but a criticism that finally rejoins all the fateful issues of language and is therefore more than aesthetic, is total. Here, however open our hospitality may be to all the voices and all the inspirations and all the traditions, we finally judge as we see things. We bring the contribution of our own perspective into the arena, into the weighing of choices, into the war of myths if such it be. So we instruct each other, challenge each other, crystallize new fronts, find unexpected allies.

In this engagement with our modern reality and its literary registers I find myself willy-nilly determined by ultimate Christian presuppositions. But this calls for clarification. Whether such presuppositions are genuinely Christian is always a prior question which should trouble the theologian-critic. Even at this basic level he should be open to instruction not only by other theologians but by his whole continuing life-experience, precisely in our modern context. For even presuppositions, not to mention doctrines, must be repossessed in every new situation.

The theologian-critic has been found especially vulnerable at two points. On one side he has often made the mistake also found in other critics of violating proper method by a prior dogmatic. Even in the domain of politics or morality it is only by a highly simplistic procedure that the Christian can pretend to assert norms directly from his doctrines or confessions. In questions of jurisprudence it is recognized that decisions and interpretations can only properly be reached by laboring with the precedents in all their complexity. The judge may not leap directly from Magna Carta or the Bill of Rights to the matter in hand. The moral theologian should not leap directly from the Sermon on the Mount to the present ethical decision. So also in the field of letters there is no shortcut for the believer.

But the theologian-critic has also been vulnerable on the other side. If his orientation has a contribution to make to the total undertaking he should be as clear and candid as possible about his ultimate criteria and maintain their cutting edge. Too often he has been uncertain about his base of operations. He has leaned over backwards to show his breadth and tolerance. This kind of protective coloring can relate to the regnant mood and horizon of current writing. Or it can relate to critical fashion. But by such acquiescence any profitable dialogue is frustrated. The modern situation with its special art forms, from the greatest to the least, from the modern classics to the popular floods in the mass-media, surely presents us with competing options and these demand discrimination at every level.

When all is said and done, one cannot finally separate life-attitudes from aesthetic judgments. Behind every poem, novel or play there is a man. Behind every critical assessment of whatever school or method there is a man. Behind the artistic production of a decade or a period there is the fathomless reality of mankind. Admitted that every art has its own refined disciplines, whose independence is to be jealously guarded; admitted that literary criticism has its own sophisticated and scrupulous procedures; yet all such rightful autonomy can only be penultimate. Art and letters are too important not to be referred back finally to what is at stake in the human story. Inevitably, therefore, fundamental perspectives will and do affect particular judgments even of detail, and all such prior visions have their rightful place in court.

III

Even when some such plausible case can be made for the uses of a theological criticism, the real crux remains. How does such a critic move properly and convincingly from his faith to his literary judgments? I do not, indeed, accept that view which insists upon the total incommensurability of divine and human things. But I agree that the theologian-critic should explain how he can pass in a persuasive way from those assurances of revelation and their corollaries which are indisputable to him to their particular application in the free market of literary discussion. It is not enough to have a stance or a perspective or some claimed world-epiphany or baptism. The *homo religiosus* cannot enter into the forum of life-decisions arbitrarily. Even the prophet and the martyr engage with the language of their contemporaries.

The difficulties if not the scandal of such a participation should be frankly recognized. After all the Christian view of the world carries with it axioms and assumptions which are widely held to be incredible today. Nor can such matters be excluded as extra-aesthetic unless we wish to dehumanize the arts and assign them that kind of immaculate autonomy which, experience has shown, only ends in their being credited after all with a religious or sacred character, whether hermetic or vatic. Life and language at whatever level cannot finally evade or deny the dimension of the sacred, and it therefore here again becomes a question of appropriate criteria. Aesthetic criticism cannot stop short of a total criticism and such ultimate sanctions should be as explicit as possible.

To suggest some of the disparities between the basis of a Christian criticism and the reality-view underlying much contemporary evaluation one could in rough fashion martial a few models or pointers, distinguishing between several levels of language.

In ordinary language, then, the Christian believes that "no sparrow falls to the ground without your Father's will," and that "even the hairs of your head are numbered"; in dogmatic language, in personal providence; in mythological language, that "in everything God works for good with those who love him, who are called according to his purpose."

In ordinary language, the Christian believes that history has meaning and that the meek shall inherit the earth; in dogmatic language that God has disclosed himself and his purpose in the historical process; and mythologically, that God has elected Israel for the blessing of the Gentiles and has chosen the "community" as the means by which a disordered creation shall be reconstituted in unity.

In ordinary language, then, the Christian believes that the health and fulfilment of human society are linked with some aboriginal pattern of atonement at the heart of things; in dogmatic terms, that the world is redeemed by the death of Christ; and in mythological terms, that on the cross Christ overcame the principalities and powers of evil.

In ordinary language the Christian believes that in life or death we are the Lord's; in dogmatic terms, in the resurrection of the body; and in mythological terms, that he that raised Jesus from among the dead will also raise us.

One could add other axioms, especially such as seem to have a special timeliness: a Christian believes in the kind of love of God that is compatible with inexorable judgment, for example on every idle word. Like the Buddha he believes that "the liar digs up his own root" (for "liar" here read the purveyor of toxic or self-flattering images, of fraudulent rhetorics). He believes in non-violence psychological as well as overt, but he also believes that inherent civil authority and its sanctions of force are ordained by God. He believes in the essential innocence and goodness of created things, and therefore of the sensuous and sexual and economic orders, as well as of the rational faculties. But he warns against daemonic crafts and towers of Babel; looks on acquisitiveness as idolatry and equates the lustful eye with adultery. He draws a sharp line down through all agitations for freedom and all claims on property, distinguishing between covenant-rights and brotherly bonds on the one hand and secular emancipationism or emulation, avidity, and invidiousness on the other.

Thus the theological critic should not compromise or disguise his disagreement with the widespread scepticism and nihilism and intoxication of our time, nor with widely regnant ideologies, programs, and attitudes with aesthetic presuppositions, all of which find expression in contemporary literature. But as in the social-ethical domains so in the field of letters, such a critic must identify himself with the givens of the occasion. That particular and austere criterion that is his can only validate itself meaningfully, even for himself, in the process, and not in some hortatory or moralistic intervention. A Christian presence in literary or artistic discussion surely involves no other law than that of the embodied Word as exemplified in both aspects of his scripture.

I would like to explore what such a proper procedure would be by selecting the first of the Christian convictions listed, that having to do with personal providence. In dealing with writings in which exposure of the self to sheer fortuity and meaninglessness is central a theological criticism will certainly not first of all indict the negative portrayal as such. It will indeed commend as truer to reality a work which recognizes disguised operations of grace in the enigmas of personal tragedy. But before all else it will ask whether the experience in question, however ambiguous, is adequately rendered. As Beckett admonishes in *All that Fall*: "Tell all! Tell all!" Does the author present the protagonist, the action, the impasse with some dense sense of all the contexts, complexities, imponderables that envelop all human situations? In artistic terms does he have at his command the palette for this kind of exhaustive faithfulness? Does he employ a full complement of the registers and manuals for a nuanced portrayal of the inwardness and ramifications of the matter?

In the case of the Book of Job – which imposes itself in this connection – meaningfulness here emerges not first of all out of the final intervention of God but out of the dialogue and the full gamut of affective-imaginative apperceptions evoked in it. The divine vindication that follows is to be seen as rhetorical strategem enforcing the postulate of faith which speaks through the expostulation and tone of the hero. The prosodic as well as the religious matrix of Job's accents are to be traced to such older texts as Deut. 32:10,

> He found [Jacob] in a desert land,
>   and in the howling waste of the wilderness;
> he encircled him, he cared for him,
>   he kept him as the apple of his eye.

The genre of the work, moreover, with its antecedents in the ancient world, governs the import of the dialogue.

But I would like to apply these considerations to two recent writings. Peter De Vries' novel, *The Blood of the Lamb*,[1] deals with the problem of meaninglessness in perhaps its most acute form, the suffering of a child. The Christian reader will sympathize with the assault on the stultifying dogma, "it is God's will," pilloried in the book. He will also respect the bereaved father's alternative: an agnostic celebration of the ephemeral beauty and delight of human intimacy in all its precariousness. He will, however, find the problem handled in a truncated way: the full octaves of imaginative and affective context and the prior ambivalences of our total human situation are missing. In literary terms these lacks can be related to the genre employed, that of the novel *à thèse*. Indeed, any satisfactory dealing with this subject-matter for our contemporary sensibility would rule out the conventional novelistic form here adopted, a form which belongs to "last year's language." Related to this incongruity is the occasional resort to the melodramatic as well as the tone and tenor which fail to move beyond the plangent to the deep diapason familiar to us in works that could be cited.

A better test case is afforded by Beckett's *All that Fall*.[2] This radio-play is all the more to the point since its title cites the 143rd Psalm, "The Lord upholdeth all that fall." I cannot agree with the view that the "wild laughter" of Dan and Maddy Rooney on recalling this text represents nothing but derision of it on the part of the author, granted that life is, indeed, lived "under the wheels." The work is greater than any such part. The incandescence of the detail, the humanity of the characterization, the irony and desperation suggested through the colloquial and the grotesque, the abysses of silence behind the words and gestures; all these suggest what we find even more movingly in the wonderful companion-piece, *Embers*, that motif of famishment and prayer, that Breughelesque *de profundis*, which keeps open the incursions of grace. A Christian criticism of the work will know how to recognize in the rhetoric what faith itself knows in extra-aesthetic wrestling with the enigmas of personal providence. If it be objected that any sound criticism can make such comments as I have made upon such writings I would reply that this illustrates the fact that a "Christian" criticism rightly carried out will coincide at many points with any grounded humanistic criticism, but, secondly, that it can also alert such criticism to the resonances of a profounder anthropology.

IV

There is one point at which the Christian or any profoundly religious perspective can introduce an important element into the assessment of the modern arts. It is not predisposed to exaggerate the importance of the contemporary, even granted the stature of the works in question. This can become a matter of far-reaching consequence in a time like ours. The critic with this perspective will certainly not take lightly the signs of the times, the creativity of the moment. It is the peculiar genius of biblical religion to assign fatefulness to every present and to attribute significance to the present act or neglect whether of life or of the imagination. But such a critic will read all the witnesses and symptoms of this "now" in a wider context.

What makes him keep his distance, despite his admiration for contemporary voices, indeed his deep involvement in their explorations, is an old wisdom that has repeatedly justified itself in riding out the gyrations of strange times, a wisdom which refers back to what Walt Whitman, no doubt in a different context, called the kelson of creation. These insights mean more than that a long history is recalled to relativize the present. They mean that the most intimate texture of contemporary work becomes subject to subtle apperceptions otherwise absent.

We find an analogy to this theme in remarks of Proust's alter ego in the closing section of the great novel. Marcel here is defending his at that time unappreciated art and questioning the reigning authorities and reputations. He suggests that the anonymous multitudes of mankind have a truer flair for what is important in literature than the current parties and schools "whose logomachy is renewed every ten years," the kaleidoscope being composed not only of the successive "modern groups," but of the social, political, and religious ideas which successively take on a momentary amplitude and prestige.

There is a greater analogy between the instinctive life of the wider public and the talent of the greater writer . . . than in the superficial verbiage and the changing criteria of the official judges.[3]

Proust's pursuit of a deeper sensibility and portrayal of society than that of Anatole France and other contemporaries suggests the detachment of a Christian discernment for whom something of Vanity Fair is found in all cultures, and something of the Cities of the Plain. In this view the fashions of criticism are part of the carnival and many of the critics represent the town criers of this or that Babylon. At short range they may have immense subtlety in dealing with the works symptomatic of the crisis, and this is a valuable service. But in a wider frame of reference, though they may see the writing on the wall at the feast of Belshazzar they are not able to decipher it.

In any period or decade the observer of current letters inevitably has his attention called to highly publicized schools, personalities, and movements which may, indeed, have undeniable significance and which rightfully demand not only his attention but often also his defense. Such movements are characteristically iconoclastic and controversial, and the works that represent them dominate the scene and focus the attention of sophisticated circles. They are important because they touch the nerve of the modern consciousness and reflect the changing sensibility of the period. There are, however, many considerations which argue for reserve on the part of the critic and point to the complexity of his task.

For one thing, without denying the fateful importance of the more searching and talented avant-garde voices of the time, we cannot but remember the cultural pluralism of our society. The modern world is made up of many communities and traditions and what speaks for one does not speak for another. The arts that crystallize the ethos of one group may not answer for another. Nor is it only a question of lag or ripeness, as though the culture moved as a whole toward only one kind of experience and sensibility. Our world with its many strata and legacies solves its inherited problems in various ways and is creative in various ways. In retrospect the more visible trends in art, and even those most rightfully authoritative for the historical moment, must take their place in a wider context. There are more permanent aspects of man than are evoked in our modern classics or evoked in other ways. The critic should be alert to this pluralism of the situation.

V

It is a special feature of our time that the shaping of critical opinion tends to fall disproportionately into the hands of the most deracinated intellectuals of our society and their forums and media of publication. We can understand such deracination and recognize that it makes possible a disabused assessment of art and life that brings its own illumination. Perhaps it is always true that in any age the most sensitive groups are likely to be disaffected with prevailing patterns and attentive to those who are in revolt. But in our present disorder this phenomenon is maximized. For in our situation a wide public even of the discerning is so unsettled as to be open to the most radically oriented of those who shape our images and our opinions. In a time of disarray the most iconoclastic voices have the most appeal. In one aspect Proust, again, accounts for this prestige of a criticism over-impressed by contemporary fashion: "It consecrates as a prophet a writer who brings no new substance just because of his peremptory tone and the scorn he affects for the school that has preceded him."[4]

One sees susceptibility to extreme opinion today especially among students. Often our faculties in the humanities lend themselves to such unbalance. Thus it has been remarked that "too many brilliant students come out knowing Kafka, but not Plato, Sartre but not Shakespeare, Black Power but not the French Revolution . . . and believing that American history began with John F. Kennedy."

There is still another consideration which weighs with the "Christian" critic who would keep some detachment from the sway of the contemporary. This has to do with certain extreme manifestations. When the revolt against tradition takes the form of blasphemy, pornography, gleeful or vindictive profanation, however justified such extremes may well appear in view of the aesthetic or moral insipidity of what is attacked, here a grounded even if sympathetic criticism will detect the symptoms of phantasy and guilt which accompany extreme deracination. The common charge that such features in the arts are motivated by a desire for attention, and thus by shock-tactics and exhibitionism, is hardly relevant to the more serious artists. Among these, moreover, wide latitude must be allowed where the engagement with such ambiguous areas is responsibly conducted. But the resort to nihilism and outrage often represents a covert displacement of self-destruction in the author and in his society. This is related to an impulse to profane our human bonds, especially with the fathers. Relevant here is the commandment to honor father and mother.

Deeply embedded in the work of Proust is the tortured theme of *les mères profanées*. In his *Gates of Horn*[5] Harry Levin has sifted out the strands of this preoccupation of Proust. The eventual compunctions of this author for his earlier cruelty to his mother had much to do with his dedication to his great task. "The years of desecration had to be atoned for by a long and testing consecration."[6] At the same time this retrospective sobering added a final moral dimension to the total vision, a legacy from his Jewish mother and grandmother. Thus, as Levin observes, the "pilgrimage has unexpectedly led from the *Almanach de Gotha* to the Old Testament."[7] But there are many writers of talent today, talent which for the moment disorients both criticism and self-criticism, whose garish impulse and whose fascination with the destructive element has never thus been chastened. Our crucial test of the artist even when dealing with the worst tyrannies of our situation is an ultimate deportment of holy fear of pietas before the final mysteries. Or, as Charles Péguy observed in his *Saints Innocents*, "All life comes from tenderness."[8] It is not only the Christian in criticism who insists on the ultimate sanctities of life. And it is not only as a moralist that he does so.

A great many modern artists and critics speak for special new strata, new kinds of men, produced by the conditions of our society: the disordered family, neighborhood, livelihood. If there is an ecological crisis which calls our attention to the balance of nature, we may say that there is a human ecological disturbance which has already for some time been determining a new kind of human breed within the wider culture. These groups have little or no memory – and what they have is highly distorted – of that older world and its continuities which are still so real for many of us. But this means that they are not capable of relating old and new or of making just comparisons. We have every right therefore to assign their witness only limited authority. Yet the forces which have shaped these more deracinated groups have of course also played upon society as a whole in our time. The dilemmas so occasioned are indivisible and the responses to them in any quarter must be taken account of.

VI

There is, finally, one major consideration bearing on the role of the Christian in criticism today or at any time. His perspective is one that assigns purpose and meaning to the human story and is confident that grace operates in the most baffling labyrinths of the life of the individual or of societies. It is here, indeed, that the charge of dogmatism seems most clearly justified, but the believer can blunt the charge by moving the discussion to the literary level and by invoking the evidence precisely of the supreme literature and literary forms provided by the charters of his faith. The Christian reads human experience and judges the monuments of time in terms of the biblical epic and its vision of providential strategies.

It is to be granted that the special nurture of the theological critic has been in only one of the main religio-cultural traditions of mankind. Yet it is one whose literary classics are interwoven with a rich variety of other religious patterns and their rhetorics. Indeed one may say that his engagement with contemporary culture has a background of three thousand years of encounter and discrimination, receptivity, and rejection, vis-a-vis the cultures of the past. But it is precisely as a man of letters that the instructed Christian, initiated into the paideia and language repertory of the Hebrew and Christian charters, may offer some credentials as an interpreter of any literature.

It is not merely a question of widening the field of comparative literature and calling attention to genres and styles often neglected. One important range of observations has indeed been opened up by Erich Auerbach in his demonstration of the influence of the Scriptures upon the history of realism and the Western understanding of reality itself. More significant is the fact that this religious tradition has from the tenth century B.C. been peculiarly identified with the word and with writing. Through successive epochs it has been associated with profound revolutions of language and with new modes of oral and written communication, whether the schooling of the laity (from the first emergence of the synagogue in the period of the Exile), or refined disciplines of commentary, or extensive translation, or the exploiting of new arts of diffusion and publication such as the codex, illustration, and printing. Thus even granted his particular commitment the theologian, like the Jewish intellectual (if he cherishes his tradition), has special habituations for opening up dimensions of reality associated with the arts of the word.

But more important than these considerations in qualifying the "Christian" critic is the concretely human character of his faith and its rhetorics. In the act of criticism it is language that we are concerned with. But from beginning to end the language of scripture is wedded to all the dynamics of human experience, to the many-layered reality of man's life whether private or social, whether historical or cosmic. Immersion in this linguistic world provides an indispensable resource for the assessment of the rhetorics of any culture or period. Quite apart from any formal theological or moral dimensions of these classics the Christian brings with him to his reading apperceptions and literary expectations which are a unique equipment for any kind of humanistic discrimination.

In the final analysis those of us who have been identified with the theological criticism would like to see all such activity merged with the one common pursuit. What properly literary illumination it may contribute should become part of the resources of any critic. At least the task of wrestling with any such perceptions falls on any interpreter of whatever confession or no confession. The case is like that of sociological criticism. There was a period in which the sociological approach to letters, indeed to all the humanities including history, was so valuable a corrective that it was proper to speak of the sociological critic or the sociological historian. When the insights in question had been, as it were, digested in the discipline as a whole there was no longer need to distinguish that particular approach.

Yet however instructive such an analogy may be, the case is not the same. The Christian approach to all cultural creativity and fabulation will no doubt continue to have its own critical perspective. The humanism associated with the Jewish and Christian vision of the world will continue to remain in productive tensions if not in contradiction with all other humanisms and anthropologies, even when in a post-Christian epoch all such traditions will have been radically restructured.

NOTES

1. New York, 1961.
2. London, 1957.
3. *À la recherche du temps perdu*, Vol. III, Pléiade ed. (Paris, 1954), pp. 893–94.
4. *Ibid.*, p. 893.
5. New York, 1963.
6. P. 439.
7. P. 442.
8. *Cahiers de la Quinzaine*, XIII, 12 (1912); *God Speaks*, trans. Julien Green (Pantheon Books, 1945), p. 66.

SPECIFYING THE SACRED

Vincent Buckley

Vincent Buckley is Professor of English at the University of Melbourne in Victoria, Australia. He is the author of Poetry and Morality (1959) *and* Poetry and the Sacred (1968). *The following essay is from* Poetry and the Sacred. *Copyright* © 1968 *by Vincent Buckley. Reprinted by permission of the author, Chatto and Windus, London, and Barnes and Noble, Inc, New York.*

It is a great pity that no one has undertaken a study of changes in the history of the word "religious", as Raymond Williams has so valuably done with the word "culture". Doubtless, such a man would have an immensely harder task than Williams, whose keyword was of comparatively short provenance, and so could be approached without a great deal of discomfort. Its difficulty may be suggested by the very fact that, while Williams had a noun to work on, I feel obliged to specify an adjective. To speak of the relations between religion and poetry would be to venture on a bogland. For one thing, everyone assumes that he knows what the word "religion" means; religion is something which you have or have not got, something that belongs to you ("what is *your* religion?") or that you would prefer to go without ("I have no time for any religion"); or it is something *to* which you belong, something by which you live, something that would remain there, unchanged, external, demanding, whether you acknowledged it or not, an institutional allegiance rather than a personal vision, and hence an institutional vision to which your relation is bound to be one of conformity rather than extension. No doubt it is these senses of the word that led Bonhoeffer to call for a "religionless Christianity"; though that term itself is so odd that one can never be quite sure. At any rate, religion in these senses hardly applies to poetry at all; or, if it does apply, it does so by analogy. It would be possible to go on using the noun, "religion", with great and rigorous cheerfulness in analysing "the issues of religious poetry", and miss the real issues entirely. But those issues are much harder to avoid when, instead of the noun, we question the adjective, "religious", which stands at the centre of a group of adjectives to suggest why they ought not to be regarded as mere synonyms or antonyms: religious, sacred, divine, supernatural, irreligious, profane, secular, natural.

Much work has of course been done on changes in religious belief and religious sensibility. There is, pre-eminently, the monumental work of Hoxie N. Fairchild, *Religious Trends in English Poetry*, which takes for its province the controversial centuries (1700–1920). There is M. M. Ross' *Poetry and Dogma*, which deals chiefly with the seventeenth century, as does Douglas Bush's *Science and English Poetry*. There is A. S. P. Woodhouse's *The Poet and His Faith*, which lives under the shadow of Fairchild's much more important work. Then there are all those works which examine the decline of a tradition or traditions. Donat O'Donnell writes of the break-up of Christendom in the modern Catholic imagination; George Steiner writes of the death of tragedy, J. B. Broadbent of the death of love poetry, J. Hillis Miller of the disappearance of God. And I have no doubt whatever that the phenomena dealt with by all these critics merge with one another in one great movement within society and the psyche. Yet it is interesting that Fairchild and Ross, for example, approach the matter in terms of the erosion of Christian dogma and, through that, the erosion of a certain symbolic or sacramental realism in the poets who were the victims of it. It is not my purpose to dispute whether such an erosion took place, or to offer a historical account alternative to theirs, but to suggest that it is time for the terms of the discussion to be widened again, to be conducted in terms of "the religious" and "the sacred" rather than in terms of "the revealed" or "the dogmatic". My interest, in other words, will be anthropological as much as doctrinal.

If these men, with their sense of doctrinal centrality, provide a less than fully satisfying guide in my present purpose, a thinker like Arnold, with his amiable anti-dogmatism, is equally unsatisfying on the other side. Indeed, when I think of Arnold's predilection for balancing comprehensive nouns, my preference for the adjective is strengthened. Arnold is willing to tell you not only what "culture" is, or even what "religion" is, but also whether this man has it or has not got it, to what extent that man approaches it or is diverted from it. However supple the play, however scrupulous the concern, the effect of this habit is to focus attention on the word rather than on the works it is apparently used to elucidate. Arnold was a religious man, as his letters and notebooks show; but his definition of religion as "morality touched by emotion" is singularly unhelpful.

He is not the only critic to hypostatise in this way. For Santayana, "religion and poetry are identical in essence, and differ merely in the way in which they are attached to practical affairs. Poetry is called religion when it intervenes in life, and religion, when it merely supervenes upon life, is seen to be nothing but poetry."[1] For A. C. Bradley, the starting-point of religion is "the experience, on the one side, of my feared or felt separation from something conceived as beyond me, much greater than I am, superior to me in mode of existence and powerful over me; and, on the other side, the experience of the removal of that separation by my submission to, or union with, this something, a removal which gives me freedom and happiness. Or, more briefly, it is the experience of freedom from evil attained by willed union with a being which is free from evil."[2]

As compared with Santayana, or even with Arnold, this will seem a large step in the right direction; but even here the word "experience" tends to suggest too static and formalised a sense of that separation and that union. To take one example only: as I shall argue, the kind of redefinition of God undertaken, however implicitly, in *Moby Dick* is an attempt to de-formalise and to render dynamic man's sense of separation from and union with the forces which overshadow his life; so that we are returned to the notion of God as mysterious, active, possessing initiative, holy and terrifying – precisely the notion taken over by Christian metaphysics from the Old Testament and available, in any case, in the New. It is as though

certain parts of a life's experience were discovered and declared as
sacred in order to suggest that the whole of life is, in some final
sense, sacred; but it also, by testifying to *God's* action and presence,
makes those areas, and that God, the Holy in relation to whom men
must bow down. To say as much as this is to anticipate my argument; but the fact is that we may have definitions of religion which,
however generous their scope, and however consistent their terms,
do a good deal less than justice to the communal experience they
refer to; and I think that Bradley's definition is of this kind. So is
Woodhouse's when, in speaking of religion in the West, he says,
"The minimal dogmatic requirement appears to be the recognition
of a power, anterior and superior to man, which serves to explain
to man himself and his universe and to give a measure of meaning
and guidance to his life, and which, therefore, becomes the object
of his worship. . . ."[3] Whether the requirement is minimal or not,
this statement of it is very flat, quite out of key with the forces it
refers to. And "explain" is surely wrong, particularly when it is
great poets we are thinking of; is Donne, for example, or is Wyatt,
or Coleridge, looking in poetry for an explanation of his universe?

When faced with such difficulties of definition, one does well to
remember that the expert in Comparative Religion, Mircea Eliade, is
more cautious in his offerings of meaning. He says, indeed, that
while the element of "the sacred" is an irreducible element in all
religious experience, he sees no point in "beginning with a definition
of the religious phenomenon".[4] The reason is clear; if he begins
with a notion of what a religious phenomen *is*, how it is shaped,
what factors produce it, or how we are to account for it, he is going
to miss, or to have no interest in, a large number of cases where
"the sacred" is manifested; the end result will be to confirm the
truncation of a concept. I feel the same about the notion of "religious
poetry"; and, although of course I have no intention of proceeding
with Eliade's far-reaching scholarly inclusiveness, I do not want
to exclude any poet *a priori*.

It is interesting that, since Blake and Wordsworth, there has been
a good deal of discussion about the religious nature of poetry; not
about the nature of "religious poetry", for that concept as a concept
has had little effective issue since the seventeenth century, but about
the religious nature, or in some cases implications, of poetry itself.
In his essay "Religion and Literature", T. S. Eliot has justly remarked

that when men of our culture speak of religious poetry, they mean something which is "a variety of *minor* poetry; the religious poet is not a poet who is treating the whole subject matter of poetry in a religious spirit, but a poet who is dealing with a confined part of this subject matter; who is leaving out what men consider their major passions, and thereby confessing his ignorance of them".[5] That this should be so is very sad, but it is chiefly the fault of those who would claim the title of "religious poet" for themselves. The discussion I am thinking of has taken place quite outside this charmed circle; and it is rich and varied in its expressions. Thus David Jones, D. S. Savage, and Auden all speak of poetry as itself a sacred act; and while Auden goes on to talk of it as specifying sacred occasions, Savage says that at least "great art . . . declares the inherent structure of the universe". That is, poetry is an act both sacred and sacralising. A. D. Hope sees it in the same terms, though he carries their implications still further. For him, poetry is

a way in which man carries out his side of the continual responsibility for maintaining the frame and order of the world, from the rising and setting of the stars, the procession of the seasons, the nature of beasts and plants and rivers and seas, the order of society and the behaviour of supernatural beings.[6]

It is hence "an act of celebration",[7] which "involves a sense of communion with those natures and participation in their processes. It is for the poet to feel himself to be not merely the mirror of nature or its commentator, but the voice of creation, speaking for it and as part of it."[8] Allen Tate in his scholarly fashion and Dylan Thomas in his ebullient way suggest the same orientation for poetry.

There are many more examples, but these few will serve to illustrate both the strongly affirmative nature and the extraordinary persistence of a hope for poetry which exists against the tenor of the age. Now, it is worth remarking that most of these men are speaking precisely as poets, not as observers of poetry; that they are speaking not of religion in poetry but of poetry as a religious act; and that they are locating the religious nature of that act neither in some thesis about the autotelic status of poetry nor in some contention about the basic themes or subjects for poetry but in terms of how the poet is brought as a religious being, concerned with human life and an actor in its drama, to create works which themselves carry his religious being, fortify creation and exist as, in a sense,

sacred spaces. No doubt some of them go back for their inspiration
to seventeenth century or Renaissance ideas about poetry; but if
they do, it is not to ideas of "sacred" or "divine" poetry that they
are resorting, but to conceptions of the poetic venture as such.
And, in any case, these conceptions had a powerful life throughout
the nineteenth century; the poets I have mentioned have immediate
as well as remote predecessors. Yeats of *Explorations* and *Auto-
biographies* stands behind them; so does the Wordsworth of the
Prefaces and Letters; so, probably, does Blake, though it is hard to
be sure; so, certainly, does Coleridge, with his view of symbolism
as characterised by "the translucence of the eternal through and in
the temporal".[9] I am not for the moment concerned to specify
precise influences, still less to outline the terms of any implicit
debate, but to stress what I have called the strongly affirmative nature
and the extraordinary persistence of this *kind* of conception of poetry.
If we are to deal fruitfully with the issue of what I earlier called
"religious poetry", it may best be done by abandoning that term, at
least in the short run (because there will be need for it later), and
speaking of a poetry which specifies the sacred. This will be in
keeping with the kinds of concern shown by the poets whom I have
mentioned, and many more whom I have not. And it will enable
me to work my way into my topic unburdened either by *a priori*
definitions or by any suggestion (which I emphatically reject) that
religious poetry is a separate and definable *genre*, or "kind", or
"mode" of poetry.

Before, then, considering at all the vicissitudes in the concept of
religious poetry over the past centuries, it is necessary to establish
a meaning for two words which, though sometimes used as synonyms,
cannot be usefully regarded as synonymous in any strict sense. The
words are "religious" and "sacred". Of the first, I propose to offer
my own definition, relying as I do so both on what the adherents of a
fully articulated religion might be supposed to accept and on what
the "ordinary man", who, as everyone insists, lives now in a secu-
larised world and does not care for religion, might mean by it if he
bothered with the concept at all. For the second, which is a term
now used more often within studies of comparative religion than
within systems or disciplines of devotion, I feel bound to rely on
definitions already established within such studies, and, specifically,
on the work of Mircea Eliade, who is perhaps the most influential

of all the "believing" contributors to the contemporary debate about the sacred and the secular, but who writes as a scientist rather than a theologian.

As I say, I cannot usefully offer a definition of "religious poetry" for two reasons; I do not believe that it is generally useful to talk about such a *genre* or category of poetry, and it is the purpose of this whole study to suggest the great variety of ways in which poetic *oeuvres* may exhibit a religious interest or impulse. But I may perhaps offer as general a definition as possible of that interest or impulse. I take it as the impulse to establish the sense of man's life and his human relationships as being connected with, or, better, bonded with forces in the universe, which have their correlations in his own psychic life and so in at least some of his chief relationships, but which cannot be accounted for *in terms* of his psychic life, are in some sense superior to him, in some sense govern him, are manifest to him in terms of power and presence, and in some sense require of him adoration, worship, and celebration. They may or may not involve the further concepts of a communal fall, personal sin, personal or communal salvation, and an eternal life lived either in personal or in communal terms. Therefore, they may or may not incite to attitudes of personal *devotion* of the sort which lie behind or within the "religious" poetry characteristic of centuries up to and including the eighteenth but which have seldom been resorted to with any poetic force since the Romantic movement. They will always, however, incite to attitudes of personal submission and responsibility, even where such a spiritual movement is not very satisfyingly completed; for the forces I speak of, in whatever terms they may be conceived (and the sustained conception of them is theology) will be religious forces only so long as they are seen as having a present relevance to questions of personal identity, meaningful action, and the inner structures of feeling. In this sense, to anticipate my argument a little, a poet like Theodore Roethke or A. D. Hope may well seem to be a more "religious" poet than many a Christian devotional poet who, however talented and serious, gives the appearance of enclosing his experience in institutional terms and conventional symbols.

It is true, however, that with the development of anthropology and comparative religion, the interest of students of religion has come to be in religious *behaviour* as a classifiable sign of this impulse and the apprehensions which it nourishes. Consequently, the word "sacred" becomes prominent in a rather different sense from that which it had in the days when it seemed natural for poets and essayists to speak of "sacred poetry" as though it were a separate literary *genre* representing and enclosing a psychic interest separable from the other interests of the person or the society. Whatever the large disagreements among scholars, I take them, from my limited reading in the field, to agree that the word "sacred" is not synonymous with the word "devotional" as a traditional Christian might even now use it, and that "the sacred" has never been in any culture a *completely* separate category. If the latter is true of primitive cultures, it is much more true of our own, in which a concept of the sacred has for great numbers of men no overt relevance whatever. Yet it seems to be an invaluable instrument for indicating what men do when they engage in religious acts.

In one of his best known works, *The Sacred and the Profane*, Mircea Eliade begins with a reference to Rudolf Otto's famous work, *Das Heilige*, translated here as *The Sacred*. Otto, says Eliade, "undertook to analyse the modalities of *the religious experience*",[10] which is an experience of God as *power*, the *mysterium fascinans et tremendum*. Such experiences are "numinous", for they are "induced by the revelation of an aspect of divine power".[11] Speaking for himself while endorsing Otto, Eliade comments that "the sacred always manifests itself as a reality of a wholly different order from 'natural' realities". Yet he is plainly uneasy; for he goes on to insist that his own interest is not in the *irrational* aspects of religious experience but in "the sacred in its entirety".[12]

It is perhaps as well that Eliade gets away from Otto's terms, for those formulations come from a particular phase of German theological thinking, and may nowadays be found misleadingly dramatic, although I do not see how they could be found completely irrelevant. Eliade's own terms may, in time, be superseded as misleadingly "scientific" or emotionally question-begging. But there is no doubt that his venture is "open-ended" in a heartening way, which is one of the reasons why I rely on him for my definition of "the sacred".

At this point of his analysis "the sacred" refers to those forces which I spoke of earlier rather than to a mode of specifying, responding to, or participating in them:

Man becomes aware of the sacred because it manifests itself, shows itself, as something wholly other than the profane. To designate the act of manifestation of the sacred, we have proposed the term *hierophany*.[13]

An hierophany is "anything that manifests the sacred";[14] and so we must get used to the idea of recognizing hierophanies absolutely everywhere, in every area of psychological, economic, spiritual and social life. Indeed, we cannot be sure that there is *anything* – object, movement, psychological function, being or even game – that has not at some time in human history been somewhere transformed into an hierophany.[15]

In each case where something is taken as an hierophany, we are confronted by the same mysterious act – the manifestation of something of a wholly different order, a reality that does not belong to our world, in objects which are an integral part of our natural "profane" world.[16]

And since "the sacred is always manifested through something",[17] whether that thing is small and simple or large and complex, the recognition of an hierophany is always a break in the continuum of experience, the homogeneity of a world, which otherwise might, and to modern men often does, appear completely "profane". But here a certain dialectic appears in Eliade's thinking, a dialectic which at some points narrowly avoids becoming a contradiction. The designation of an hierophany is a break in the profane continuum, and so the designated or designating object seems completely other than the profane; but it also takes place in objects "which are an integral part of our natural 'profane' world", and, far from abolishing their actuality, enhances it. There is in every hierophany "a paradoxical coming-together of sacred and profane" which "really produces a kind of breakthrough of the various levels of 'experience' ".[18] Therefore, while "the sacred" is an absolute category, "the hierophany" is not; or, to put it another way, the sacred as designating object is never completely able to manifest the sacred as that which is designated:[19]

Obviously there are no purely religious phenomena; no phenomenon can be solely and exclusively religious.[20]

This is, of course, true in the sense that the behaviour of religious men may be of interest to people besides them, and may be analysed in terms different from those chosen by them; a sociological or juridical account, for example, may be given of it; it may be studied by people like Eliade himself. But it is also true in the sense that the sacred object is ever completely transformed by its sacred use; it remains within the environment, manifestly still part of the environment, in the whole of which it may be taken as suggesting a certain potency. That is, it shows both a movement into the world of common experience and a movement within the common experience to transcend or complete itself. And it is in this second sense that it becomes useful in the analysis of the varieties of religious poetry: not because it establishes a category of poetry separate from all other categories, but because it shows a movement within the world which the poet deals with and recreates, a movement which the poet himself might prefer to speak of in other than religious terms. Furthermore, it is true (and here again the relevance to poetry is obvious) that sacred things can become "an object of veneration or fear according to the circumstances (for the sacred usually produces this double reaction)".[21] We see this quality most markedly in poets like Wordsworth and Yeats, and in a novelist like Melville. "Veneration and fear" justly expresses the remarkable equipoise in the recognition of superhuman forces which we find at many crucial places in their work. But that it *is* an equipoise, and not merely an ambivalence, is seen in the fact that "fear" and not "dread" is the word that commends itself to us when we think of those passages. "Dread" seems more appropriate to certain passages of Coleridge and Hopkins, poets temperamentally inclined to feel those forces as bearing down on them and even judging them rather than as offering themselves for a complete response. And personally I am interested to notice that, when I think of the very diverse cases of Donne, Smart, and Blake, I do not feel inclined to use even the word "fear".

Leaving such dualities, however (and I mention them at this point to make it clear that an hierophany is not a simple and unequivocal event in nature), I return to Eliade, who is prepared to maintain that the acts of religious man can *never* be fully expressed in terms of his own aspiration to self-completion but always involve the recognition of and response to forces outside him, and superior to him, which prompt to his self-completion:

We must not forget that for religious man the supernatural is indissolubly connected with the natural, that nature always expresses something that transcends it. As we said earlier: a sacred stone is venerated because it is *sacred*, not because it is a *stone*; it is the sacrality *manifested through the mode of being of the stone* that reveals its true essence. This is why we cannot speak of naturism or of natural religion in the sense that the nineteenth century gave to those terms; for it is "supernature" that the religious man apprehends through the natural aspects of the world.[22]

I quote these passages not because I want to use a show of some-one else's "scientific" method to support an ideology of my own, but for the following reasons: First, that since I have tried to supply a definition of "the religious impulse in poetry" broad enough to include poets who are certainly not devotional poets, whose work does not at all lend itself to theological exegesis and does not incite either themselves or their readers to worship of an easily identifiable, traditional God, I need a further term which will enable me to both link them with and distinguish them from poets who are "believers" in the traditional sense; and Eliade's use of "the sacred" provides that term. Second, the works of many poets particularly since the height of the Romantic movement not only allow for but positively invite or demand analysis in terms which point to their religious quality, but avert theological or doctrinal treatment. Third, since that time, which I take to be a crucial one for my study, even the Christian poets, like Hopkins, Eliot, and Lowell, may be more helpfully approached in the broader terms than in doctrinal categories. Fourth, the more intensively one focusses on a quality in the poetry that one feels it necessary to call "religious", the more important it is that one should provide oneself with a means of avoiding sheer subjectivity.

I confess that Eliade's language of "the sacred" does not satisfy me entirely; for one thing, his use of it does contain the dialectic, verging on contradiction, to which I pointed before; and for another, the repeated use of it is likely to suggest, and to be misleading in suggesting, that "the sacred" is a special and separable category of experience. It would be a great pity if having, through the process of historical development, got rid of the notion of sacred or religious divine poetry as a special separable category of *poems*, we lapsed into the complementary weakness of regarding it as a special, separable category of experience or apprehension *within* a poem. I think it as important not to presume too readily on the homogeneity of the sacred within the poet's imagination as to refuse to presume on the profane homogeneity of the world. Yet, after all, we need *some* language other than the jargon of "poise", "health", "paradox", and so on in which to present our responses to a poetry which has already been written and which, as it were, opens out to be responded to in terms other than those we use for our everyday relationships.

I do not think it tendentious to maintain that the religious impulse, as I have broadly defined it, persists in a remarkable and perhaps astonishing way in poetry, so that we may say that, even in a desacralized society like our own, there are some poets who, *as a mode of life*, concern themselves with estimating, defining, and recreating manifestations of the sacred. In fact, in a heavily desacralized society there may be a few poets whose emphasis on this activity will be more intensive and exclusive than it would have been in a society more habitually open to the sacred dimensions of life. Herbert is plainly a religious poet in a sense in which Theodore Roethke is not; his religious poetry is a poetry doctrinal and devotional in a way Roethke would not even aspire to; yet it would not be completely vacuous to say that Roethke's religious concerns are as intense as Herbert's; nor would it be foolish to ask if Herbert's concerns were more exclusive than Roethke's. The question certainly points to the fact that for Roethke, as for other modern poets, religious apprehensions are inseparable from poetry, or, perhaps more accurately, that for him religious apprehension, what we may even call the religious venture, is implicit in the very poetic act. It is in those terms that he participates in the world and in language. To say this is to suggest, in Eliade's terms, that he is not using poetry as a means of forming a personal religion of nature, but that he is, rather, extending and completing in language a contact with the world which is religious in its nature.

Roethke is not alone in this. In fact, we may almost specify a contemporary poetic type by using these terms; although in doing so we are not necessarily specifying a poetic category. And it is interesting that such a concern should persist and take new forms in a historical period of which the following three phenomena seem to be increasingly characteristic.

First, there is the rise of anthropology and comparative religion which, relying on all sorts of technological and procedural aids, open up to scrutiny a great number of cultures in which the similarities, often most surprising, and the dissimilarities of religious experience may be studied. In fact, among certain no doubt restricted groups of people, the evidence made available by these disciplines is sometimes taken as a new kind of proof for the existence of God or, at least, of "the supernatural". It is in this context, which has to do so noticeably with the continuance of poetry, and perhaps of painting, as art forms, that terms like "the sacred" come to be used as aids to description and interpretation. If they are not yet much used in the criticism of poetry in England, that is perhaps a sign of English reluctance either to lead literary criticism outward to conclusions which might be taken as ideological ones or to meddle with forces in life which are better treated with reserve. Nevertheless, the work is being done in fields other than literary criticism, and unless poetry becomes as desacralized as society has become, it may come to be found necessary in literary criticism also.

Second, there is the remarkable and accelerating debate among Christians about the relevance of a concept of the supernatural, the misleading nature of the word "religious" in dealing with Christianity, and the relation of the sacred with the secular. On the one hand we have Bonhoeffer's famous talk about a "religionless Christianity", which is coming to be more and more echoed in all the Christian communions. My own habits of mind are such that I find the reference unintelligible; but at any rate the fact that the term was coined at all suggests that many people within those communions find the religious pressures of Christianity so strong that a special formula has to be used to repel them.

Then too we have attempt after attempt to dissociate Christianity from any notion of the numinous to be found in non-human nature and from any identifiable sense of the sacred. The debate about this matter is already under way, in England as elsewhere. We find books like Ronald Gregor Smith's *Secular Christianity* and Harvey E. Cox's *The Secular City*, whose tendency is clearly enough suggested by their titles, in effect opposed by Brian Wicker's *Culture and Theology*, in which the author argues for the importance of the sacred and for ways of re-establishing and recreating it not simply as a concept but as a mode of participation in the world. On the one side, the basic image of life is that of the atomised individual cleaving in faith to an absent God, or that of the modern city, not organic-seeming like (say) Florence or Dublin but so formalised and institutionalised as to seem to constitute its own world; on the other side, the basic image is that of a non-human world and a human community being remade towards some state which is seen as a final one and so as having, even in the present, a character which can only be called eschatological. Christian commentators are coming increasingly to suggest that the Incarnation has, so to speak, assimilated God to the historical process, so that there is no world outside history which can be the object of religious aspiration; but this notion, so variously approached, has not yet been subjected to the analysis which would reveal its implications. We find also the insistence, by now associated with the name of Bishop John Robinson, that to "demythologise" Christianity involves de-supernaturalising it in accordance with the demands of a de-supernaturalised world. So there is the widespread phenomenon of a religious faith which is wary of words like "religion" and a Christianity which asks nothing better than to dispense with concepts of the sacred and of transcendence.

Third, arising out of the facts of the world in which they live, there are poets who wonder whether poetry is an atavistic survival, in certain types of psychic structure, which it would be as well to dispense with as soon as possible. A mode of life which is no more than a prolonged acting-out of a regressive syndrome is not only uncomfortable to its first victim, the poet, but confusing to its other victims, his readers. I have had the matter put to me in just these terms – by a poet, of course – and, like many other poets, I have wondered the same thing myself. Yet it is this very wondering that may be the fantasy. And poetry persists, is resorted to for a variety of purposes by an astonishing number of people in our soicety. Given its difficulty, its persistence is most suggestive. It might be thought, for example, that the very self-doubt of the poet is a testimony to, if not a proof of, his almost unwillingly persistent commitment to the writing of poetry as a sacred act and an aspiration to self-completion.

For poetry is an art and act which combines the forming of a verbal statement with the completion of a rhythmic movement both on the page and from within the psyche; and it usually does so by heightening imagined or observed particulars to the condition where they have a force as symbols. If this art and act are atavistic, they are also surprisingly difficult and complex. In fact, they serve something of the purpose of a sacralising act; they are resorted to in order to set aside certain experiences or places or people or memories as representatively revealing ones – in however attenuated a form, sacred ones. That some of the people for whom the making of these acts is in effect a mode of life often wonder about their efficacy is a sign not of the weakness but of the strength with which they inhabit their modes of thought and feeling. It is particularly paradoxical that this should be so during the years when the religious "believers" are trying to "purify" their faith of all such habits.

NOTES

1. *Poetry and Religion* (New York, 1900), p. v.
2. Quoted by Fairchild, Vol. II, p. 280.
3. *The Poet and His Faith* (Chicago, 1965), p. 2.
4. *Patterns in Comparative Religion*, Meridian edition (Cleveland and New York, 1963), p. xiv.
5. *Selected Essays* (London, 1932), p. 390.
6. *The Cave and the Spring* (Adelaide, 1965), p. 14.
7. *Ibid.*, p. 15.
8. *Ibid.*, p. 16.
9. *Political Tracts of Wordsworth, Coleridge, Shelley*, edited by R. J. White, p. 25.
10. *The Sacred and the Profane:* Harper Torchbook Edition (New York, 1961), p. 8.
11. *Ibid.*, p. 9.
12. *Ibid.*, p. 10.
13. *Ibid.*, p. 11.
14. *Patterns in Comparative Religion, op. cit.*, p. xiv.
15. *Ibid.*, p. 11.
16. *The Sacred and the Profane, op. cit.*, p. 11.
17. *Patterns in Comparative Religion, op. cit.*, p. 26.
18. *Ibid.*, p. 29.
19. A distinction which Eliade himself never seems clearly to make, though his analysis requires it.
20. *Patterns in Comparative Religion*, p. xiii.
21. *Ibid.*, p. 13.
22. *The Sacred and the Profane, op. cit.*, p. 118.

4

VOICE AS SUMMONS FOR BELIEF: LITERATURE, FAITH, AND THE DIVIDED SELF

Walter J. Ong, S.J.

Walter J. Ong, S.J. is Professor of English at St Louis University. Among his many publications are Frontiers in American Catholicism *(1957),* Ramus: Method, and the Decay of Dialogue *(1958),* In the Human Grain *(1967), and* The Presence of the Word *(1967). The present essay is reprinted with permission of the Macmillan Company from* The Barbarian Within *(1962), by Walter J. Ong. Copyright 1954, 1955, 1956, 1958, 1959, 1960, 1961, 1962, by Walter J. Ong.*

Memory believes before knowing remembers. Believes longer than recollects, longer than knowing even wonders.

William Faulkner, *Light in August*

Everything that we believe, we believe either through sight or through hearing. Sight is often deceived, hearing serves as guaranty.

St Ambrose, *Commentary on St Luke*, Book IV, Chap. v.

A Presence is never mute.

Pierre Teilhard de Chardin, S.J., private notes.

I

Any discussion of literature and belief must at some point enter into the mystery of voice and words. In a sense every one of man's works is a word. For everything that man makes manifests his thought. A dwelling or a spear tip communicates even when communication is not particularly intended. A building or a tool, we say, "shows" thought. In this, it is a kind of word, a saying of what is in one's mind.

In the fine arts, communication is even more intense, for the *raison d'être* of works of the fine arts is some sort of communication. As a "word," a painting may be polysemous and mysterious. Yet it remains something that some person has projected outside himself and made accessible to others. It externalizes something conceived within the artist – although not fully conceived, indeed, until it was in some way externalized – in order that this something may be assimilated into another or others, or at least may be available for such assimilation.

In this a painting is both like and unlike a word. For, if a word is an externalization, it is not so external as this. A word can live only while actually issuing from the interior, physical and psychic, of the living individual. As soon as it has passed to the exterior, it perishes. Returning toward its speaker, a word is not a word, but only an echo. "Words, after speech, reach/Into the silence." No spoken word can exist in its entirety all at once, but only bit by bit.

On the other hand, in so far as words are formed within us, they are destined for externalization. One might conjecture about intelligences with ineffable private words which remain forever media of interior contemplation and cannot be projected to the exterior. But the fact is that our natural interior words or concepts are not of this sort. If we can conceive a thought within ourselves, it is the sort of thing our fellows – the more perceptive ones, anyhow – can enter into. If we can think it, others can, too. Depth analysis has made it more evident than ever that there is no private language, even of inarticulate symbols. In so far as we speak to ourselves in any way, others are capable of sharing our thoughts. To conceive something interiorly is to process it for externalization.

If a painting is in some sense a human word, an exterior saying of something conceived interiorly, much more is a work of literature a word. For it is not only, as a totality, a word, but the stuff of which it is compounded is words. The canvas and oils and ground clays and salts with which a painter works are not of themselves means of expression, although they can be made so. But the words with which a speaker or writer works are themselves means of expression, and, no matter what we do with them, this they must remain.

This fact, banal enough in itself, is occluded by our present tendency to think of literary works as objects. Under one of their aspects, they are objects, of course. As a painting or sculpture or even a dwelling, while essentially an object, is also in a more subtle sense a word, so a literary work, while consisting of words and being in its own totality a word, is also in a more subtle sense an object. But it is well to remind ourselves how subtle this sense really is. Would an illiterate society, where verbal expression could be given no vicarious existence in space through writing or printing, be able to think easily of songs or orations as objects?

In a society where the only known word is the pure, evanescent spoken word it is easier to think of objects as words than it is to think of words as objects. This is the mentality revealed in the Old Testament and even in the New. It is the mentality of the primitive peoples studied by Benjamin Lee Whorf and others. Even in John Donne's day, when typography was established but had not laid so tight a hold on society as it has in the days of neoscholasticism and the New Criticism, a poem, circulated in manuscript, was associated with rhetoric rather than with an artifact. Literature was expression. "The play's the thing," says Hamlet. But it is not a "thing" in the sense of an object. It is a "thing" to move the "conscience of the king." Moving or persuading was one of the offices of rhetoric.

II

When we say a literary work is a "word," we mean that it is some thing which is said or spoken. In our typographical culture, of course, this saying or speaking must be understood in a special sense. For in such a culture the great bulk of literary production never finds its way out of the silence of the manuscript or the printed page. Probably the only persons who actually pronounce aloud the words of novels or of most poems written today are proof-readers, whose experience while reading proof, whatever else it may be, is hardly literary; and, alas, most of what is written never gets so far as the proof-reading stage. Nevertheless, in an acceptable sense silent writing is a form of speaking, as silent reading is a form of hearing.

Speaking and hearing are not simple operations. Each exhibits a dialectical structure which mirrors the mysterious depths of man's psyche. As he composes his thoughts in words, a speaker or writer hears these words echoing within himself and thereby follows his own thought, as though he were another person. Conversely, a hearer or reader repeats within himself the words he hears and thereby understands them, as though he were himself two individuals. This double and interlocking dialectic, so beautifully described by Louis Lavelle in *La parole et l'écriture*, provides the matrix for human communication. The speaker listens while the hearer speaks.

The fact that the speaker listens to himself and the hearer speaks to himself shows that communication is not effected between individuals related to each other as we might imagine a broadcasting station and a receiving set to be. In wireless transmission there is a center of emission and a center of reception, one active, the other passive, and there is movement of impulses from one to the other. Because it has this simple structure, broadcasting is not at all communication in the human sense. It is an aid, a tool of communication. In the human situation, matters are quite different. The center of emission is a kind of receiving center, too, and cannot emit its words properly unless it is at the same time receiving them. Similarly, the receiving center has to be a kind of center of emission, for it receives its words by imagining them as emitted. One consequence of this is that it is fallacious to imagine that words are capable of being reduced to impulses.

Every human word implies not only the existence – at least in the imagination – of another to whom the word is uttered, but it also implies that the speaker has a kind of otherness within himself. He participates in the other to whom he speaks, and it is this underlying participation which makes communication possible. The human speaker can speak to the other precisely because he himself is not purely self, but is somehow also other. His own "I" is haunted by the shadow of a "thou" which it itself casts and which it can never exorcise. In *The Secret Sharer*, that strangely existentialist story from a pre-existentialist age, Conrad's hero is painfully aware that the refugee from justice whom he has secreted on board his ship is his double, a symbol of his own interior division and of his alienation from himself. The stranger-double is somehow there in the captain's own cabin because the captain himself feels himself a stranger on his own ship, and this because he is a stranger to himself in his own soul. The same double is party to the captain's conversations with other men. When a visitor from another ship, come aboard to look for the refugee, speaks too low, the captain explains, "*As . . . I wanted my double* [concealed in the cabin] *to hear every word*, I hit upon the notion of informing him [the visitor] that I regretted to say that *I was hard of hearing*" (italics added). It was essential that the double participate secretly in the conversation. But to effect this participation, the captain had to attest a deficiency in his own powers of communication.

Conrad's profoundly symbolic tale is a kind of allegory of human existence. It reveals a rift, a limitation inside our own beings, but a rift which opens its own way to salvation – for it is a rift which comes from our bearing vicariously within ourselves the other with whom we must commune, and who must commune with us, too, and thereby compensate for the rift, the limitation, in our persons. The other within must hear all, for he already knows all, and only if this other, this *thou*, hears, will *I* become comprehensible to myself.

A literary work can never get itself entirely dissociated from this I-thou situation and the personal involvement which it implies. For a literary work to exist in the truest sense, it does not suffice that there be code marks, which we know as letters, printed on paper. A drawing can exist on paper, in space, in a way in which a literary work cannot. A drawing can be assimilated in an instant, at a glance. For a literary work to be what it really is, words must move in sequence, one after another, in someone's consciousness. The work must be read or heard, re-created in terms of communication touching an existent person or persons over a stretch of time.

The manner of this literary communication is, of course, complicated in the extreme. As compared with real dialogue between two persons, a literary performance – a story or a poem or a play – has a special objective quality, signalized by the fact that the author himself stands outside the work, as Shakespeare's own person stands outside his plays. In this way the literary work is like a drawing. It is in a sense something that the author has extruded and thereupon left. This same impression is not given by the words spoken in a personal conversation in which persons find themselves actually involved through the process of daily living. The words in such conversation are less exteriorized.

The symbol of the exteriority of a literary creation is the mask, for in such a creation the author does not communicate directly but through a kind of covering or disguise, fictitious persons or characters, who are more or less in evidence and who speak his works. As T. S. Eliot remarks, poetry "is not the expression of personality, but an escape from personality." A literary work is a sign of special alienation, for wherever we have literary creation some sort of mask inevitably appears. In *The Sound and the Fury* Faulkner nowhere emerges as Faulkner in the way he does in his Nobel Prize speech. The bard who sings the ballad is not the same person who sits down to eat afterwards. The courier who brings news by word of mouth is. The orator, being partly creative, both is and is not the same.

In the case of the drama, the communication is still more complicated by another echelon of persons coming between the writer and his audience, the actors themselves. Actors are real persons, but they perform not as the persons they are, but as persons they are not. They have at times worn masks, to show that they are not themselves, but something other. Yet, is it not highly indicative that the word for mask, *persona* (that-through-which-the-sound-comes), has given both to the ancients and to us the word for person? It is as though this ability to take on the rôle of another shows the actor's own humanity, shows that the other is already within him, and is, indeed, the shadow of his most real self. Ortega y Gasset points out that the brute animal is pure *alteración*, pure "otheration," in the sense that he cannot enter into himself. Man is not pure "otheration," because he can enter into himself – and yet, by the same token, he can find in himself and recognize by contrast the echoes of the personal other, the "thou," the alienation or *alteración* which is there. Thus acting a rôle, realizing in a specially intense way one's identity (in a sense) with a someone who (in another sense) one is not, remains one of the most human things a man can do. No brute animal can act a rôle. Unable to recognize himself, he finds it impossible to recognize what by contrast with self is other. By the same token, he has nothing against which to set a rôle so that it is a rôle.

III

Voice is the foundation for rôle-playing among men in the sense that the use of voice and its understanding, as we have seen, forces man to enter into others. From this point of view, it is not strange that as literature develops in the course of history, rôles become more manifold and more complex. Homer's Odysseus plays a great many rôles, but how many more are played, and played designedly, by the modern Ulysses, Leopold Bloom? And how many more, still, are played by the voice whom the reader hears – it does not matter here whether or not he knows that the work is by James Joyce – narrating the story *Ulysses*? Over and beyond all the other rôles in which it is involved (those of Bloom and all the other characters) is the voice playing the rôle of mocker, making fun of itself?

Whatever the answer, a rôle cannot exist outside a context of belief, and it is my purpose here to discuss how it is that, since voice demands rôle-playing, taking the part of the other within who is not ourselves, it demands belief as well, and how it is that belief is thus not something superadded to communication and thought, but something endemic to all human thinking, so that the question of belief and literature is really a specific variant of the general question concerning belief and communication in general, and ultimately concerning belief and human thought itself. All human intellectual activity implies belief because it implies faith in the possibility of communication and faith in someone with whom we can communicate.

Here one must make the well known distinction between belief as opinion and belief as faith. Essentially, as Gabriel Marcel points out, belief as opinion is belief *that* and faces toward what it is concerned with as toward an object or "thing" or "fact" (a truth considered as thing), as when I say, "I believe that tomorrow will be rainy," or "I believe that this book would sell well." Belief as faith, on the other hand, is belief *in* and faces toward a person or persons, as when I say, "I believe in Matthew," or "I believe in God." Belief as opinion is impersonal and should be impersonal, for its whole rationale is its "objectivity." Even if it is concerned with a person, it treats the person "objectively," not as someone to commune with but as an object to be measured. Thus, "I believe that Matthew is a competent reporter." Belief as faith, on the contrary, is personal in cast, and must be.

However, despite these contrasts between opinion and faith, it is no accident that the term "belief" is used for both, since opinion and faith are indissolubly related by the commerce they carry on with each other. Thus, although belief as faith basically is belief *in* a person, it is also possible to believe *in* a thing or an object by giving it a personalist cast. Thus, "I believe *in* this book" erects the book into more than object. It makes of it a cause, with all the personal issues which this involves. It throws down the gauntlet on behalf of the author, whereas "I believe that this book would sell well" does not necessarily do so. Conversely, to believe *in* a person (belief as faith) involves a certain belief *that* what he says (in so far as he understands and controls it) is true.

Moreover, it appears that any belief *in* (belief as faith) not only is directed toward a person but also involves in one way or another his truthfulness, his "word." This is shown in part by the fact that one cannot believe in a liar as a pure liar (if such a man can exist). But something more profound than this negative example is involved. For belief in a person is ultimately an invitation to the person to respond. As Gabriel Marcel has pointed out in *The Mystery of Being*, belief in a person may include all sort of beliefs *that* varying from mere conjectural opinion (thus I believe that my friend will act considerately) to the acceptance of the truth of something of which I do not have direct knowledge (thus belief in God includes the acceptance of the existence of God as a truth, belief *that* God exists). But belief in a person includes also much more than this. To believe *in* God is to look for a response from Him. The construction of our expression and thinking with the term "in" – a construction found in many languages other than English – is significant here. It suggests that somehow in believing *in* someone, we enter into him. He is not merely an "object" of belief with whom our belief terminates. He is an interiority into whom our belief penetrates and with whom it enables us to commune. The expression suggests the same interpretation of I and thou which, we have seen, underlies all human communication.

This brings home to us the fact that all communication – and, indeed, all our thinking, which is learned and developed only through communication with others – goes on in a context of belief.

For when we speak, we invite response. If I expect no response, no Yes, no No, no riposte of any sort, at least internal, I do not normally speak at all – unless I am losing hold on myself, am distraught, or am not in my right mind. Now, any expectation of response is in some way a declaration of belief in the person or persons to whom I address myself. It is recognition of a presence to whose word I can, in turn, attend, and in whom I can thus believe through the acceptance of what he has to say.

Since belief, either as opinion or as faith, includes some sort of acceptance or commitment without full "objective" evidence, belief as faith, or belief *in*, surpasses belief as opinion, or belief *that*. Belief as opinion moves toward knowledge of objects, but, since it has not sufficient contact with objects to amount to full knowledge, it is essentially deficient and vulnerable. Belief as faith moves toward knowledge and love of persons, and since persons cannot be known as objects at all, no matter how intimately they are seized, the lack of "objective" evidence here is not the liability that it is in the case of belief as opinion.

This situation can be restated in terms of the way in which belief as opinion and belief as faith differ with regard to their relationship to words. Belief as opinion tends to do away with words in so far as it is ordered to "objective" knowledge, which has to do with things which do not speak. Belief as faith, on the other hand, since it has to do with persons, tends not to eliminate words but rather dwells in words and feeds on them, since they are manifestations of persons. Furthermore, in so far as communication with persons is better, more human, and, we might add, holier than contact with objects, belief as faith outclasses belief as opinion. Opinion is styled belief because it can be thought of as analogous to belief as faith. But belief as faith is simply belief in its purest form. For, short of direct observation, the best contact we can have with objects and "facts" is not opinions about them gleaned from imperfect evidence but faith regarding them – that is, knowledge derived from our acceptance of the word of other persons who have this knowledge by direct observation.

Of the knowledge which individual men have today, almost all of it is grounded in faith. The knowledge of scientists themselves is almost all grounded in faith, well founded and rational faith in the reports of their fellow scientists, but faith nevertheless. Of the scientific knowledge which any man has, only a tiny fraction has been achieved by his own direct observation. For the rest, he has good reason to believe *that* it is true because, within the limits of their competence, he believes *in* his fellow scientists reporting on their work or reporting reports of the work of others. Thus, even in the most "objective" of fields, in actuality the word of persons is more pervasive than factual observation. Science itself cannot live save in a network of belief. Even in science, where fact is more determinative, presence is nevertheless more pervasive than fact.

IV

Against this background, the question of belief in literature can be raised. A survey of current writing in English on this question shows that it is pretty well all concerned with literature as involving belief *that*. The grounds of the question are staked out in terms of Coleridge's "willing suspension of disbelief," so that the problem becomes, as in Richards' *Practical Criticism*, How can one who does not share Donne's Christian faith enter into his sonnet "At the Round Earth's Imagined Corners Blow"? Or, to adapt Richards's terminology, How can one share Donne's beliefs emotionally while not sharing them intellectually?

This focus of the question of belief in literature is legitimate. However, we must remember that it considers belief as concerned with a kind of object or "thing," excised from any personal context. The notion of response to a presence, manifested by voice, drops out entirely, although such response seems intimately a part of literature. Objects cannot elicit response to a voice in the way in which persons can, and when we treat belief in terms of the object of belief exclusively, response becomes attenuated to behavior, and its correlative is not voice but stimulus in the Pavlovian pattern of stimulus-response. It is significant that Professor Richards not only concerns himself with "willing suspension of disbelief" but also, perhaps not entirely out of line with Coleridge's thinking even here, regularly discusses literature in terms of the way words "behave," as though words were not cries but "things," visible objects. We have a right, of course, to speak of words in terms of this analogy, but let us not forget that it is an analogy.

Without attempting to deal with the question of belief on these grounds, I should like to set it up on other grounds and to examine it there, not with a view to providing utterly conclusive answers but to improve our perspectives and to reveal how limited some of our common views of this problem really are. Let us recall that in the last analysis, any utterance, even a scientific utterance, is the manifestation of a presence, which cannot be "grasped" as an "objective" of knowledge can be, but only invoked or evoked. The most abstruse mathematical theorem remains always and inextricably within this framework of utterance, for it originated as something communicable and remains always something which someone *says* to others or, in special cases, to himself. But, since in the case of scientific utterance the vocal element is minimized, we can treat such utterance readily as an object and speak with ease of "grasping" or "not grasping" it, as we might an object. Thus, we grasp or we do not grasp the meaning of the formula $E = mc^2$. But we know how difficult and unconvincing it is to apply the notion of "grasp" to a poetic work. The notion can, of course, be applied to some extent. We can speak of "grasping" *Hamlet* or *The Marriage of Heaven and Hell* or *Absalom, Absalom!* But so to speak is not very satisfactory, not convincing. It seems much more real to speak of the response which these works evoke from us. The "evocative" quality – which is to say, the "calling" quality – is paramount in a work of real literature. Literature exists in a context of one presence calling to another.

This is a context of faith, no matter how much there may be in an individual work which, outside the work, we can know by direct evidence. Indeed, here faith achieves a special intensity (and simultaneously a special attenuation) in so far as the voice which invokes us as present and evokes our response is in a way more a pure or self-subsistent voice because of the "objective" quality of the literary work as such, its detachment from the poet, who as an individual is disassociated from the work by his literary mask. There is a special kind of dialectic at work here. In so far as the work is objectified, set apart from the existent writer who gives it being as a kind of well wrought urn is detached from its creator, its evocative effect becomes more poignant. Thus Yeats went to the Japanese Nō plays for "more formal faces," explaining that "a mask [even taken metaphorically] . . . no matter how close you go is still a work of art." Joyce's progress from *Stephen Hero* through *A Portrait of the Artist* to *Ulysses* and *Finnegans Wake* is progress from personal involvement to artistic detachment, and, as the masklike detachment grows, the evocative quality of the work, its pull on the sensibilities of the reader, grows. Because Poe can never achieve so great a detachment, because his personal problems and neuroses show through – to those, at any rate, for whom Poe's English is their native language, as it was not for Baudelaire and Mallarmé – the evocative quality of his work remains less poignant than that of Joyce or, to take another American, that of Faulkner.

We might ask why this is. If voice is an invitation to response, in what sense can the invitation become more insistent when the speaker wears a mask? To see what is involved in this question, one must consider the peculiar conditions of person-to-person communication, which is implemented by the use of voice. Human persons are of themselves distant from one another in the sense that they cannot enter entirely into one another's consciousness. The sense of distance attending on personal or I-thou relationships has been elaborated by recent writers such as Lavelle, Heidegger, and Buber, but once it is stated it needs no great explanation, for we live with this sense all the time. In dealing with another person, I am always dealing with one whom I cannot entirely fathom and with whom I cannot enter into direct communication quite like the communication I enter into with myself. His sense of self remains outside my direct awareness, and yet I can feel its aura and know that there is some interiority with whom I am dealing.

My contact with this interiority is mediated by exterior phenomena which implement commerce between interiors. This commerce is most readily maintained by voice. Voice is the least exterior of sensible phenomena because it emanates not only from the physical but also from the divided psychological interior of man and penetrates to another physical and psychological interior where, as we have seen, it must be re-created in the imagination in order to live. Unlike a picture, it lives by its contact with these interiors – when they are gone, it is gone.

Still, for all this interior orientation, even a voice is an exterior something. It achieves its effect through an exterior medium. Our way of hearkening to one another, and thus our sense of presence, necessitates a kind of breakthrough. We penetrate into a "thou" through a something which is neither "I" nor "thou," through a medium over which the acting emanating from one person exercises an effect on another. Even direct physical contact involves an externalizing medium, for our body is, in a sense, not so much ourself as is our consciousness. Even in its interior, our body is somehow the "outside" of us.

The exteriority attendant on communication is what gives point to the mask in dramatic performance and, analogically, in all literature. Although it modifies the presence which manifests itself most poignantly in voice, of itself the mask is not vocal, but a medium manifest in space. It does not modify the voice of the character (presence, person) as the mute modifies the sound on a violin. Even though masks may occasionally affect voice projection, to do so is not the mask's primary function, for it is patently objectified as a visual phenomenon and produces its characteristic effects by being seen. It stands for that in the person-to-person situation which is non-vocal, non-communicative, non-personal, remote, alienated.

In the preliterate world, where the eye is especially subservient to the ear, masks themselves are felt as belonging rather more to the world of voice than they are today, or perhaps are caught up more thoroughly into the world of voice, and aesthetic distance tends to disappear. For the Wintu, Dorothy Lee has noted, Coyote, Buzzard, and Grizzly Bear are bewilderingly man-and-animal. Although the wearer of a wolf mask among primitives is not a wolf, he somehow really participates in wolfness. In this situation, where the object-world is not clearly differentiated from the world of voice and person, belief has not the depth of meaning it enjoys in a civilized society, for the same reason that science itself has not: the two are confounded with each other, for the dialectic which sets them apart with some precision has not yet sufficiently progressed.

This seems to have been the state of affairs with the very early Greeks in their ritualistic use of masks. Later, with the great tragedians, real characters appear, and the masks worn become devices establishing aesthetic distance, *alteración*, limited more definitely to the universe of space. For space separates; whereas voice unites. As this evolution takes place, the number and complexities of roles, and of literary forms, proliferate. The means of controlling and differentiating characters and forms have been developed as the tension between the vocal and the visual grows. For this tension the mask is the symbol, or in a later day costume and make-up, a mitigated form of mask.

As the tension between visual and vocal grows, and with it the use of the truly dramatic character and the formalized separation of drama from life, there grows also, paradoxically, an awareness of the foundation in real human existence for dramatic character. A character in a drama is a person set off, advertised as other. Yet this state of being-set-off, this remoteness in the midst of intimacy, is found in real life, too, and experience of drama teaches us to recognize the fact. Each man is always in some degree a mask to other men, more consciously so today because of the progressive reflectiveness which mankind develops in its passage through history.

The sense of being-set-off is not annihilated by intimacy. Indeed, it is heightened and realized in its fullness through intimacy because of the very interiority which makes possible intimacy between persons. As a unique and induplicable individual abiding in the depths of your own interior consciousness, you are in a way more other to me than even inanimate objects are; and this despite the fact that I can carry on a diaglogue with you and cannot carry on a dialogue with inanimate objects. For in assuring me of my closeness to your consciousness, this dialogue assures me also of the uniqueness of your consciousness and of its ultimate inviolability – of the fact that, naturally speaking, I can never know what it is to be you, can never share this ultimate experience of yourself with you. Of course, I cannot know what it is to be an object either – a rosebush or a canary – but neither can the object know what it is to be itself, so that this lack of knowledge on my part does not prevent a quite full knowledge of the object. Object-being includes no experience of self to be shared. What uniqueness the object has is reflected from the outside. In the case of a person, however, his experience of his unique self is constitutive of his most intimate self. Yet it is this very experience that intimacy cannot share.

V

These considerations throw some light on what happens to the personal charge carried by a voice in the case of a work of literature – of poetry, let us say, to take a relatively pure instance of literature. In a poem, the voice is there, but "objectified" in such a way as to mask the real person who uttered it in the first place and any other real person who utters it after him. A poem thus advertises the distance and remoteness which, paradoxically, are part of every human attempt to communicate, and it does this in so far as it is under one aspect "objective," an "objective correlative," objectlike, which is to say, non-vocal. But under a certain aspect only, for under another it is not objectlike since it is attempting to communicate very hard indeed.

Given the effective drive toward communication, the more the remoteness between the voice which, working within this drive, really creates the poem (that is, the voice of the writer) and those who hear or read it, the more evocative the work becomes. The drama is the most evocative and personal of all literary forms. In it living persons on a real stage really speak to one another; and yet, here the remoteness between point of origin and point of assimilation has actually been increased because the number of masks has been increased; in a performance of *Othello*, besides the mask or masks which Shakespeare as author wears, there is the mask of a character which each performer wears and which makes him precisely a *dramatis persona*, a person or mask in the drama. The reason for the corresponding heightening of effect seems to be the fact that all communication takes place across barriers, or is an attempt to crash through barriers, namely, the barriers which bar the ultimate compenetration of the "I" and the "thou." Provided that communication is going on, the interposition of further barriers has a tantalizing effect. It teases us to more vigorous attempts, sharper alertness, greater efforts at compassion or sympathy. One thinks of the poignancy achieved by the device of the wall in the story of Pyramus and Thisbe.

But certain other parallels might be adduced to show the intensification of the personal charge by the interposition of a mask or other barrier. A major one is in the religious history of Judaism and Christianity, where, moreover, the connection becomes evident between person and mask on the one hand and faith on the other. Compared with Aristotle, who thought it impossible that God should concern Himself at all with human affairs, Hebrews and Christians know God in a highly personal fashion. Yet they know Him by faith, which is in a kind of mask, "through a glass darkly." Moreover, in the Christian dispensation God reveals Himself more personally to man when the Second Person of the Trinity, whose personal name is the Word as well as the Son, takes to Himself a human nature which masks His divinity. His passion, where even His human nature is seen through the mask of death, is memorialized in the Eucharist, where the human and divine natures of the Word are both masked under the appearances of bread and wine, which also, by symbolic separation of His Body and Blood, masks His human death itself. But this "masking" only heightens the personal relationship between God and man, for through the Eucharist the personal union of Christians in the Person of Christ and thence in the other two Persons of the Godhead is realized and perpetuated. Although not applied to what we are discussing here, this sense of the Eucharist is highly operative in Christian tradition. It accounts for a favorite name of the Eucharist, Holy Communion, that is, Holy Togetherness. Its implications are elaborated by St Thomas Aquinas and other theologians, who point out, moreover, that the consecration of the elements in this sacrament of sacraments is effected not by any sign in space, but by *words* given us by the Word of God. The whole setting for this series of masks is one of communication of the most personal sort, in a universe of words and of faith, where sight is always at one or more removes from full reality.

VI

The masks in literature are generally assumed by one party to communication rather than by both. The playwright and the actors, who are the communicators, assume the masks – the playwright a metaphorical one and the actors real ones or their equivalent in costume and make-up. By contrast, the hearer is present in his own person. Were he to put on a mask, he would become a part of the play, a *dramatis persona*. As it is, although the actors and the play may enrapture him, carry him somewhat out of himself, they do not make him into a quasi-other person. The act on his part which corresponds to the masking on the part of the communicators is simply his act of belief, in the sense of faith; and belief here is not at all tantamount to opinion. One has no "opinion" that Sir Laurence Olivier is Hamlet, and no "opinion" that Ophelia's death is real. Belief *that* is relatively meaningless here. This belief is more radically belief *in*, and such belief is not pretended.

But belief in whom? In whoever are the persons behind the masks. In the actors and the playwright all together. The act of faith, or belief *in* is an invitation to them to respond as persons, to give themselves in and through truth. While there is also a certain faith in the audience which playwright and actors both have, a belief *in* the audience, an invitation to the audience to respond – for this faith, as we have seen, accompanies all human communication – nevertheless this faith of the playwright and the actors is less obviously faith than that of the audience. The reason is the curious one-way nature of artistic communication, the fact that no real dialogue takes place, that the audience itself has no occasion or opportunity to speak. The audience's response is hidden, as the act of faith on the part of the playwright and actors is correspondingly hidden. The response of the playwright and actors, on the other hand, to the audience's faith is the play itself, which is far from hidden since the audience's act of faith is quite obvious.

In response to the audience's act of faith the playwright and the actors give themselves in and through truth. How the truth is contained in the words of the play – or, *mutatis mutandis*, in the poem or other pieces of literature – and, indeed, what the truth in question really is, may be a very mysterious matter. This is to be expected. The truths arrived at by faith, natural as well as supernatural, are not noted for readily admitting of clear-cut statement or of clear-cut assimilation nor for being entirely evident to everyone, even to those of good will. They often submit reluctantly or not at all to full articulation, for they have to do most intimately with persons to whom we address ourselves. If they are neatly articulated, they are taken not on their own evidence but on the evidence of a person to whom we address our act of faith; and it is hard to articulate a person. For a person whom we are addressing nature provides us no distinctive word while we are addressing him save the strange noun-substitute or name-substitute or pro-noun "thou," which is not a name at all but changes its entire meaning with each different person we apply it to.

Our belief in a play or a poem is thus an invitation to the persons involved in composing it and presenting it to us either to say something worth our while or to betray our trust in them as persons. It involves a kind of openness to them and to their meaning at all levels, to what Professor Philip Wheelwright in *The Burning Fountain* styles "depth experience." If certain details of a poem seem unacceptable to us in terms of belief *that*, the voice of the poem, coming through the mask of its speaker (as well as through the masks of any characters he may have introduced) teases us on, so that beneath any disagreement with detail there persists the conviction that something worthy of assent is being said, into which the otherwise unacceptable detail may somehow be fitted. If we cannot believe in Prospero as a real magician, we can believe that the playwright is using him to convey some further word or truth to us.

In *La parole et l'écriture* Louis Lavelle makes much of the "world" as language. For communication to be possible there must be a world shared by our individual consciences so that by naming the objects in this world we can break through our solitude and communicate with one another. When a child believes that he knows something as soon as he can name it, he is not entirely wrong. For when he can name it, he can use it for what it is worth, as a means of communicating with others. That which is neither you nor I, once it is known, becomes a link uniting you and me. This is true not only of the natural world which we apprehend through our senses, but also of poetry and of literature in general. Poetry is often involved and mysterious, but by its very existence within our ken it is destined to communicate. Indeed, its communication is in one sense communication *par excellence*, the most intimate communication. John Stuart Mill's notion, romantically rooted, that poetry is something which is overheard is a not too happy attempt to deal with the intimacy which poetry can effect: so intimate is the union of hearer and poet that it is as though the hearer as other were not there. The opinion sometimes expressed that poetry or art in general is basically not communicative at all is connected with the dialectical situation in which estrangement (the mask of the poet) and intimacy (achieved when the mask is somehow penetrated) are so strangely compounded.

If a poem is likened to an object in the world, it must be likened to an object already named, processed for purposes of communication, if named with a quite mysterious name. "Poetic truth," which seems so difficult to bring to earth, to isolate, to state clearly, and which is also so strangely intimate, has its roots in a sense of communion with other persons, persons perceived through masks, yet somehow decidedly there, who have believed in us enough to invite us to this uncommonly intimate response and in whom we, in turn, are called on to believe.

We come to the conclusion that any belief *that* involved in literature is subservient to belief *in*, that the most basic meaning of belief in literature has to do not with belief in the sense of opinion, which regards objects and facts (truths treated as objects), but with belief in the sense of faith, which regards person-to-person relationships, invitations and response, and truth with reference to these relationships. This conclusion is, I believe, nowhere more strikingly evident than in the situation which has obtained for some years in twentieth-century poetry. The withdrawal of the serious poet (or of the serious artist generally) has been commented on *ad nauseam*. Withdrawal from what or into what? Into himself, we are told. Yet we are faced with the striking fact that serious readers of poetry today favor no other type of poetry so much as this poetry of withdrawal. The conclusion would seem to be that readers like nothing better than to follow the poet into his retreat. Everybody wants to be alone together; and this is not strange. There is no doubt that in our age, which has evolved, among other things, a mass culture and mass media of communication, intimacy is also in many ways better served than it has ever been before. Certainly the human race is more conscious of itself as a whole and has developed its dialogue about intimacy and communication more than at earlier periods in human history. We have a more highly perfected vocabulary and more advanced means of articulation about this subject than ever before. However aware earlier man may have been of persons and of the "I-thou" situation, the philosophy known as personalism is a twentieth-century creation, just as thoroughly a product of our age as technology or television commercials. In this climate belief *in* becomes very meaningful. In terms of belief as we have viewed it here, the serious modern reader wants to believe in his poets more than ever before. This would seem to indicate that in the age of television voice is in some ways regaining a prestige over sight, that we are at the end of the Gutenberg era.

5

HOLD ON HARD TO THE HUCKLEBERRY BUSHES

R. W. B. Lewis

R. W. B. Lewis is Professor of English and American Studies and Master of Calhoun College at Yale University. He is the author of The American Adam: Innocence, Tragedy, and Tradition in the Nineteenth Century (*1955*), The Picaresque Saint (*1959*), Trials of the Word: Essays in American Literature and the Humanistic Tradition (*1965*), *and* The Poetry of Hart Crane (*1967*); *and he has edited several volumes of critical essays. The following essay was first published in the* Sewanee Review (*Vol. No. 3, Summer, 1959*). *Copyright by The University of the South. Reprinted by permission of the author and the* Sewanee Review.

The search for religious elements in literature, especially in American literature, has become a phenomenon in recent years that would have startled and bewildered Matthew Arnold, who did not have this sort of thing in mind at all. An increasing number of books address themselves to the subject, courses and symposia are given over to it, and I believe a university department or two have been established to make the undertaking permanent. Some of the work, like some of the workers, displays a high degree of cultural relevance; but in general practice the study of "religion and literature," as the phrase usually is, exhibits several rather disturbing oddities, the first of which is implied by the phrase itself. It is theologically correct but aesthetically perilous: in a way which might ultimately damage the theology. Absolutely speaking, as between religion and literature, religion no doubt comes first; but in the actual study of a particular literary text, it probably ought to follow, and follow naturally and organically and without strain – for the sake of the religion as well as the literature. Or so I shall try to suggest. We may perhaps recall the remark made to Emerson by an old Boston lady who, talking about the extreme religious sensibility of an earlier generation, said about those pious folk that "they had to hold on hard to the huckleberry bushes to hinder themselves from being translated." Their instinct was as sound as their impulse was proper.

I

It was characteristic of Emerson to have quoted those words, for he knew well enough that his own hold tended to slip from time to time. He was articulately dedicated to the actual; he embraced, as he said, the common and explored the low and familiar, both in life and in literature. But the Over-Soul drew him like a magnet, and he was regularly prone to premature translation into the vast, un-individuated realm of the One. The atmosphere he found there was invariably sunny and smiling; and it is by stressing the sunshine and disregarding the translatability, that Randall Stewart, in *American Literature and Christian Doctrine*,[1] is able to condemn Emerson to the sixth circle, the place reserved for the burning tombs of the heresiarchs. "Emerson is the arch-heretic of American literature," says Professor Stewart, "and Emersonism [sic: a foreshortening rhetorically equivalent to the phrase Democrat Party] the greatest heresy. By no dint of sophistry can he be brought within the Christian fold. His doctrine is radically anti-Christian, and has done more than any other doctrine to undermine Christian belief in America." There is a kind of health in the hardness of Professor Stewart's saying. But I confess that it has for me a pointless irrelevance which it would not be easy to measure, though it may be important to define.

Professor Stewart's little book is amiably unambiguous in state-ment, and engagingly direct in style; it is sprinkled with nice personal reminiscences of a long and honorable academic life for which many of us have cause to be grateful. The book belongs, in its slender way, to the number of studies which have sought to examine the whole of American literature from a single organizing viewpoint; and in this respect it follows a path opposite to the one followed by Frederick I. Carpenter in *American Literature and the Dream*[2] – a neglected work, in which Emerson appears as the high priest and dream purveyor rather than the arch heretic. But Professor Stewart's title is radically misleading, just as his method is revealingly – one is tempted to say, importantly and usefully – ill advised. By Christian doctrine, Professor Stewart means Protestant doctrine; by Protestant doctrine, he means American Puritan doctrine (in a manner that rather confirms than refutes the contention of the great Protestant historian of dogma, Adolph von Harnack, that there can be no such thing as Protestant dogma); by Puritan doctrine, Professor Stewart means very simply the doctrine of Original Sin; and by the doctrine of Original Sin, it is no longer clear what he means, since the matter has grown too small to be visible. He seems to mean even less, so far as one can make out, than T. E. Hulme meant thirty-five years ago, when he said – in a sentence that has done as much harm to the cause of cultural good sense as any that one can rapidly remember – that "dogmas like that of Original Sin . . . are the closest expression of the categories of the religious attitude." Separated from the rich theological framework within which it historically evolved, the concept of Original Sin is not much of a concept at all; it is more an image of unredeemably depraved human nature shivering somewhere in the void. In any case, this is the image that provides the single instrument by which Professor Stewart gauges the value of American writers from Edwards to the present. By the use of it, he denounces the villains, those who seem unaware of Original Sin (Paine, Franklin, Jefferson, Emerson, Whitman, Dreiser, Lewis), and salvages the elect (Edwards, Hawthorne, Melville maybe, James, Eliot, Hemingway, Faulkner, Warren). But the writings of both heroes and villains suffer a sort of total defeat. The latter are blown into oblivion by the author's rumbling southern rhetoric; and the former are blotted out behind an enormous OS, as Hester Prynne's image was lost behind the gigantic A reflected in the convex surface of the shining armor.

In Professor Stewart's case, the translation was effected before the huckleberry bushes were ever taken hold of. The actualities of the works in question – their actions, their words, their concrete embodiments, their sensuous images, their characters, their incidents – seem to have evaporated before a single glance descended on them. This is the likely consequence of the doctrinal approach to literature. If Professor Stewart had taken a more generous view of Christian doctrine, he might have composed a more interesting book; but I am not sure that it would have been a more pointed and purposeful book, or that it would have done better service to the field of literature or of religion; for the issue of priority would still remain. This issue is whether one scrutinizes literature for its univocal formulations of particular historical doctrines one cherishes or whether one submits for a while to the actual ingredients and the inner movement and growth of a work to see what attitude and insight, including religious attitude and insight, the work itself brings into being. Emerson continues to be a valuable case. Proceeding from Emerson's words as he uttered them, Newton Arvin – who is anything but a sophist, and is on the contrary one of America's most intelligent, tactful, and scholarly critics – has managed to bring Emerson some slight way "within the Christian fold."[3] Emerson, Mr. Arvin says, did after all have a knowledge of evil and an awareness of human sin; his famous cheerfulness was for the most part an achievement, a matter of discipline and hard intellectual choice. But Emerson could not convey his conceptions in the theological vocabulary available to him, because it was not comprehended within that vocabulary; and he was not in command of the vocabulary which could, in fact, convey it. He set it forth in tropes and figures, in shadings and insistences, in asides and repetitions of his own; and he emerged with a view of evil so profoundly different from that of his contemporaries that of sin itself he has seemed to have been simply and blissfully unconscious. For Emerson's sense of the problem was surprisingly similar to the older and more really traditional Christian attitude: the one that held firm from St. Augustine to the Reformation: the view of evil as non-being, as a privation, as a negation and an absence of good. Emerson normally preferred to talk about something rather than nothing, about being rather than non-being and affirmation rather than negation; he lacked the special taste and affection for evil of so many modern intellectuals. But (here I am pushing Mr. Arvin's argument beyond anything he would wish to claim for it) it might be salutary to reflect that, as regards the doctrine of sin, it is Hawthorne who was the heretic and Emerson

who was working toward the restoration rather than the under-
mining of Christian belief in America.

Emerson did not knowingly aim at the restoration of anything:
except of the soul's fresh and immediate perception of certain aspects
of the universe, getting rid of the linguistic and institutional clutter
in which those aspects had gone stale, and relating them anew to the
instant of experience. "They only who build on Ideas, build for
eternity. . . . The law is only a memorandum. We are superstitious,
and esteem the statute somewhat: so much life as it has in the character of living men is its force." That is Emerson's authentic voice, or
one of his authentic voices: the voice of a man disentangling the
Idea from the historical record of it, and allowing it again to invi-
gorate the present. But it is a suggestive and representative accident
that, in pursuit of that aim, Emerson's metaphysical gaze lighted
just occasionally and without historical awareness upon the essences
of certain moral and religious doctrines that had been given their
fullest elaboration in pre-Reformation Christian theology. It is
this essential (or, may one say, essentializing) quality in Emerson
that should dictate the method and scope of any significant religious
inquiry into his writing; and it is this quality that relates him as an
American of his time to his most talented contemporaries.

The same faculty for arriving by mistake at the very heart of some
ancient doctrine, long since smothered by Calvinism, is observable
in the two Henry Jameses, and to a greater or lesser extent in Hawthorne and Poe. The elder James, for example, wrestling in New York
with the secret of Swedenborg, emerged with his own version of the
Augustinian concept of the *felix culpa*, the notion that the fall of
man was a happy and a fortunate event. Not a syllable of James
consciously echoes either St. Augustine or the medieval *Exultet*
which celebrated the fortunate fall; nor was his statement of the idea
(Adam's fall was "an every way upwards step indeed, pregnant with
beatific consequences") buttressed by the traditional theological
scheme that lent some measure of logic to the paradox. But there
he was, driven by his personal intellectual momentum and his
private tropes, at the naked center of the old doctrine. Henry
James, Jr., is a much more complex and awe-inspiring case, deserving
lengthy analysis elsewhere. Here let us say only that either James is a
cultural miracle, or else he had devoured (as seems distinctly im-
probable) almost all of Aristotle, St. Augustine, St. Thomas, St.

Bonaventura, and Dante Alighieri. And as to Poe, his root idea, according to the persuasive essay by Allen Tate,[4] the one idea he did not merely "entertain" but which actually pushed and bedeviled him was the grand old heresy of attributing to human beings the intellect and imagination that God had reserved for the angels. It is a heresy, to be sure, but one form of it was indispensable to the scholastic thinking of the twelfth century, and in particular to St Anselm, of whom Poe is unlikely to have heard. And so on.

The American Protestant analyst, if sufficiently limited in viewpoint, is apt to miss these strange appearances and theological throwbacks. He tends to go at the business wrong way round, looking for unmistakable recurrences of key terms and neglecting the cumulative suggestive power of the terms or images or special private meanings of the individual writers; while the doctrine accidentally echoed or latent in the work inspected may not be a part of the American Protestant stock in trade. Hawthorne tried out *his* version of the fortunate fall by having Kenyon, the sculptor in *The Marble Faun*, broach it to conventionally Protestant Hilda; and "Oh, hush!" she tells him, shrinking away "with an expression of horror," saying that she could weep for him, she is shocked beyond words, his "creed" makes a mockery "of all religious sentiments . . . [and] moral law" – that is, the sentiments and the law drilled into her back in New England. Kenyon hushes.

II

I have probably not escaped, in the preceding few paragraphs, from seeming to honor in Emerson, Hawthorne, and the others their rediscovery of "pieties that are older and more solid than the Puritan ones"; but, much as I respect those older pieties, the pieties of age-old Catholic Christianity, that is not precisely what I am trying to do. It *is* what is attempted in *American Classics Reconsidered*, from which the last quotation above is taken. This book, edited by Harold C. Gardiner, S.J.,[5] brings together essays by ten Roman Catholic writers on the major American men of letters in the early and middle nineteenth century. It is by no means a work of systematic expropriation. The intellectual standards are Catholic ones, and the approach is explicitly theological; but there is a reasonably sustained effort to deal with the writers as writers and as Americans, and very little effort to scold or convert them. "Quite literally, I think," says Michael F. Moloney in a creditable essay on Thoreau, "[Thoreau] went out to Walden Pond to write a book. . . . He went . . . to strike a blow in defense of the poet's right to existence. . . . He must be evaluated primarily as a creative artist rather than as a thinker." Mr. Moloney does so evaluate him; yet it is a sign of a certain uneasiness, as of one who has muddled a little the right order of the goods, that Mr. Moloney's title is "Christian *malgré lui.*" The phrase luckily has almost nothing to do with the essay's content; for if it were Mr. Moloney's intention to Christianize Thoreau despite himself, it would be a serious misdirection of energy. A similar sense of strain is detectable, or seems to me to be, in most of the other essays; and I shall offer some hints about the possible reasons for it, by looking in some detail at the essay by Joseph Schwartz on Hawthorne.

The latter is not necessarily the best contribution to the book. Although the volume is almost inevitably uneven, the level of critical and scholarly accomplishment strikes me as pretty high. The treatments of Longfellow, Poe, Melville, and "the literary historians" are perfunctory, perhaps the writers in question are perfunctory themselves, like Longfellow, or because they have been drained of blood, like Melville, by the interminable critical surgery of the past few decades. (I digress to wonder with a certain anxiety how long the relatively small store of American literature is going to survive the writing about it, and especially the writing about the whole of it. Our production has fallen badly behind our consumption, as Henry James foresaw seventy years ago when he told a summer school on "the novel" at Deerfield, Massachusetts, that "We already talk too much about the novel in proportion to the quantity of it having any importance that we produce.") But the long analysis by Robert C. Pollock of Emerson's "single vision," for example, is a work of genuine scholarly composition; it composes something (a view of reality), and it is about the effort to do so. Mr. Pollock makes good overt use of Charles Feidelson's brilliant *Symbolism and American Literature* to clarify Emerson's long struggle "to free men from the delusion of a split universe, which, as he knew, had reduced human life to a fragmented state." Perhaps, Mr. Pollock presents Emerson as achieving too completely what Emerson only succeeded in aiming at, and when he says that Emerson "steadfastly refused to recognize any split between the higher and lower worlds," he may have chosen the wrong verbal. What Emerson refused was to accept a split that he did recognize; he remains, in fact, America's most knowing and moving portrayer of the failures of connection in human experience – of the appalling lack of context, in modern times, for action and for judgment.

In addition to the chapters on Emerson, Thoreau, and Haw-thorne, several other items in *American Classics Reconsidered* are to be commended. They include Ernest Sandeen's sometimes awkwardly phrased but compassionate and suggestive examina-tion of Whitman ("He must accept even the social and moral out-cast because he himself is an outcast asserting his claim to be accepted"); Alvan S. Ryan's intelligent survey of Orestes Brownson and his dialectical involvement with New England idealism; Charles A. Brady's informed and even loving study of the life and writings of James Fenimore Cooper – in my opinion, the most valuable as well as readable essay in the book, rather unexpected considering not Mr Brady but James Fenimore Cooper, and rising to a poetic evocation of Leather-Stocking as a godlike figure similar to Oberon and Herakles ("Hawkeye and Chingachgook . . . become twin numina, two great *genii loci*, two waiting presences, tutelary deities of the American continent, joining hands in amity over a coil of motives and cross-purposes, the Green Man and the Red Manitou");[6] and Father Gardiner's brief introductory chapter, which establishes the theological perspective and makes up for a debatable salute to Colin Wilson's *The Outsider* by citing the special relevance, for his volume, of Charles Feidelson's book.

Father Gardiner urges, in his introduction, that "modern criticism would do well to minimize somewhat its preoccupation with tech-niques and return to more theological approaches." With that advice, I am personally very largely in agreement, up to what is for me a crucial point. And it should be added, especially on the evi-dence of this volume, that *most* Catholic writers, unlike *some* Protestant writers, are aware that in the theological approach some account must be taken of God. There is an extraordinary contem-porary intellectual reluctance to utter the name of God, or even to allude to God in any definite way at all: a phenomenon peculiarly notable in books and courses on religion and literature. This is a current characteristic of the highest significance, though it does not, I believe, mean that God is dead in the consciousness of the present time (the report of God's death has been very much exaggerated). It means something rather different, my main suggestion about which I shall shortly and belatedly come round to. But in much of the purportedly "religious writing" of the day, God is treated, if at all, in the manner dramatized time and again by Graham Greene (who is, I am aware, a Catholic of sorts) – as a married man's mistress, someone who must never be mentioned openly, is only thought about with a far corner of the mind, and is met briefly and on occasion in dark and hidden places, for illicit reasons. God, in short, is associated primarily with the sometimes titillating modern sense of sin and guilt. Hence it is that the entire range of Christian doctrine can be narrowed down to a belief in Original Sin, and Emerson, who had a more sublime view of the universe and its creator, dismissed as a corruptive influence on young minds and one who made the better cause appear the better. Even certain American forms of Roman Catholicism, I am told, are not always free of this bleak reductive tendency. But Father Gardiner's volume of essays is. When Michael F. Moloney wants to distinguish between Thoreau's humanistic mysticism and that of an authentically Christian religious mystic, he says rightly and flatly, "Man is Thoreau's primary concern, not God"; and Father Gardiner's own list of the great issues that he regards as central to the theological approach includes "the indwelling of God in the soul" as well as "the nature of sin and responsibility and the role of free will in responsibility." It also includes "[God's] Providence and salvific will . . . detachment from created goods, the communion of saints . . . and the real and proper 'divinity of man.' "

Those terms (especially "salvific," which I had to look up, and which means "tending to save" and is listed as obsolete) are not ones that an outsider in the non-Wilsonian sense can feel very easy with. But that they partake of a comprehensive and unmistakably theological vocabulary is hardly open to doubt. What is open to doubt is not the value of a theological approach to literature, but the value of approaching this particular body of literature with any set of terms and doctrines that has been fully and finally elaborated, historically, once and for all. That is just the question perhaps unwittingly pushed into prominence by Joseph Schwartz, in his essay on Hawthorne: an essay in this case appropriately titled "God and Man in New England."

Mr Schwartz begins with the proposition that "the history of literature has been an attempt to put such abstractions ["free will, the natural desire for God, fatalism, and providence"] into concrete statements for the benefit of mankind"; and hence that it is proper to seek out in Hawthorne his concept of "the moral and religious character of man." The crux of the problem may be right there. Mr Schwartz's principle runs counter, of course, to the most influential critical convictions and prejudices of the past few decades, according to which literature does not "put abstractions into concrete statement," but, rather, generates a special kind of idea by the special processes of the creative imagination. The basis of those critical convictions has been the observation that modern literature, at least, can be shown to be doing just that: which has led to the suspicion that maybe the greatest literature in all ages has been up to the same poetic business. Hawthorne is an uncommonly tangled and contradictory case. From time to time, he most certainly did put abstractions into concrete form, and his notebooks let us watch him as he does so. But at other moments, he seems rather to have begun with a particular image or incident and to have allowed it to expand in his mind till it reached its maximum suggestiveness.[7] Similarly, while the conclusion of "The Artist of the Beautiful," published in 1844, declares that the symbol which makes beauty perceptible becomes at last of little value for the artist who has "possessed himself . . . of the reality," the conclusion of "The Antique Ring," published a year earlier, argues that the artist "can never separate the idea from the symbol in which it manifests itself." The two statements have different contexts, and they are not strict opposites in any case. But they illustrate the magnificent hedging of which Hawthorne was a master, and which was radically necessary in the cultural circumstances in which he found himself. The same thing shows up still more revealingly in his habit of dramatizing a humane resistance to the metaphysical and theological concepts he has at the same time splendidly acknowledged. So, at least, I read tales like "The Birthmark" and "Ethan Brand," neither of which would readily yield their full and echoing discordance to the critic which searches for the abstractions made concrete in them.

Mr. Schwartz knows, at any rate, the right abstractions to look for: the conception of God and of God's relation to man. As he attempts to make these things visible, he (I think persuasively) disengages Hawthorne from the legend of an uninterruptedly Puritan ancestry. Militant orthodoxy seems to have vanished from the Hawthorne family by the mid-eighteenth century; Nathaniel's mother, who had exclusive charge of him from the time he was four, was an unemphatic Unitarian; Hawthorne was never, on the evidence, indoctrinated or proselytized; and when he arrived at Bowdoin, he gravitated instinctively toward persons "of the same noncommital temperament." Mr. Schwartz draws the picture of a man with a strong religious impulse and an intense religious curiosity who yet had the opportunity of choosing the forms in which his sense of religious experience might get itself articulated and who disliked and distrusted all the forms available to a nineteenth-century New Englander – all the gradations of orthodoxy and the varieties of "liberal Christianity." He then makes too little of the form Hawthorne finally did choose for his purposes: the form of the narrative art.

If he slights that eventuality, it is probably because the art of narrative does not appear to Mr. Schwartz as one of the forms accessible to the religious impulse. For a person to whom none of the modes of Protestant Christianity in the nineteenth century were satisfying, only one other religious mode – Mr. Schwartz seems, not unnaturally, to assume – could be possible. He becomes explicit only at the moment when he relates Hawthorne's account of Donatello's "way to the Lord" to a sermon by St. Thomas Aquinas for "The Feast of Saint Martin," and expresses "amaze[ment] at Hawthorne's knowledge of Catholicism as it affected a character drawn from that tradition." The religious pattern which Hawthorne is here found to be slowly fulfilling is the pattern of traditional Catholicism. Central to that pattern and to Hawthorne's fiction as studied by Mr. Schwartz is the image of a God of love and of hope.

It is useful counterbalance to the occasional description of Hawthorne as presenting a hopelessly depraved human nature cowering away beneath the imminent chastisement of a cold angry deity. And for about half of his essay, Mr. Schwartz holds on pretty hard to Hawthorne's huckleberries, to the human and artistic elements sensibly at work in the notebooks and some of the earlier stories: but then the process of translation sets in, and nothing further hinders it. The remainder of Hawthorne's writings, including *The Scarlet Letter* and *The Marble Faun*, are translated out of their unique existence into the (for those writings) deforming emphases of Catholic Christianity. An entire interpretation of *The Scarlet Letter* rests on the theory that "Dimmesdale's fundamental weakness . . . is his failure to recognize that God is a God of love" – an excellent notion for a psychoanalytically trained confessor to try to inculcate into a real-life Dimmesdale, but not the one central to the realized stress and strain of the novel itself. And a bundle of quotations about "the promises of a blessed eternity" and "O beautiful world! O beneficent God!" leads Mr. Schwartz to identify Hilda, who sometimes does talk like that in *The Marble Faun*, as "winningly virtuous." Hilda comes at us in fact, from the fictional context she inhabits, as a girl so bloodlessly virtuous as to be well-nigh terrifying, and partly because of the way she talks. That Hawthorne, or a part of him, thought of Hilda as such is indicated by his references elsewhere to his belief that the words "'genteel' and 'lady-like' are terrible ones," and to "the pure, modest, sensitive and shrinking woman of America – shrinking when no evil is intended, and sensitive like diseased flesh that thrills if you but point at it."

This is not to say merely that Hawthorne reveals more fertile contradictions in his work than Mr. Schwartz acknowledges; it is to say, rather, that the contradictions that give Hawthorne's work its particular mood and movement are not entirely translatable into traditional Christian terms – because they are moving away from rather than toward a demonstration of the relevance of those terms. Like Emerson, Hawthorne was largely free of the exact religious formulas of his own time (though he regarded them more closely, and always with a fascinated and creative scepticism). Hawthorne's gaze, too, in its curious range and freedom, rested betimes upon the essence of some central pre-Puritanical piety – an image of God, perhaps, a deep conviction about human responsibility. But those elements remained unrelated except in the quick of Hawthorne's imagination; they were unfortified by anything like a theology, much less a definitely Christian theology. There is no dramatic use (I do not say, no mention) in Hawthorne of the determining items in such a theology – no use whatever of the idea of an intermediary between man and God: of Mary, of the Holy Ghost, and, most crucial of all, of the figure and role of Jesus Christ. There is an important sense in which Hawthorne was not a Christian writer at all.

Hawthorne's view of religious experience is to be found only by following the actual evolution, in each work and from one work to the next, of his persistent images and patterns of relationship. I am not making one more pedantic defense of the absolute integrity of literature; I am trying rather to say something about American and modern literature and the forms of religious expression in our times. As regards Catholic *or* Protestant Christianity, as in his relation to any other major historical development, Hawthorne was neither an outsider nor an insider: he was an in-betweener. His writings and his habitual concerns and response lie somewhere in between the Christian epoch and an epoch (our own) which, with due modifications, we have to call post-Christian; and Hawthorne's imaginative energies bent forward, not backward. The direction in which he was bending is made clearer by his logical successor, Henry James; for James is probably the representative or at least the introductory figure in the post-Christian epoch.

James was post-Christian in somewhat the way that Virgil seems to us pre-Christian – James could dimly remember about as much of the substance of Christianity as Virgil could dimly foresee. The two men stand at opposite ends of the most enormous cultural curve in Western history, and almost everything they wrote had to do with their sense of where they stood. Each was beautifully shaken by premonitions of some gigantic disaster and by opaque hopes of an eventual transformation scene in the affairs of the cosmos. James's fiction, R. P. Blackmur once remarked in a singularly tantalizing sentence, was his reaction to "the predicament of the sensitive mind during what may be called the interregnum between the effective dominance of the old Christian-classical ideal through old European institutions and the rise to rule of the succeeding ideal, whatever history comes to call it." To the phrase "sensitive mind" in Mr. Blackmur's remark, I should like to add "religious imagination"; for James was, I believe, a religious writer, and his fiction was increasingly caught up in the web of circumstances investing and indeed creating the relationship between man and God.

James never put it that way: he was American and modern. Both the human and the literary problem of the present epoch was summed up by Merton Densher in *The Wings of the Dove*, when, trying to make good his lie to Maude Massingham about having been on his way to church on Christmas morning, he asked himself miserably, "To what church was he going, to what church . . . *could* he go?" He went, finally, to the Oratory on Brompton Road, but we must not make too much of that decision, any more than Merton did. It was no more than a transient effort to find a traditional Christian form in which to acknowledge what Merton had long before realized was nothing less than a religious experience. That realization was compounded altogether of Merton's sense of Milly Theale and of the course and meaning of his relationship with *her*. It was this that was "too sacred to describe," just as it was the genuine sacredness of the relationship that James had spent some seven-hundred-odd pages in describing: or, rather, in creating. The creation is achieved while carefully avoiding any direct utterance of the name of God; we have instead the names of Milly Theale, Merton Densher, and the others. This is the point of a reverent witticism made by a friend of mine who, when asked whether he thought that Milly Theale is a Christ-figure, replied, "No, but perhaps Christ is a Milly-figure."

It was, in short, characteristic of James, as representative of the post-Christian epoch, to have conveyed his religious sense by intensifying the human drama to the moment where it gave off imitations of the sacred. And it was characteristic of him to have done so almost exclusively by the resources of the narrative art, generating the "vision" *within* the developing work of art, and with almost no help from and perhaps very little knowledge or recollection of the traditional Christian doctrines. (Hence, by the way, the strange and baffling quality – strange and baffling, at least, for those who probe them from a systematic theological viewpoint – of James's mainly self-begotten symbols.) It was toward the Jamesian position and method that Hawthorne and his contemporaries were heading in an earlier generation. Perry Miller was luminously right when he claimed, in his introduction to *The Transcendentalists*, that Emersonian transcendentalism was "a religious demonstration" in which, however, the persons concerned put their cause into the language of literature rather than of theology. But it must always be added that when that is done, as I have suggested elsewhere, something happens to the cause as well as to the language. There is a deep propriety in searching for religious elements in works of literature, since that is where they often appear with the greatest urgency in the modern epoch; but there is a certain impropriety and perhaps an irrelevance in searching for historically grounded doctrinal elements. Christianity itself may very likely *not* be a historical phenomenon, or at least not in any decisive manner a purely historical phenomenon.

But its institutions and its vocabulary are historical phenomena, and they may in some instances become as unusable for our present religious purposes as Anglo-Saxon is to our linguistic ones. The analogy is intended to be reasonably precise, for in both cases some very important use yet remains. James is representative in this respect as well, for he is post-Christian in the sense of coming after and making scant dramatic use of the finished frames of doctrine: while various essences of Christianity continue to work in his prose and to color and flavor the forms he finds and the forms he creates in human experience.

NOTES

1. Baton Rouge, La., 1958.
2. New York, 1955.
3. "The House of Pain," *Hudson Review*, 12 (1959), 37-53.
4. "The Angelic Imagination," in *The Man of Letters in the Modern World* (New York, 1955), pp. 113–31.
5. New York, 1958.
6. Like Henry Bamford Parkes, in an extremely valuable essay published in *Modern Writing* No. 3 (New York, 1956), Mr. Brady emphasizes the organic continuity between Leather-Stocking and the hard-eye private detective of recent years, affirming the claims of morality in the midst of cross-purposes more frightful and treacherous than any Leather-Stocking knew of.
7. Ronald Gray's little book on Kafka (Cambridge, 1958) traces in scrupulous detail an analogous development in the composition of *The Castle*, and manages thereby to demonstrate the relative unsoundness of the Christian or Jewish doctrinal attack on that novel.

PART TWO: LITERATURE AND ITS RELIGIOUS DIMENSIONS

6

THE IDEA OF MAN IN LITERATURE

Erich Auerbach

After immigrating to the United States in 1947, Erich Auerbach taught for a brief period of time both at Pennsylvania State University and Princeton University before joining the faculty of Yale University. He was Sterling Professor of Romance Philology at the time of his death in 1967. Among his many publications, Professor Auerbach wrote Mimesis: The Representation of Reality in Western Litera-ture *(trans. Willard Trask, 1953),* Scenes from the Drama of European Literature *(1959), and* Literary Language and its Public in Late Latin Antiquity and in the Middle Ages *(trans. Ralph Manheim, 1965). The following selection, Chapter I of* Dante, Poet of the Secular World *(trans. Ralph Manheim, 1961), by Erich Auerbach is reprinted by permission of the University of Chicago Press. Copyright © 1961 by The University of Chicago.*

Ever since its beginnings in Greece, European literature has posses-sed the insight that a man is an indivisible unity of body (appearance and physical strength) and spirit (reason and will), and that his individual fate follows from that unity, which like a magnet attracts the acts and sufferings appropriate to it. It was this insight that enabled Homer to perceive the structure of fate. He created a charac-ter – Achilles or Odysseus, Helen or Penelope – by inventing, by heaping up acts and sufferings that were all of a piece. In the poet's inventive mind an act revealing a man's nature, or, one might say, his nature as manifested in a first act, unfolded naturally and inevitably into the sum and sequence of that man's kindred acts, into a life that would take a certain direction and be caught up in the skein of events which add up to a man's character as well as his fate.

The awareness that a man's particular fate is a part of his unity, the insight embodied in the maxim of Heraclitus cited above,* enables Homer to imitate real life. Here we are not referring exactly to the realism that some ancient critics praised in Homer and others found lacking in him,[1] for those critics were concerned with the probability or credibility of the events he narrates. What we have in mind is his way of narrating. Regardless of their plausibility, he makes them so clear and palpable that the question of their likelihood arises only on subsequent reflection. In the ancient view, a narrative of a fabulous or miraculous event is necessarily unrealistic. The view I am taking here is that the portrayal can be convincing regardless of whether such a thing has ever been seen or of whether or not it is credible. We recall, for example, a Rembrandt print representing the apparition of Christ at Emmaus; it is a successful imitation of life because even an unbeliever, struck by the evidence of what he sees, is compelled to experience a miraculous event. That realism, or to cast aside a word that is ambiguous and has undergone so many changes of meaning, that art of imitation is to be met with everywhere in Homer, even when he is telling fairy tales, for the unity, the *sibi constare*, or constancy, of his figures justifies or produces the things that happen to them. In a single act the poet's fantasy creates the character and his fate. Observation and reason play a part; they enrich the scene and arrange it; but observation can do no more than register the chaotic abundance of the material, while reason tyrannically cuts it to pieces, unable to keep pace with the shifting appearances. Homer's inventive gift carries within it a conviction that neither observation nor reason can wholly justify, although everything in his work supports it; the conviction that every character is at the root of his own particular fate and that he will inevitably incur the fate that is appropriate to

* The maxim referred to is Heraclitus' "A man's character is his fate" – Ed. note.

him. But this means appropriate to him as a whole, not to any one
of his attributes; for his attributes, taken in the abstract never coincide with the figure as a whole. What can be represented in poetic
terms and what demands belief on the part of the reader, is not that
good things happen to a good man and brave things to a brave man,
but that the fate of Achilles is Achillean; the epithets δῖος, "godlike,"
or πολυμῆτις, "astute," carry meaning only for those who know
what they contain of Achilles' character.

Thus Homeric imitation, which the ancient critics called mimesis,
is not an attempt to copy from appearance; it does not spring from
observation, but like myth from the conception of figures who are
all of a piece, whose unity is present even before observation begins.
Their living presence and diversity stem, as we can everywhere
perceive, from the situation they inevitably get involved in, and it is
the situation that prescribes their actions and their sufferings. Only
then, when the conception is established, does naturalistic description set in, though there is no need for the poet to summon it; it
comes to him quite spontaneously. The natural truth or mimesis of a
Homeric scene such as the meeting of Odysseus and Nausicaa is
not based on sharp observation of daily events, but on an *a priori*
conception of the nature and essence of both figures and the fate
appropriate to them. It is that conception which creates the situation
in which they meet, and once the conception is there, the narrative
that will transform the fiction into truth follows of its own accord.
Thus Homer's portraiture is no mere copy of life, not only because
he tells stories that could never happen in real life but because he
has a conception of man that experience alone could not have
given him.

Tragedy grew out of the epic myth; but in developing a form of
its own, distinct from the epic, it concentrated more and more on the
actual decision; a man and his destiny are laid bare in the moment
when they become wholly and irrevocably one – the moment of
doom. In Homeric epic a man moves toward his fate in a gradual
process of clarification and the hero's end need not necessarily come
into the story. Classical tragedy, on the other hand, discloses the
end of his career, when he has left all diversity behind him and no
escape is possible; deciphered and manifest, his disastrous fate
stands there before him like a stranger; fear grips his innermost
being; he tries to defend himself against the universal which is

destined to engulf his individual life; he flings himself into the hopeless final struggle against his own daemon. That struggle, which
stands out most clearly in Sophocles, is such that those who enter
into it lose a part of their individual nature; they are so caught up
in their extreme plight, so carried away by the final struggle, that
nothing remains of their personality but their age, sex, position in
life, and the most general traits of their temperament; their actions,
their words and gestures are wholly governed by the dramatic situation, that is, by the tactical requirements of their struggle. Nevertheless, Greek tragedy left its hero a good deal of his individuality;
especially in the opening scene, when he still stands there firm and
intact, he shows the particular, contingent, earthly side of himself
with reality and dignity; and even later on, after the breach between
his individuality and his fate, when the universality of his fate
becomes more and more manifest, he still retains, whether con-
vulsively clinging to it or heroically sacrificing it, the characteristic
form of his vital will. But here there is no place for the epic spontaneity which at every moment derives colorful new forms from the
concordance of the two elements of his unity. Formerly, in his epic
life, man's individuality was enriched by each new turn of his fate,
but here he has grown hard and rigid and poor in color and detail.
He resists his all too universal doom, yet runs to meet it; all that
remains of him is what is most universal, a man on the way to his
doom, squandering and exhausting his store of vital energy, which
can no longer bear fruit.

In the Sophist Enlightenment the character lost its unity; psychological analysis and a rational interpretation of events dispersed
the compelling power of destiny. The form of the tragedy was
preserved only with the help of technical devices: often an arbitrary,
empty, and mechanical plot contrasted irritatingly with subtle
psychological perception. At the same time comedy with its observation and imitation of daily life, its rationalist caricatures, just or
unjust, of everything that was unusual, began, though with ups and
downs, to gain the support of the enlightened public and to discredit
the notion of *a priori* unity of character.

That was the situation when Plato developed his critique of
imitative art. Plato scorned his own feeling for sensuous reality and
his own poetic talent, and in his conception of a strict, pure utopia,
condemned the indiscriminate emotion aroused by art. The results

of his long meditations on the subject are set forth in the tenth book of the *Republic*: if the empirical world is second in rank, a deceptive copy of the Ideas, which alone have truth and being, then art, which concerns itself with the imitation of appearance, is still lower in the scale, a clouded, inferior copy of a copy, third in respect to truth: τρίτον τι ἀπὸ τῆς ἀληθείας;[2] it is addressed to the lower, irrational part of the soul; there poetry and philosophy have always been in conflict, a poetry must be excluded from the philosophical Republic. He grants a limited value to the non-imitative arts, which are disciplined by a firm tradition and make no concession to changing, deceptive appearances; they, he holds, can serve to fortify civic virtue in the philosophical state. But that only underlines his basic condemnation of all truly creative art.

However, Plato's teachings did not destroy the dignity of imitative art – on the contrary, they gave it a new impulse that was to endure for many centuries and assigned it a new aim. Not that Plato was not serious in his view. Neither his praises of inspiration in other dialogues, nor the mimetic art he himself practised so consummately and for which indeed he was criticized,[3] can alter our belief that this passage represents his essential attitude which, despite his own poetic disposition, despite dangerous trials and temptations, had taken form in the pure perfection of his theory of ideas. Yet the influence of his words was colored by the memory of a man who had spoken them. In various ways he had praised phenomenal beauty as a stage on the way to true beauty; it was through him that artists and lovers of art first began to reflect on the presence of the Idea in the appearance of things and to yearn for it. It was Plato who bridged the gap between poetry and philosophy; for, in his work, appearance, despised by his Eleatic and Sophist predecessors, became a reflected image of perfection. He set poets the task of writing philosophically, not only in the sense of giving instruction, but in the sense of striving, by the imitation of appearance, to arrive at its true essence and to show its insufficiency measured by the beauty of the Idea. He himself understood the art of mimesis more profoundly and practised it more consummately than any other Greek of his time, and apart from Homer he had greater influence as a poet than any other poet of antiquity. The figures in his dialogues are represented in their innermost individuality; the dialogue itself is shot through with movement and actuality; the most abstract disquisition becomes a work of magic, whose sensuous color, in every receptive mind, merges with the subject matter and seems to become one with it. It is false, indeed it is quite impossible, to look upon the poetry in Plato as a kind of subterfuge or delusion from which we must free ourselves in order to arrive at the true meaning of his thought. Plato's love of the particular was his way to wisdom, the way described in Diotima's monologue. It achieved such unique expression because for him man's universal τέλος, or end, did not conflict with the individual nature and destiny of men, but was shaped and expressed in them. The unity of essence and destiny is set forth in the myth recounted by Er the Pamphylian who stood before the throne of Lachesis and beheld how the souls of the dead chose their destinies before returning to new life[4] – for each soul retained its individual character, which death had not destroyed. Plato's art is pious; it is a supreme expression, confirmed and purified by reason, of the mythical consciousness of destiny. Herein and in the power of the soul to partake of the beauty of the Idea, the dualism of the Platonic system is transcended. The influence of this Plato, who introduced philosophy into art and laid the foundations for a more profound and at the same time more accurate perception of events, lived on in the minds of future generations. The enriched perception embodied in his art also springs from his philosophical attitude. In the dialogue form that he created there is, strictly speaking, no encounter with fate, no dramatic situation; even in the Socrates trilogy – the *Apology, Crito, Phaedo* – the encounter with fate is no more than a background. In its place truth becomes the judge; in the quiet movement of the dialogue, men of all ages pass before the judgment seat of truth, constrained, like the souls passing before the judges of the underworld in the myth that Socrates relates at the end of the *Gorgias*,[5] to lay bare their willingness, devotion, resolution. Here the soul must prove its courage and nobility, its inherent truth, as the body must prove its strength and skill in an athletic contest, and although these secret, intangible things are disclosed in terms of appearance, of the most manifest sense perception, they seem at the same time to be weighed in scales of the utmost precision and defined as it were by an art of measurement.

Thus it is not surprising that the philosophical theory of art should find not its end but its beginning in the Platonic critique of imitation. The theory of Ideas in itself contained the germ of a transformation whose significance for the fine arts has recently been set forth by E. Panofsky.[6] Then, little by little, thinkers concerned with a philosophical justification of the arts moved the Platonic Ideas or archetypes, from the supra-celestial realm to the soul, from the transcendent to the immanent world. The object which the artist imitated underwent a similar change, passing from the empirical world to the soul, for it was held that what the artist imitated could not be the real object – for if it were, the work of art would not be more beautiful than the immediate object – but the image in his soul, which is nothing other than the immanent Idea, the ἐννόημα. Now the imitated object and the truth, which Plato had distinguished so sharply, met in the soul of the artist, and the higher perfection which to Plato's mind could be encountered only in the supra-celestial realm, was imputed to the immanent Idea in contrast with actuality and, later on, with the work itself as well. Consequently the notion of mimesis underwent an extreme spiritualization which, though rooted in Plato's theory of Ideas, produced a result diametrically opposed to Plato's teachings, that is, a belief in the sublimity of art; and ultimately – in Plotinus, who accentuated the contrast between the archetype in the soul of the creative artist and the materialized work, which could never be anything but a veiled copy – this same process gave rise to a new dualism and a new problem.

The first important step in this revision and application to art of the theory of Ideas is Aristotle's aesthetics: its influence on the historical development of the theory is great, but it is less significant than the Platonic theory itself for those who seek to investigate the respective parts played by sensibility and metaphysics in actual works of art. The doctrine of the self-realization of the essence in the phenomenon, whereby the individual formed thing becomes reality and substance, gave imitation a new philosophical justification; all the more so since Aristotle, in his formulation of change, or process, as the entrance of form into matter, had in mind human artistic creation as well as the organic process. In artistic activity, the form, the εἶδος, is in the soul of the artist, and herein we see the relevance to the theory of art of the above-mentioned transference of the Ideas to the immanent world. Accordingly Aristotle, in opposition to Plato, expressly defends poetry as a *poietic* philosophy, which in tragedy, its highest form, arouses and overcomes certain emotions, and thus, far from being harmful and demoralizing, purifies the soul.

Tragedy is thus more philosophical than historiography, which is a pure copying of events, because in tragedy the individual gives way to the universal, and contingency to probability. Thus Aristotle, by his doctrine that the Idea is actualized in the formed particular, rehabilitated the formed particular as an object worthy to be imitated. But since, opposite to the creative εἶδος of the artist, the formed object reverts to matter, it follows that the artistic imitation is more perfectly formed than its empirical model and hence higher in rank. These principles, however, spring solely from rational insight into the individual occasion, not from participation in its essence, not from the process, that Plato must have experienced, of losing oneself in reality and finding oneself again. Aristotle did not try to fathom the part of actuality which resists rational formulation, but dropped it as having neither law nor purpose. To his mind what could not be explained was mere contingency, the inevitable resistance of matter, and as such occupied the bottom-most rank in his metaphysical order of the universe. Compared to the dualism of Plato's "two worlds," this dualism of form and matter seems easily bridged – for each empirical thing points to the process by which it will be transcended. But when applied to events, it implies – and indeed this is the conception underlying Aristotle's ethics – that something utterly contingent and alien can befall man; for what reason cannot resolve is τὸ οὐκ ἄνευ, or the *sine qua non*, of pure matter, or contingency. Such a conception is only natural to a man of Aristotle's cast of mind, who judges destiny by the rational concept of justice, but – quite unlike Plato's doctrine of two worlds, which dismissed happening as illusion, yet left room for the mythical illumination of happening – it is diametrically opposed to the tragic view of fate. Certain of Aristotle's ideas concerning the poet's relation to real happening, as set forth in the *Poetics*, follow from this attitude. He states very clearly that reality must not be represented as it comes to us, in its apparent disorder and disunity, and his view in this matter was taken as a norm for centuries to come. To his mind the disorder and disunity of actual happening do not stem from the inadequacy of the eyes that look upon it, but are present in happening itself, so that the poet must create a happening superior to actual happening and tragedy must present a correction of actual events. Thus he opposes the universality of poetry to the particularity of history and expressly bases the unity of tragedy not on the hero, who can be assailed by disparate events, but on the rationalized fable which, he declares, can be independent of the character. This view led Aristotle to a system in which poetic possibilities are almost too rigidly departmentalized and restricted; it exerted a decisive influence on subsequent theory and by and large marks a limit which the poetics of the ancients was never to surpass. The only significant exception is Plato; we recall the richly meaningful scene at the end of the *Symposium*, in which Socrates tries to explain to Agathon and Aristophanes, both half-asleep, that one and the same man ought to be capable of writing both comedies and tragedies.[7]

A rationalistic negation of fate was the prevailing attitude of antiquity from Aristotle to the triumph of Christianity and the mystery religions; that was just as true of the Stoics who, in their necessary order of the world, equated reason with nature, as of the Epicureans with their metaphysical concept of freedom; and both those philosophies culminated in an ethical ideal which insulated the individual against his fate. The wise man is he whose equanimity nothing can disturb; he overcomes the outside world by refusing to participate in it, by subduing his emotions.

Late Greek rationalism is the dominant attitude in the Roman poetry and poetic theory of the Golden Age; that applies to Cicero as well as to Horace or Seneca. Only where the destiny and mission of Rome were involved, in Virgil and in Tacitus, did the creative imagination overcome the fatelessness inherent in the philosophical style of the age, and then there emerged an image of actuality as an *a priori* unity. Virgil has been greatly misunderstood and underestimated by the younger generation in Germany; the fault lies in a comparison with Homer based on two misconceptions; on the one hand these young men rashly identify Homer with a primitive stage of development, while on the other they distrust Virgil because of the over-cultivated, "classicist" period in which he lived, as though more refined conditions of life and liberation from crude anthropomorphic forms of religion were a fundamental obstacle to poetic creation. That prejudice has blinded many men's hearts to the consummate magic of Virgil's poetry, its purity of feeling, and above all to the spiritual rebirth it betokens. This peasant's son from northern Italy, whom the most reserved of his contemporaries and even the political leaders of the day regarded as a favorite of nature and looked upon with a kind of loving awe, combined a deep attachment to the Italian soil with the highest culture of his time. Those two elements were so fused in him that his rural traditionalism seems to be the quintessence of a perfect culture, while his cultivation gives the impression of a profound natural wisdom, at once earthly and divine. The experience of his youth and an intuitive sense of the forces at work in his time combined to mould in him a belief in the impending rebirth of the world. Seen in terms of the philosophy of history, the fourth Eclogue, in which he celebrates the birth of the child and the dawn of a new era, this poem of inspired learning which encompasses the eschatological conceptions of all the civilized peoples of the ancient world, really has the significance that the sage error of the Middle Ages attributed to it. What utterly distinguishes Virgil's conception from all the eschatological traditions he employs,[8] is not merely his art, with which he raises the obscure, scattered, subterranean and secret widom of the Hellenistic Mediterranean countries to the broad light of day; it is rather the fact that for him all that dark wisdom took on a concrete form in the hoped-for and already dawning world order of the Imperium. These are the roots of his poetic and prophetic power. The character and the fate of the pious Aeneas, who out of affliction and confusion made his way through temptation and danger toward his allotted destiny, were something new to ancient literature. The idea that a man should pursue a definite sacred mission in the earthly world was unknown to the Homeric epics; ascent through many degrees of trial was indeed a familiar motif in the Orphic and Pythagorean mysteries, but it was never connected with a concrete career on earth. Aeneas is conscious of his mission; it was revealed to him by the prophecy of his divine mother and by the words of his father in the underworld, and he takes it upon himself with proud piety. The prophecies of Anchises and the glorification of the Julian line may strike us as insipid flattery, but only because Virgil's formula has too often been abused for unworthy and trivial purposes. Virgil's view of the world follows the truth of historical development as he saw it, and it endured and exerted an influence far longer than he could have foreseen; he was indeed a kind of prophet, or else the word has lost its meaning. And into the history of the world he wove the first great love story in a form that remains valid to this day. Though not successful in every detail, as a whole it is a masterpiece and for the European literature of love, a basic model. Dido suffers more deeply and poignantly than Calypso, and her story is one example of great sentimental poetry known to the Middle Ages.

Thus for European literature Virgil was in many respects an important innovator, and his influence extended far beyond literature. He was the mythologist of Europe's most characteristic political form, the creative synthetist of Roman and Hellenistic eschatologies, and the first poet of sentimental love. He was the first of his cultural sphere to transcend the fatelessness of late Greek philosophy and to see the *a priori* unity of the character in his fate. True, there is an uncertainty in his theological attitude, for what he glorified was an earthly institution, and the union of religious currents that he exploited poetically aimed at more than that; in his picture of the other world – an after-life at the service of Rome's greatness – the traditional doctrines of purification and transmigration are not developed quite consistently; his realm of the dead is merely an artistic instrument, and as in all the ancient conceptions, the souls of the departed have only a partial, diminished life, a shadowy existence.

The historical core of Christianity – that is to say, the Crucifixion and the related events – offers a more radical paradox, a wider range of contradiction, than anything known to the ancient world, either in its history or in its mythical tradition. The fantastic march of the man from Galilee and his action in the temple, the sudden crisis and catastrophe, the pitiful derision, the scourging and crucifixion of the King of the Jews, who only a short time before had wished to proclaim the Kingdom of God on earth, the despairing flight of the disciples, and then the apotheosis, based on the visions of a few men, perhaps of only one, a fisherman from the lake of Gennesaret – this entire episode, which was to provoke the greatest of all transformations in the inner and outward history of our civilized world, is astonishing in every respect. Even today, anyone who tries to form a clear picture of what happened is deeply puzzled; he cannot but feel that myth and dogma gained only a relative ascendancy in the books of the New Testament and that the paradoxical, disharmonious, perplexing character of those events erupts at every turn.

The frequently adduced comparison[9] with the death of Socrates helps to bring out our meaning. Socrates, too, died for what he believed and he died of his own free will. He could have saved himself; he could have escaped before his trial or taken a less intransigent attitude at it, or have fled afterwards. But he did not wish to: serene and untroubled, he died surrounded by his friends, the earthly dignity of his person undiminished; this was the death of a philosopher and of a happy man, whose destiny seems to confirm and fulfil our human sense of justice; his enemies are anonymous figures, representing the special interests of the moment, of little importance to their contemporaries and of none at all to posterity; the fact that they held the power merely gave Socrates a last welcome occasion to fulfil and reveal himself.

Jesus, on the other hand, unleashed a movement which by its very nature could not remain purely spiritual; his followers, who recognized him as the Messiah, expected the immediate coming of the Kingdom of God on earth. And all that was a lamentable failure. The multitude, on whom he must for a moment have exerted a considerable influence, remained in the end hesitant or hostile; the ruling groups joined forces against him; he was compelled to hide at night outside the city, and in his hiding place he was finally betrayed by one of those closest to him, arrested in the midst of confused and vacillating disciples, and brought before the Sanhedrin. And now the worst of all: the disciples despaired and fled, and Peter, the root and eternal head of Christendom, denied him. Alone, he faced the judges and suffered his disgraceful martyrdom, while the multitude was permitted to mock him in the most cruel way: of all his followers, only a few women witnessed his end from afar.

Harnack[10] called Peter's denial of Christ "that terrible leftward swing of the pendulum" and believed that in conjunction with the memory of the transfiguration (Mark 8:27-29), it provided the psychological basis for the vision of St. Peter on which the Church was founded, for it may, he says, "have resulted in an equally violent swing to the right." But the denial and vision of Peter, this evident paradox, are only the most conspicuous example of the contradictory character that dominates the story of Jesus from the beginning. From the very first it moves between malignant scoffers and boundless believers, in an atmosphere strangely compounded of the sublime and the ridiculous; the admiration and emulation of his disciples do not prevent them from misunderstanding him frequently, and their relations with him are marked by constant unrest and tension.

In entering into the consciousness of the European peoples, the story of Christ fundamentally changed their conceptions of man's fate and how to describe it. The change occurred very slowly, far more slowly than the spread of Christian dogma. It faced other obstacles that were harder to overcome: resistances which, insignificant in themselves, were impervious to the political and tactical factors that favored the acceptance of Christianity, because they were rooted in the most conservative element of a people's being, namely the innermost sensory ground of their view of the world. To that view of the world the apparatus of Christian dogma could be adapted more easily and quickly than could the spirit of the events from which it had grown. But before we enter into the history of this change and the phenomena it produced in the course of time, let us try to describe the nature of the change.

The story of Christ is more than the *parousia* of the *logos*, more than the manifestation of the idea. In it the idea is subjected to the problematic character and desperate injustice of earthly happening. Considered in itself that is, without the posthumous and never fully actualized triumph in the world, as the mere story of Christ on earth, it is so hopelessly terrible that the certainty of an actual, concretely tangible correction in the hereafter remains the only issue, the only salvation from irrevocable despair. Consequently, Christian eschatological conceptions took on an unprecedented concreteness and intensity; this world has meaning only in reference to the next; in itself it is a meaningless torment. But the otherworldly character of justice did not, as it would have where the classical spirit prevailed, detract from the value of earthly destiny or from man's obligation to submit to it. The Stoic or Epicurean withdrawal of the philosopher from his destiny, his endeavor for release from the chain of earthly happening, his determination to remain at least inwardly free from earthly ties – all that is completely un-Christian. For to redeem fallen mankind the incarnated truth had subjected itself without reserve to earthly destiny. That was the end of the eudaemonism which was the foundation of ancient ethics: as Christ had taught by his presence on earth, it was the Christian's duty to do atonement and suffer trials by taking destiny upon himself, by submitting to the sufferings of the creature. The drama of earthly life took on a painful, immoderate, and utterly un-classical intensity, because it is at once a wrestling with evil and the foundation of God's judgment to come. In diametrical opposition to the ancient feeling, earthly self-abnegation was no longer regarded as a way from the concrete to the abstract, from the particular to the universal. What presumption to strive for theoretical serenity when Christ himself lived in continuous conflict! Inner tension was insuperable, and, like acceptance of earthly destiny, a necessary consequence of the story of Christ. In both cases man's individuality is humbled, but it is, and must be, preserved. Not only is Christian humility far more compelling and more concrete, one might almost say more worldly, than Stoic apathy, but through awareness of man's inevitable sinfulness, it also does far more to intensify man's awareness of his unique, inescapable personality. And the story of Christ revealed not only the intensity of personal life but also its diversity and the wealth of its forms, for it transcended the limits of ancient mimetic aesthetics. Here man has lost his earthly dignity; everything can happen to him, and the classical division of genres has vanished; the distinction between the sublime and the vulgar style exists no longer. In the Gospels, as in ancient comedy, real persons of all classes make their appearance: fishermen and kings, high priests, publicans, and harlots participate in the action; and neither do those of exalted rank act in the style of classical tragedy, nor do the lowly behave as in a farce; quite on the contrary, all social and aesthetic limits have been effaced. On that stage there is room for all human diversity, whether we consider the cast of characters as a whole or each character singly; each individual is fully legitimated, but not on any social grounds; regardless of his earthly position, his personality is developed to the utmost, and what befalls him is neither sublime nor base; even Peter, not to mention Jesus, suffers profound humiliation. The depth and scope of the naturalism in the story of Christ are unparalleled; neither the poets nor the historians of antiquity had the opportunity or the power to narrate human events in that way.

We have already said, and indeed it is well known though seldom stated in this connection, that the mimetic content of the story of Christ required a very long time, more than a thousand years, to enter into the consciousness of the faithful, even of the peoples early converted to Christianity, and to reshape their view of destiny. What first penetrated the minds of men was the doctrine, but in the course of the struggle with other revealed religions, with Hellenistic rationalism and the myths of the barbarian peoples, the doctrine itself underwent a change and even the story of Christ was resorbed in a sense by the shifting requirements of the struggle. The necessity of adapting it to the mentality of various peoples to which the doctrine was carried in polemics or missionary sermons involved a number of metamorphoses, each one of which destroyed a fragment of its concrete reality, and in the end little remained of the doctrine but a sequence of dogmatic abstractions. But the reality was never wholly lost; the gravest threat came early, from Neo-Platonic Spiritualism and its Christian heresies, and once that was overcome, what was essential was saved.

NOTES

1. For example, *Περὶ ὕψους*, ix. 13.
2. *Republic* x. 602.
3. *Athenaeus* xi. 505b.
4. *Republic* x. 617f.
5. *Gorgias* 523–24.
6. *Idea* ("Studien der Bibliothek Warburg," No. 6 [Leipzig, 1924], pp. 1–6.
7. Cf. George Finsler, *Platon und die aristotelische Poetik* (Leipzig, 1900).
8. Cf. Eduard Norden, *Die Geburt des Kindes* ("Studien der Bibliothek Warburg," No. 3 [Leipzig, 1924]).
9. Recently adduced by Eduart Meyer, *Ursprung und Anfang des Christentums* (Stuttgart and Berlin, 1921–23), III, 219.
10. "Die Verklärungsgeschichte Jesu, der Bericht des Paulus (I Cor. 15:3ff.) und die beiden Christusvisionen des Petrus" (*Sitzungsbericht der Preussischen Akademie der Wissenschaften, Phil.-Hist. Klasse*, 1922).

7

HAMLET'S MOMENT OF TRUTH

Preston T. Roberts, Jr.

Preston T. Roberts, Jr. was instrumental in founding the Theology and Literature program at the Divinity School of the University of Chicago. He is currently Visiting Lecturer in the field of Theology at the College of the Holy Cross. Professor Roberts' writing has been devoted chiefly to the areas of Greek and Renaissance tragedy, modern literature and theology, and American literature. This essay first appeared in The Journal of Religion, *Vol. 49, No. 4, October 1969.* © *1969 by The University of Chicago. Reprinted by permission of the author,* The Journal of Religion, *and the University of Chicago.*

Hamlet is without doubt one of the most interesting and important of all Shakespeare's plays. There is something intensely lyrical about *Hamlet* that somehow in all the other plays is missed. In some sense Hamlet and his "problems" are Shakespeare and his problems. For every man has his Elsinore, even if he be no prince. For this reason, Hamlet is apt to remind us of ourselves as well. We become interested in *Hamlet* because the play reminds us of certain aspects of our own lives. We also tend to be interested in our lives in part because they keep reminding us of Hamlet and his problems. The relationship between literature and life is this complex and profound.

From the point of view of theological content and literary structure, *Hamlet* stands intermediate between the ancient and the modern world. It is at once a Greek-Skeptical and a Hebraic-Christian kind of dramatic tragedy. It points back and forward, embracing the whole sweep of Western culture and civilization. Everything that is Greek, Hebraic, Christian, or Skeptical by way of theological content is expressed with impressive literary clarity and force.

What is Greek before us and within us perceives and responds immediately to *Hamlet* as the picture of man's suffering nobility. From a Greek point of view, Hamlet's story is the story of an almost perfectly good and noble man who is destroyed by a vastly more imperfect world. His tragedy is therefore pitiful and terrifying. Horatio's fond farewell, "Good night sweet prince," is a perfect consummation of this Greek motif.

What is Hebraic in us perceives the passion of Job. Hamlet is not asking for grace or for mercy. The presence of piety, righteousness, and justice would suffice. From a Hebraic point of view, Hamlet's problem is to banish his feelings of self-pity and to go forth to meet life with overwhelming religious and moral force. He is willing and yet somehow unable.

What is Christian in us sees Hamlet reenacting the Passion of Christ, coming full circle from the heroic ideal, through the tragic vision, to a sense of peace even as he stands in the midst of the ardors of youth and the harvest of tragedy.

And what is Skeptical in us interprets Hamlet as the first and perhaps the greatest of all the modern Skeptical tragic heroes who doubt the very character of life, who are overwhelmed by a sense of inner despair and melancholy, and who are destroyed as much by an inward boredom and violence as by zest for life. From a Skeptical point of view, it can be said that Melville's Pierre, Dostoevsky's Ivan, Eliot's Prufrock, and Joyce's Stephen Daedalus and Richard Rowan reenact the passion of Hamlet.

The tension between Greek-Skeptical and Hebraic-Christian motifs provides the problems of and suggests the solutions for the difficulties which define this play. *Hamlet* begins with the Trinity – almost literally framed by Father, Son, and Holy or unholy Ghost. *Hamlet* ends with the melancholy despair of the gravediggers scene. The whole story of Western theology and literature is retold at some point or moment in between. And it is not clear which motif finally defines the events and meanings of Hamlet's story.

In any case, Hamlet is a most complex topic. I do not hope to remove all of the many difficulties that have attended efforts to understand this play. I shall simply endeavor to restate the problems and the classical theories that have arisen in connection with them, with particular emphasis upon certain aspects that are sometimes neglected or ignored. These aspects suggest a general line of solution. I shall begin with a statement of the problems that have arisen in connection with the play. I shall proceed to a statement of the many kinds of theory that have been projected in an attempt to resolve the problems. I shall end with my own concrete interpretation of wherein its principle of life consists. These three steps are from detail to generality. *Hamlet* is one play that deserves both close scrutiny in a literary sense and general gaze in a theological and philosophic sense.

In the Elizabethan theatre *Hamlet* was, of course, given without breaks. The five-act division is an emendation by Shakespeare's editors. For purposes of analysis and emphasis the play breaks somewhat more naturally into three movements. The first movement is from the beginning through Hamlet's acceptance of the Ghost's command. The second movement is from Hamlet's assumption of his "antic disposition" to his forced departure for England. The third and final movement is from his return to the tragic duel that is the catastrophic end. Some of the problems of the play arise in connection with one or more of these inner movements or parts. Some theories are vitiated by the fact that they speak about the play as a whole apart from these three parts; others by speaking about these three inner parts apart from the play as a whole. The critical problem is to hold the balance of whole and part a bit more evenly. I shall proceed from the problems special to each part to the theories that have arisen to explain the whole. But a brief summary narration and description of each of these three inner movements is necessary here at the outset in order that some of the more crucial details of the play may be in view.

The opening scene of the first movement presents Horatio and Marcellus encountering the Ghost. In this scene the Ghost is silent, visible, and armed. Moreover, he is seen and described. These details are important because they prove that the Ghost is real and is Hamlet's father. These facts are in turn important because Hamlet's cautious and testing behavior later in the play means very different things if we do or do not believe that the Ghost is real. There is a generic contrast in this first scene between the outer

"There's something rotten in the state of Denmark" and the inner "'Tis bitter cold, and I am sick at heart." The first refrain is a foil to the second. This is important because this play is to be concerned with the inner rather than with the outer world. The focus of interest and attention is to be upon one man's inner moral and religious life rather than upon the necessities of a political or social order that stands without. Bernardo's simple refrain in fact sounds forth the haunting motif of the entire play – sickness in the heart. This first scene is also filled with theological and religious symbolism – the hovering Ghost (holy or unholy, as the case may be), Marcellus's invocation of the religiousness of the dawn and of that season "Wherein our Savior's birth is celebrated," and even Peter's betrayal of Christ:

> BERNARDO: It was about to speak, when the cock crew.
> HORATIO: And then it started like a guilty thing
> Upon a fearful summons.

This theological and religious symbolism is important because it foreshadows the seriousness of the themes with which the play is to deal. As in the case with the "state of Denmark," the simple piety may be or may become a foil to Hamlet's skepticism. But it nonetheless reminds us that Hamlet is a young Christian as well as a pagan prince, and that his skepticism will be struggling with an inner as well as an outer world of inherited belief.

This first movement contains two other crucial scenes: the council scene among Claudius, Gertrude, and Hamlet in the presence of the court; and the scene on the battlements in which Hamlet encounters the Ghost, receives its command, makes his oath, and assumes his strange and ambiguous "antic disposition." The only other scene in this first part introduces the subplot centering around Polonius and his son and daughter, Laertes and Ophelia.

The council scene is crucial, for in it we receive our first impressions of Claudius and Gertrude and learn of the grief and shame with which the dark and mourning Hamlet has been beset by his father's death and his mother's hasty remarriage. The final Ghost scene is crucial, too, because a large part of the meaning of the play turns upon the peculiar character of the Ghost's command and the special nature of Hamlet's oath and "antic disposition."

By the end of this first movement the stage is set. It begins with the imminence of the Ghost, boding ill within and without. It ends with Hamlet's "wild and whirling words" as he accepts the command and assumes his "antic disposition." From beginning to end this first movement is dominated by two factors – Hamlet's "initial condition" within and the Ghost without. Moreover, all of the minor elements in the play have been presented: the peculiar strength and weakness of Claudius by means of the generic contrast between his revelry in the council scene on the one hand and his wise invocation of the theme of "the death of fathers" on the other hand in that same scene; the strained and special kind of relation Hamlet sustains to his mother; and the generic contrast between Hamlet on the one side and Fortinbras and Laertes on the other – the one brought out by the talk of the soldiers on their watch, the other by means of the contrast between Claudius's refusal to permit Hamlet to return to Wittenberg and his immediate granting of permission to Laertes to go to Paris. From a dramatic point of view, movement 1 has accomplished the many things any first movement of a play must accomplish: invocation of the atmosphere and tone of the play as a whole, exposition of the background or the relation between what "happened" before the play and what is about to happen in it, definition of both the initial situation and the first complications in the action, and the foreshadowing of future events.

Movement 2 extends from Hamlet's acceptance of the command through his forced departure for England. This is the heart of the play. Apart from the gravediggers scene and the final "Good night sweet prince," all of the scenes that have affected mankind so deeply occur in this middle movement: the scene with the players, the nunnery scene with Ophelia, the "play within the play" scene, the scene with the "King at his prayers," the "closet scene" with Gertrude, and the Fortinbras soliloquy. This movement is dominated by Hamlet's "madness," feigned, real, or both; Hamlet's inactivity; and the increasing liveliness of Claudius's suspicions, issuing into the final counterplot. The "play within the play" scene is crucial, for in it Hamlet verifies the "goodness" of the Ghost and the veracity of his commands. Just as crucial are the scene with the king at his prayers and the closet scene with Gertrude, for in these Hamlet betrays each aspect of his father's command immediately following its verification. He fails both to "remember me" and to "leave thy mother to heaven." The generic contrast between the triumph of the "play within the play" scene and the poignant despair of the closet scene and the Fortinbras soliloquy is the deepest fact concerning movement 2.

The third and final movement is from Hamlet's return from England to the end. This movement begins with Ophelia's mad scenes and ends with Horatio's "Good night sweet prince." In between are Ophelia's drowning, Laertes' return, the gravediggers scene, Hamlet's acceptance of the challenge, and the duel. Apart from the mad scenes and the final resolution, the deepest things in this last movement are the melancholy of the gravediggers scene and the poignancy of Hamlet's many asides to Horatio.

Each of these movements is haunted by subtle difficulties and complications. Any theory of the play as a whole must do justice to all three movements. Each must receive a vivid and forceful interpretation, internally intelligible and externally clear with reference to the other parts and problems. And no problem connected with any one of the parts must fail of interpretation. In short, any general theory of the play must arise out of, illustrate, and issue into solutions of those problems special to the three parts.

The problems of the first movement concern Hamlet's initial condition, the peculiar character of the Ghost and of his command, Hamlet's oath in the cellarage scene, and the "antic disposition." The problems of the second movement turn upon the interpretation to be given to specific scenes: the nunnery scene, the "play within the play" scene, the scene with the king at his prayers, the closet scene, and the Fortinbras soliloquy. The problems of the last movement concern Ophelia's madness, the gravediggers scene, and Hamlet's many asides to Horatio.

The first problem of movement 1 is the nature of Hamlet's initial condition or state of mind. Among other things, this is the famous problem of the relation between the Hamlet before the play and the Hamlet in the play. Many a famous theory of *Hamlet* as a whole turns upon this question, notably T. S. Eliot's theory. Eliot argues that the thoughts and feelings of the Hamlet in the play are all in excess of the facts we are given or can infer concerning the Hamlet before the play. He finds an imperfection here of which the larger imperfection of the play as a whole consists.

This first problem is intimately related to the other three – the character of the Ghost and his command, Hamlet's oath in the cellarage scene, and his "antic disposition" or madness, feigned or real.

The key to this first movement is to be found in the fact that the Ghost of Hamlet's father dramatically dominates the entire first movement. Hamlet's initial condition cannot be understood apart from it. Hamlet is already in mourning and sick over his mother before the Ghost appears. The revelations of the Ghost deepen both aspects of Hamlet's problem. The conjunction of his initial melancholy and despair with the impelling force and ambiguous character of the Ghost suffices to account for all of his thoughts and feelings. There is nothing in excess of the facts. The Ghost appears *in medias res*, complicating an already complex situation. Moreover, the Ghost appears on the stage to Horatio and Marcellus before it appears to Hamlet. This is important because it assures them and us, the audience, of the ghost's complete physical reality. Moreover, it is specifically identified as the Ghost of Hamlet's father. The Ghost is as serious and impelling a force in the action as the plague at the beginning of *Oedipus Rex*. Other things being equal, the Ghost commands and demands action of Hamlet. In the first scene, Horatio in fact performs a function very much like the chorus in Greek tragedy. He and Marcellus give the typical Elizabethan attitudes toward the Ghost – the skeptical and the pious – in much the same way as the Greek chorus gives typical Greek attitudes toward oracles and dreams. The whole range of Elizabethan attitudes is compressed carefully into the various characters: Horatio, the skeptic; Marcellus, the good Catholic; and later Hamlet, the Protestant from Wittenberg. The Ghost is a good ghost from the Catholic point of view. He is delayed from purgatory, something pious being unfinished in his life. The Ghost is to be respected. Hamlet voices the Protestant point of view. Good or evil can come of ghosts. They may well be feared because they haunt the human scene with guilt.

The opening scene of *Hamlet* is in fact the most interesting and important of them all, approached in brilliance only by the opening scene in *Lear*. The opening scene is a microcosm of the macrocosm. The little phrase of Bernardo's in the eighth line is a précis of the entire play: "'Tis bitter cold and I am sick at heart." Sickness is to be the main theme of the entire play. And Hamlet's sickness, like Bernardo's, is to be a mystery to the end, a mystery to himself, others, and to the audience. And yet, also like Bernardo's, it is to be a mystery in the best sense, unambiguously ambiguous. There is a contrast between the externalities of this first scene and the internality of the rest of the play. The scene establishes the probability that Hamlet will be more acted upon than acting, just as Lear is more sinned against than sinning. It also establishes the theme of the play – the "death of fathers." The theme of the play is the disillusion of a son with reference to the image of a father who was great. The Ghost's appearance and command are a deadening blow, and his mother's present life is a still deeper profanation. By virtue of the nature of the father's appearance and the odd character of his command, Hamlet's initial condition of grief and melancholy is deepened. Hamlet increasingly finds himself incapable of doing what is commanded of him, whereas in life there was nothing Hamlet would not do for his father. He reacts appropriately to a terribly ambiguous sequence of situations, with too much rather than too little feeling. His life becomes overwhelmed with feelings of futility insofar as it becomes a mere function of events apart from meanings. There is a tension between secular and religious morality. The secular aspect is Greek and Skeptical. The religious aspect is Christian and Hebraic. Hamlet is intermediate between.

It is important to notice the way Shakespeare concentrates all levels of belief in the audience upon the Ghost. Coleridge's theory of a willing suspension of disbelief allegorizes a physical fact – the physical fact that the Ghost's real presence provides the framework and impelling force of the play. The opening scene is saturated with concrete theological and moral meanings. The play was written when the dominant religious character and mentality were still medieval and yet were evolving into the Renaissance and Reformation. The tension is among medieval Christian theological ideas, modern Catholic and Protestant attitudes toward the duel and incest, and Greek and Skeptical ideas. In this connection, it is important to remember that there were two sides to the Renaissance – the skeptical side and the optimistic side. Reinhold Niebuhr speaks of the latter, whereas the corrosive self-scrutiny of Hamlet is the former. Hamlet is the counterpart in literature of Descartes, Hume, and Kant in philosophy.

The second problem in movement 1 concerns the peculiar character of the Ghost's command. Revenge and "remember me" are one part of it. "Taint not thy mind" and "Leave thy mother to heaven" are the other. There are many things the Ghost might or could have said but did not. These are the things Hamlet wants and needs to know. Was Gertrude an accomplice to the deed? Had adultery occurred before as well as after the death of his father? Hamlet eventually betrays and fulfils both sides of the command. The betrayal gives poignance to the closet scene. The fulfillment accompanies the final catastrophe and resolution. The Ghost's command has an absolute character on one side and is conditioned on the other. Both sides demand explanation and justification, and yet Hamlet receives none.

The third problem in movement 1 concerns the peculiar character of Hamlet's oath in the cellarage scene and the nature of his "antic disposition" at the end. The middle part of the play is the primary concern of critics. And it is the heart of the play. But in a way we may be most moved by the first and last parts. Unless these early problems are resolved, particularly the flavor of the early soliloquies, we cannot understand why Hamlet does not kill the king at his prayers. It is obvious very early in the first movement that Hamlet loses interest in Claudius and is worried about something else. Vengeance is not his problem or his motive. The oath is peculiar because Hamlet is obviously in a mood of violently "sore distraction." But the violence of the oath indicates that it is in part something to which he is driven. Moreover, insofar as Hamlet employs this "antic disposition" as an instrument to allay Claudius' suspicions, it fails.

In summary, the first movement confronts Hamlet with a set of circumstances which are curious, involved, and strained. They are curious because a ghost has to inform Hamlet about them. They are involved because the Ghost confronts Hamlet with a double command: "Remember me" and "Taint not thy mind" or "Leave thy mother to heaven." The circumstances are strained because Hamlet's uncle is now his stepfather and the usurper of his throne as well.

The problems of the second movement center upon the interpretation of specific scenes. The general problem, if any, concerns Hamlet's failure to use his advantages against Claudius. The act ends with Hamlet in chains and sent off to England. In the middle Hamlet enjoys his greatest triumph – "the play within the play." This second movement has two general lines of action: on the one hand Hamlet seeks to verify the goodness of the Ghost and the validity of its disclosures. This movement leads to and ends in the play-within-the-play scene, which verifies both. The other line of action consists of Claudius's increasing suspicion and eventual counterplot. This movement leads from the Rosencrantz and Guildenstern subplot to the forced exile in England. The crisis of the second movement comes in the scene with the king at his prayers and the closet scene. In the first Hamlet fails to kill the king; in the second he violates the negative side of his father's command. It is also in the closet scene that Hamlet impulsively kills Polonius behind the arras. This might have been the king. In fact, Claudius gains complete command. The Fortinbras soliloquy brings the entire second movement to an end, also foreshadowing the melancholy mixed with resolution in the final movement.

It is very significant that Hamlet acts impulsively, or with too great subtlety and reflection, or not at all in this middle part. Examples of excessive subtlety on Hamlet's part are the play within the play scene and the nunnery scene. Especially in the latter does Hamlet make tremendous demands upon Ophelia's nature, demands that issue into a poignant and tragic end. Examples of impulsive action are the stabbing of Polonius in the closet scene and the leaping into the grave near the beginning of movement 3. At all three levels – inactivity, impulse, and reflection – Laertes and Fortinbras function as foils to everything Hamlet ought and should like to be but for some strange reason is not and cannot be.

The end of movement 2 accomplishes a complete reversal in the state of affairs. At the beginning Hamlet had knowledge whereas Claudius stood in ignorance. Now Hamlet has completely lost his advantage and is being sent off to England and to his death. The turning point in terms of plot was the scene with the king at his prayers. If Hamlet had acted at once he would have gained everything. Failing to act, he loses all. The turning point in terms of character is the closet scene, in which Hamlet betrays the other side of his father's command.

The final movement is the most interesting and important from a theological point of view. Of all parts, the final movement is most baffling. The general problem is the kind of resolution of his problems to which Hamlet may be said to have come in the end. It is not enough to insist upon the final insolubility of Hamlet's problem or the mysteriously inscrutable depth evoked by atmosphere and tone. What can be said in positive terms is that the plot of *Hamlet* involves something more than the story of the defeat of his moral and religious struggle. The final fact is not that Hamlet is destroyed by sickness and despair. The despair is qualified, and the sickness is in a sense and to a degree healed. Something there is in these last scenes that insists upon speaking of resolution. The deadening inner paralysis of the earlier two movements is overcome. To be sure, there is recognition and resignation in a Greek sense. But there is discovery and reconciliation in the Christian sense as well.

Hamlet makes two kinds of penetrating remarks in this final movement – brief soliloquies and highly lyrical asides to Horatio. Shakespeare appears to be trying to emphasize the human nature of Hamlet in this last movement and in an incredibly simple way. From a Skeptical point of view, all we have is premature old age, a wasting away in the face of weariness and despair. From a Christian point of view, Hamlet is coming full circle, from the herioc ideal of youth, through the tragic vision, to religious longing and religious peace.

The final problem of the play is thereby this: does he or does he not solve his problems in the last movement? Is his last look of final penetration one of despair or one of faith? If he resolves his doubts and his despair, does he solve them simply by giving up his intellectual, moral, and religious quest? Is fatalism his final word – the notion that no man does or can think seriously about life, since every man finally just has to let the chips fall where they may? Does Hamlet solve his problems in his own terms? Does he remain in a way youthful, heroic, and bright? Even if Hamlet learns that one cannot make the world over according to one's heart's desire, still does he not witness life as essentially redeemable in principle and in fact redeemed at certain points and moments? The answer must reside in Hamlet's brief soliloquies – penetratingly sincere as they are – and in his poignant asides to Horatio:

It will be done; the interim is mine;
And a man's life's no more than to say "one".

But thou would'st not know how all's sick here about my heart; but it is no matter.

Sir in my heart there was a kind of fighting
That would not let me sleep; me thought I lay

Worse than the mutinies in the bilboes. Rashly, –
And prais'd be rashness for it, let us know,
Our indiscretion sometimes serves us well
When our deep plots do pall; and should teach us
There's a divinity that shapes our ends,
Rough-hew them how we will.

. . . is't not perfect conscience
To quit him with this arm? And is't not to be damn'd
To let this canker in our nature come
To further evil?

. . . The hand of little employment hath the daintier sense.

He that is not guilty of his own death shortens not his own life.

Not a whit, we defy augury; there's a special providence in the fall of a sparrow.
If it be now, 'tis not to come; if it be not to come, it will be now; if it be not
now, yet it will come: the readiness is all. Since no man has ought of what he
leaves what is't to leave betimes? Let be.

If there be a resolution in these brief soliloquies and asides, it is
indeed a rare one. There is something awfully strained, poignant,
and melancholy about it. In a way Hamlet never does find a way out
of his moral and religious problems. Resignation and acceptance,
in the sense of ignoring or forgetting, are a large part of his response.
"Readiness is all." This final readiness to act, no matter what, when,
where, or how is without reasons, intellectual or emotional. It is not
impulse or reflection, for both have failed. Nor is it the inactivity of
hesitation. Something new has evolved. Out of sickness and despair,
there has come a new life, something beyond submission and
acquiescence. It is the feeling that the course of events will in some
sense illustrate the meanings of life – the faith that redemption in
fact will come once and for all.

And yet this final resolution resists easy statement. One can distort
it in the name of Greek and Skeptical fatalism or in the name of
Christian optimism. What keeps Hamlet alive and endows him with
his readiness is neither Skeptical disillusion nor Christian faith,
hope, trust, and love. The final look is not quite as reduced as the
one or as full-blown as the other. In this sense Hamlet stands intermediate between Greek and Skeptical theology on the one hand and
Hebraic and Christian theology on the other. He does not deny
redemption in principle or in fact.

But there is resolution. For Hamlet goes out to meet the course of events and accepts his implication in them forcefully, not just bitterly or joyfully. His dying phrase is, "I had a story to tell." If there is no resolution, Hamlet reenacts the story of the Greek tragic hero who defies circumstances with the integrity of his soul or a modern Skeptical tragic hero who gives up or acts out of indifference. Hamlet in the end is too poignant to be heroic in a Greek sense, bitter in the modern Skeptical sense, or joyful in the Christian sense. There is a religious seriousness and gravity about Hamlet's readiness, but it is as short of joy as it is beyond sheer agony. Hamlet is not restlessly heroic and impulsive in the end as he was at the beginning. Nor has he been completely overwhelmed by sickness, despair, and melancholy. The final look is intermediate.

There are many general theories of *Hamlet*. I shall briefly consider the strengths and weaknesses of the more interesting and important of them before stating that understanding of the play which is my own.

The theories fall rather naturally into two groups: external and internal. The external kind of theory seeks to resolve the difficulties within the play by means of evidence external to it; the internal kind of theory by means of evidence within the play.

Of the external theories, I shall consider three.

First of all, there is the literary theory that speaks of the sources of Shakespeare's play. Everything that is difficult and complicated in *Hamlet* can be accounted for by reference to the fact that it is a recasting of a ready-made play. The imaginative envisagement of the character afresh and the indebtedness to the borrowed story are not completely reconciled, and in the ensuing conflict the latter is usually sacrificed to the more pressing claims of the former. Consequently, the minor characters of the borrowed story and its plot suffer most. And Hamlet's character also suffers some obscurity, if not inner contradiction, in the end. His madness in the old play is a mere feigned device, born of a deliberately assumed antic disposition that may protect him against the pressure of outer circumstance and gain time. Shakespeare's fresh insight calls for madness born of sore distraction – the desperate device employed by a haunted, sickened, and passionate figure caught in tremendous inner moral and religious conflict. The inwardness at the heart of the new play casts the externalities of the old play to the periphery in principle. But they remain in fact.

To be sure, in this play, as in other plays, Shakespeare makes capital out of the tension between the old play and the new; but in this case the reconciliation is not entirely happy. He is unable to turn it fully to his advantage. In the end the character of Hamlet is not fully dramatized, for Shakespeare does not submit it to the final discipline which would make it an integral part of the play. The key to *Hamlet* is to distinguish the old from the new.

Closely related to this theory are the theories which refer to the fact that Hamlet is both an original creation and a stock character – the conventional Elizabethan "melancholy man" and a conventional Senecan tragic hero made over in the image of Elizabethan nobility.

The strength of this kind of literary theory is that it reveals how central Hamlet's character is – "the marrow of the play" – and exhibits how crucial the distinction between pretense and tragic reality is in the initial scenes of the play, especially in the early soliloquies. The weakness, apart from the theoretical difficulty of solving a play by means of external aid, is that it solves the problems of the first movement only and fails to provide a theory of the other parts or of the play as a whole.

Third, there is the dramaturgical theory which speaks in terms of Shakespeare's development as an artist. According to this theory, Shakespeare's method of characterization is not fully mature. He attempts to give the central character a heightened and intensified spiritual life beyond that enjoyed by figures in his historical plays or early tragedies. His only means to this end are the aside and the soliloquy, the former providing lyrical intensity and the latter providing an enlarged epic scope and power. Shakespeare has not fully mastered either device. This explains why Hamlet's soliloquies are virtually inexhaustible matter for meditation, and why an added dimension of spirituality struggles to realize itself through them. But they are not fully worked into the plot – the interplay of character with character, and of character with situation.

The strength of this theory is that it reminds us that Shakespeare was a dramatist rather than just a playwright, that he pushed beyond the conventionalities of his theatre and his own mastered materials and methods. The weakness is that some of the difficulty of *Hamlet* is inherent in the subject matter and therefore inescapable and important.

The third kind of external theory speaks of the lyrical, personal, and autobiographical elements in the play. It refers to the author behind the work. There is Dover Wilson's theory that Hamlet is a close personal friend – the Earl of Essex, and there is T. S. Eliot's theory of an intractable emotional stuff Shakespeare could never fashion into art or externalize and objectify by his art.

The strength of these theories is that they remind us that there is an intensely lyrical aspect to *Hamlet*. The weakness is again theoretical or methodological. That is to say, the theory commits the intentional fallacy. There is an inability to account for the parts and the play as a whole as well.

Of the internal theories, I shall consider eight. They fall very conveniently into two groups: those which stress character and those which stress circumstance. All of the internal theories seek to account for Hamlet's general inability to act. The one finds the reason outside him, the other inside. The key to the suspense of the play resides here – in the real and unreal reasons presented for this fact. Claudius speaks of excessive mourning, Polonius of a mad love for Ophelia, the queen of her hasty remarriage to the king. And Hamlet presents as many more, both feigned and real. Critics and actors are somehow fated to add their own.

Of the internal theories which stress circumstance, I shall consider two.

First is the "obstacle" theory, which suggests that Hamlet's inability to act arises merely from external difficulties. For example, Hamlet cannot find a way both to kill the King and to survive himself or to kill the King and confront the world with public justice rather than merely private vengeance. Hamlet waits upon a chance to get at the king apart from the protection afforded by his guards. The cause of delay is not irresolution, melancholy, madness, or any such deadly inward disability. It comes from a positive desire to marshall evidence whereby he can accuse and convict the king of his guilt in the world's eye. Hamlet has to delay because his ghostly evidence is more apt to prove his own madness than the king's guilt. His madness is therefore a conscious and deliberate device used to protect his life, gain time, and postpone action until circumstance is ripe.

This theory may survive until the scene with the king at his prayers. At that point it completely collapses. Moreover, it is shaky long before that fatal point. Hamlet fails to mention any such

external difficulties. He is more bent upon convincing himself
of the ghost's difficulties. He is more bent upon convincing himself
of the ghost's goodness and veracity than upon convincing the world.
He has it in for the king for private as well as for public reasons. His
constant cry is that he has "the cause and will and strength and means
to do't." Moreover, he has the favor of the people, whereas Claudius
does not. With the king at his prayers Hamlet has everything to
gain and nothing to lose. The scene destroys this theory completely.
Something is here beyond its ken.

This theory's only strength is that it points up the fact that
Hamlet is not so rash and foolish as to give up his life wantonly
and that he does have a concern for the world's eye. The theory is a
function of the old play. All the reworking is in a different direction.

The second circumstance theory is the political theory that
Hamlet, no less than every Shakespearean hero, no matter how
lonely and set apart from his surroundings, acts as a party of a
definite social order. The play involves the realization, not of an
isolated individual only, but of society itself. Whatever is rotten in
Gertrude and Claudius reaches as far as Denmark does. Hamlet's
tragedy is a function of his inability to establish normally coherent
relations with his social order – a task he passes on gratefully and
honestly to Fortinbras in the end. Hamlet's situation involves "a
political environment" as Dover Wilson argues. Part of Hamlet's
desperate uneasiness springs from the fact that Claudius is Denmark's king; the state as well as an individual is betrayed. Hamlet
has awe for his father as king. The purgation at the end is social and
political. This element in the play was obscured by the Romanticists,
who failed to see that no dramatic conflict can be projected apart
from a moral, political, and social order.

The weakness of this theory is that Shakespeare carefully soft-
pedals the political element in the play. We become aware of it by
implication. There is the foreboding of a "strange eruption in the
state," but this is ironically misleading. The sickness is within, not
without. Fortinbras just skirts the edge of the play. As Harley Granville-Barker observes, "Shakespeare stops short of enlarging the
play's action beyond the bounds of personal conflict. . . . For if
once these wider issues took the stage the more intimate ones would
lose, by comparison, their intensity and force. The sanctities are
more inward and deep than the outer order of the state."[1]

Intermediate between the circumstances and character theories of *Hamlet* is A. C. Bradley's famous theory that Hamlet is not "naturally or normally such a man" as he is in the play, "a man who at any *other* time and in any *other* circumstance than those presented would have been perfectly equal to his task; and it is, in fact, the very cruelty of his fate that the crisis of his life comes on him at the moment when he cannot hope to meet it, and when his highest gifts, instead of helping him, conspire to paralyze him."[2] Bradley's theory thus conjoins character and circumstance and is a profound version of the Greek theme of man's suffering nobility and its consequent pity and terror. It is one of the strongest themes and theories of the play.

Of all the character theories, I shall briefly consider six. They fall into two groups: those which stress the conscious and those which stress the unconscious elements in Hamlet's character.

The first and most notorious of the theories emphasizing unconscious elements is the so-called medical theory of Hamlet. According to this theory, Hamlet suffers from the ills to which one of the four kinds of temperament and physiology in the world are subject. He is the melancholy man. This is the famous doctrine of "humours."

More formidable is the Freudian theory of Hamlet. Freud stresses the Oedipus-like complex to which Hamlet is subject, with closely related homosexual and narcissistic tendencies.

The Freudian theory is powerful because Hamlet's mother has made him sick at heart. He is sick with her world and then with his own. The sanctity of life has been dealt a blow. The sexual element in the play is strong. And yet this is more than a case study in abnormal psychology. The weakness of the theory is that Hamlet is an introspective being, understanding himself in a poignant and ironical way. His irony is not captious, bitter, or driven. It is directed against himself.

There are four theories stressing conscious elements of Hamlet's character.

First of all, there is the Romantic theory that Hamlet's inner desperation springs from a nature too finely strung and gently disposed to be able to perform the ugly deeds life sometimes asks and requires. This is the sentimental Hamlet. This theory is unjust to the vigor and masculinity of the actual Hamlet, making him an object of contempt rather than of pity and terror.

The strength of the theory is Granville-Barker's portrait of what he calls "the intrinsic Hamlet," the Hamlet of before the play, the more normal Hamlet persisting beneath all the abnormalities that in part bring on his doom. One can document specifically how Shakespeare carefully "contrives to give us some refracted glimpses of a more normal man," who delights in "the thing that does not matter" and delights in it for its own sake, who has a warm generosity for his friends, who is above all gentle, modest, and open in nature, who passionately admired his father and loved Ophelia, and who had an unaffected fondness for Horatio. This is another version of exquisite sensibility, suffering nobility.

Second, there is the philosophic or intellectualist theory of *Hamlet*. This is the theory rendered famous by Coleridge and Schlegel, who saw Hamlet's tragedy as issuing from excessive reflection. The cause of delay is irresolution, and the cause of irresolution is an excess of the reflective or speculative habit of mind. Hamlet generally intends to obey the Ghost, but "the native hue of resolution is sicklied over with the pale cast of thought." He is said by Schlegel to be "thought-sick." "The whole of the play is intended to show how a calculating consideration which aims at exhausting as far as human foresight can, all the relations and possible consequences of a deed, cripples the power of acting. . . . Hamlet is a hypocrite towards himself; his farfetched scruples are often mere pretexts to cover his want of determination. . . . He has no firm belief in himself or anything else. . . . He loses himself in labyrinths of thought."[3] Hamlet is felt to have had no sense of fact, since every event becomes an idea rather than a deed. He thinks "too precisely upon the event." All his deliberation and analysis dissipate his resolve and paralyze his ability to act, so that when he does finally act he acts without thought and by impulse. Only when he obliterates thought can he act at all. The real tragedy lies in an unbalanced nature wherein thought and action are disjunct.

The weakness of this theory is that the Hamlet in the play is not thus one-sided in nature. Far from being a man of inaction, a timid, weak or reflective creature, he was, Fortinbras tells us, a most practical man who, had he been put on, would have proved himself most royally. Hamlet is eminently capable of acting. A more fierce melancholy than reflection is involved. He is not undone by sheer thought as such. His inactivity arises out of passionate involvement.

His thoughts are bloody. They are driven and haunted. His irony is involved, not detached. His wit is frenzied, seeking relief. His speculation and fancy hover about something eating away his heart and mind.

The strength of the theory is that Hamlet *is* bothered by something between thought and action. Coleridge and Schlegel have a finger on the problem, but their solution is wrong.

Third, there is the moral and religious theory of *Hamlet* that sees Hamlet's delay arising from the restraint of conscience and the constraint of moral and religious scruple. But it is clear in the play that Hamlet assumes he ought to avenge his father and craves to do so. He may doubt the veracity of the Ghost, although this doubt may be a dodge. But he never doubts the moral and religious obligation once it is verified. Hamlet rebukes and chastises himself for failures – behavior inconsistent with the theory. His moral and religious outrage are at his squandering of a calling, not his questioning of it.

Fourth, there is the skeptical and agnostic theory that Hamlet is overwhelmed by a sense of the essential uncertainty and incompleteness of man's life. According to this theory, Hamlet's recognition scene involves a movement from one kind of unhappy misery to another. His reversal is from bad to still worse fortune. This is a formidable theory because the Skeptical motif in the play is very strong.

My own theory of *Hamlet* is intermediate between the last two. *Hamlet* is at once a Hebraic-Christian and a Greek-Skeptical kind of dramatic tragedy. Shakespeare holds these two motifs in tension through the play, from beginning to end. Insofar as the Hebraic-Christian motif is dominant, we feel Hamlet's moral guilt and religious sin. Insofar as the Greek-Skeptical motif is dominant, we feel his suffering nobility and piteous abnormality. The one roots the tragedy in character, the other in circumstance. The flaw in the Hebraic-Christian motif is Hamlet's conscious and unconscious idolatry – his idolatrous impatience with himself and others, his passion to have the events and meanings of life come together too simply or all at once. His flaw in the Greek-Skeptical motif is his finitude and his melancholy despair. He is finite because he is more implicated in the course of events and meanings than a wise man should be. He is in despair because he dreams of a fulfillment within the course of events which he is powerless to bring about or do.

Under the aspect of the Greek-Skeptical motif he moves in the last act from ignorance to the bitterness of truth and from normality to the sadness of complete indifference and despair. Under the aspect of the Hebraic-Christian motif the recognition scene in the last act involves a movement from his knowledge of guilt and sin through repentance and faith to new hope and courage. The reversal of fortune is from misery to happiness, even as he stands deep in tragedy, rather than a simple fall from happiness to misery or from high to low estate. Neither of these motifs is a foil to the other. Each stands out in its own right. The whole genius of the play in fact consists in the way Hamlet persistently refuses a simple image of suffering nobility or piteous abnormality on the one hand or a simple Hebraic-Christian image of idolatrous impatience on the other.

In theological terms, Hamlet stands between the moral and the religious stages of life.[4] In the first movement we see the aesthetic immediacy of his youth broken by pathos. In the second movement we perceive the heroic, ethical seriousness of his oath undercut by irony and humor. In the third and final movement we perceive Hamlet's incipient religiousness shattered in part by despair. He witnesses no insistently particular or unambiguous redemption in fact.

In more literary terms, Hamlet stands between the tragic and the comic hero. In tragedy, the tragic hero perceives the gap between what could or should happen and what in fact occurs. In comedy, the comic hero perceives the gap between what men are and what they claim or attempt to be. In both instances, there is a purification of the understanding by the emotions, or of the emotions by the understanding. But Hamlet refuses or is denied the consolations of both. He does not witness that release that can come of laughter or of tears.

The final effect of the play is neither pity and terror nor judgment and forgiveness. It is rather a sad and poignant melancholy reminiscent of and foreshadowed by Bernardo's "'Tis bitter cold, and I am sick at heart."

A more concrete way of expressing my constructive theory is to say that *Hamlet* is the story of a very young man who tries to become his father's son but without doing violence to his own given nature in the process of doing so. Hamlet makes three attempts to become his father's son. The first two fail miserably. Only the third succeeds, and even it is hard pressed and only narrowly carries the day. What is fascinating is the way Shakespeare dramatizes the shifts in life-attitude from initial heteronomy at the beginning of the play, through autonomy in the middle, to theonomy at the end.[5]

In the first part or movement of the play, Hamlet tries to act in a heteronomous or other-directed way. He attempts to be abjectly obedient toward his father. This is the most short-lived of his efforts. It is almost over before it begins. This attempt starts with his acceptance of his father's command in his oath and ends with the "O, what a rogue and peasant slave am I!" soliloquy. This attempt itself receives vivid expression in the following statement as he takes his oath:

> . . . Remember thee!
> Yes, from the table of my memory
> I'll wipe away all trivial fond records,
> All saws of books, all forms, all pressures past,
> That youth and observation copies there;
> And thy commandment all alone shall live
> Within the book and volume of my brain.

The sound and more autonomous or self-determined attempt begins with the "rogue and peasant slave" soliloquy and ends with the Fortinbras soliloquy. In this attempt Hamlet is extremely active but tries to act only when things make sense to him. In the middle of the play we have the Renaissance Hamlet – bright, witty, and self-assured – trying to shake life down to size or to grab life by the nape of the neck. He has fun with the players, gives Ophelia a very hard time, and refuses to leave his mother alone. But his actions in the middle of the play fail because they play into Claudius's hands and make him more and more suspicious of Hamlet.

The third and final attempt is theonomous or God centered in the sense that Hamlet takes the risk of faith. He decides to do the best that he can do and leaves it up to God to thwart his actions if they turn out to be evil. His faith that God has the last word to say in human affairs is expressed most vividly in the passage which begins with the affirmation that there is a special providence in the fall of a sparrow.

Hamlet's moment of truth comes near the end of the play in a statement he makes to Horatio: "If it be now, 'tis not to come;

if it be not to come, it will be now; if it be not now, yet it will come: the readiness is all." This is one of the most structural passages in the entire play. Its meaning turns on what is taken to be the antecedent of the little word "it." In the context it may mean death, and a very strong case can be made for this possibility. But it may also mean "moment of truth" – the moment when the events and the meaning of life come together in a decision. In any event, this reading is what makes a Christian interpretation of the play possible.

NOTES

1. Harley Granville-Barker, *Prefaces to Shakespeare*, 2 vols. (Princeton, N.J.: Princeton University Press, 1946), 1:24–96.

2. A. C. Bradley, *Shakespearean Tragedy* (London: Macmillan Co., 1904), p. 107.

3. Bradley, p. 105.

4. This particular typology of the spheres of human existence – aesthetic, ethical, and religious – is taken from the work of Sören Kierkegaard. See his *Concluding Unscientific Postscript* (Princeton, N.J.: Princeton University Press, 1941).

5. This typology of life attitudes – autonomy, heteronomy, and theonomy – is taken from the work of the late Paul Tillich.

8

MEDITATIVE POETRY

Louis L. Martz

*Louis L. Martz is Douglas Tracy Smith Professor of English and
American Literature and Master of Saybrook College at Yale Univer-
sity. He is the author of* The Poetry of Meditation (*1954*), The
Paradise Within (*1964*), *and* The Poem of the Mind (*1966*). *The
following essay, with only slight modification, is from* The Meditative
Poem: An Anthology of Seventeenth-Century Verse, *by Louis Martz.
Copyright © 1963 by Louis Martz. Reprinted by permission of
Doubleday & Company, Inc.*

What is a meditative poem? It is a kind of poem that occurs in
various periods of the world's history; but for the seventeenth
century, it is enough to say that the meditative poem is one that
bears a close relation to the practice of religious meditation in that
era. The relationship is shown by the poem's own internal action,
as the soul or mind engages in acts of interior dramatization. The
speaker accuses himself; he talks to God within the self; he approaches
the love of God through memory, understanding, and will; he sees,
hears, smells, tastes, touches by imagination the scenes of Christ's
life as they are represented on an inward, mental stage. Such imaginative, introspective meditation has its roots in the Middle Ages,
when every aspect of the later practice may be found at work, but
in scattered forms, chiefly designed for those who had entered into
religious vows. The special achievement of meditation during the

sixteenth and seventeenth centuries lies in two developments: first, the manifold tactics of medieval meditation were developed into a unified and widely accepted method; and secondly, this way of meditation was viewed and taught as a practice within the reach of every man, as the Jesuit Edward Dawson clearly demonstrates in the short treatise – *The Practical Methode of Meditation* (1614). It is important, first of all, to consider the implications of this method in some detail.

Dawson's treatise, written at the peak of the period's intense concern with the "art of meditation," sums up the central principles that had gradually come to dominate the meditative life of the Continent, primarily through the influence of the *Spiritual Exercises* of Ignatius Loyola. Dawson's treatise is in fact a paraphrase of the *Spiritual Exercises*, with adaptations and extensions prompted, as he says, by "approved Authors and experience." What he gives here is the essence of the advice for meditation that was being offered by spiritual counselors throughout Europe, as well as by the underground priests in England, such as Dawson himself. At the same time this advice was being offered in dozens of popular treatises on meditation that were circulating in thousands of copies throughout Europe, and in England as well.

Signs of the impact of this Continental art of meditation upon England have been explored in my study, *The Poetry of Meditation* (Yale University Press, 1954; second edition, 1962); for present purposes, it is enough to rely primarily on Dawson's neat and compact treatise, which shows by its blunt, simple, "practical" manner the way in which the art of meditation might become part of the everyday life of everyman. The matter-of-fact tone of the treatise, indeed, helps to convey its central and pervasive assumptions: that man, whether he will or not, lives in the intimate presence of God, and that his first duty in life is to cultivate an awareness of that presence. Thus arises the whole elaborate ceremony of meditation: the careful preparation of materials the night before; the "practice of the presence of God," as it was called, before actual meditation; the preparatory prayers; the preludes; the deliberate, orderly operation of the "three powers of the soul" – memory, understanding, will; and the conclusion in "some affectionate speach" or colloquy with God or the saints, in which "wee may talke with God as a servant with his Maister, as a sonne with his Father, as one friend with another, as a spouse with her beloved bridgrome, or as a guilty prisoner with his Judge, or in any other manner which the holy Ghost shall teach us." The aim of meditation is to apprehend the reality and the meaning of the presence of God with every faculty at man's command. The body must first learn its proper behavior during the ceremony: hence the detailed advice on whether to kneel, or walk, or sit, or stand. The five senses must learn how to bend their efforts toward this end: hence the elaborately detailed explanation of the Jesuit "application of the senses" to the art of meditation. Everyday life must come to play its part, for the meditative man must feel that the presence of God is here, now, on his own hearth, in his own stable, and in the deep center of the mind: thus "we may help our selves much to the framing of spirituall conceites [thoughts], if we apply unto our matter familiar similitudes, drawne from our ordinary actions, and this as well in historicall, as spirituall meditations." That is to say, analogies from the world of daily actions must be brought to bear upon the history of the life of Christ, as well as upon such matters as the problem of sin and the excellence of the virtues.

Among all the varied ways of using the senses and physical life in meditation, the most important, most effective, and most famous is the prelude known as the "composition of place." This brilliant Ignatian invention, to which the Jesuit *Exercises* owe a large part of their power, is given its full and proper emphasis by the Jesuit Dawson: "for on the well making of this *Preludium* depends both the understanding of the mystery, and attention in our meditation." Whatever the subject may be, the imagination, the image-making power of man, must endeavor to represent it "so lively, as though we saw [it] indeed, with our corporall eyes." For historical matters, such as events in the life of Christ or a saint, we must visualize the scene in the most vivid and exact detail, "by imagining our selves to be really present at those places." In treating spiritual subjects we must gain the same end by creating "some similitude, answerable to the matter." Thus, for the Last Things, Death, Judgment, Hell, and Heaven, the similitude may be created by imagining the scene in detail, by creating, for example, a likeness of one's self on the deathbed, "forsaken of the Physitians, compassed about with our weeping friends, and expecting our last agony." But the similitude may also be much more figurative: the word "similitude," in seventeenth-century usage, could refer to any kind of parable, allegory, simile, or metaphor. Thus Dawson, discussing the preparation for meditation, suggests that we should "begin to take some tast of our meditation" before the actual performance begins, by stirring up the "affections," the emotions, appropriate to each meditation: "Which we may performe more easily," he adds, "yf we keep in our mind some similitude answering to the affection we would have." And later he suggests that, among several dramatic ways of strengthening these affections, we may sometimes proceed by "faygning [imagining] the very vertues in some venerable shape bewayling their neglect." Thus too he notes that, in the opening similitude for the meditation on sins, "we may imagine our soule to be cast out of Paradise, and to be held prisoner in this body of ours, fettered with the chaines of disordinate Passions, and affections, and clogged with the burden of our owne flesh." In short, this insistence upon "seeing the place" and upon the frequent use of "similitudes" in meditation invites every man to use his image-making faculty with the utmost vigor, in order to ensure a concrete, dramatic setting within which the meditative action may develop. Upon the inward stage of that scene or similitude, the memory, the understanding, and the will may then proceed to explore and understand and feel the proper role of the self in relation to the divine omnipotence and charity. Thus heaven and earth are brought together in the mind; and human action is placed in a responsive, intimate relation with the supernatural.

Only one important qualification needs to be added to the advice of Dawson. In the Ignatian way, he insists that every meditation must begin with some vivid "composition," but we should not be led to expect that every meditative poem will begin with some vivid scene or symbol. Many do so, directly or implicitly, with the speaker present, for example, at some scene in the life of Christ; but many meditative poems also begin simply with a brief, terse statement of the problem or theme to be explored:

> Why are wee by all creatures waited on?

> Why do I languish thus, drooping and dull . . .
> Come, come, what doe I here?

> I Sing the *Name* which none can say,
> But touch't with an interiour *Ray*,
> The *Name* of our *New Peace*, our *Good*,

Our *Blisse*, and supernaturall *Blood*,
The *Name* of all our Lives, and Loves.

What Love is this of thine, that Cannot bee
    In thine Infinity, O Lord, Confinde,
Unless it in thy very Person see,
    Infinity, and Finity Conjoyn'd?

Such openings, though not mentioned by Dawson, are advised by
other writers for abstract topics, particularly by St. François de Sales,
who notes, "It is true that we may use some similitude or comparison
to assist us in the consideration of these subjects," but he fears that
the making of "such devices" may prove burdensome, and thus for
the meditation of "invisible things" he advises one to begin with
"a simple proposal" of the theme.[1] A meditative poem, then, will
tend to open in any one of three ways: (1) with a vivid participation
in some scene in the life of Christ or a saint; (2) with a "similitude,
answerable to the matter," that is, with some imaginary setting or
metaphorical representation; (3) with a "simple proposal" of the
issue to be considered.

With the event or theme thus firmly presented within a "recollected"
mind fully aware of the presence of God, the meditative action
of the three powers of the soul begins to develop each "point"
(usually three) into which the long process of meditation (usually
lasting an hour) has been divided during the period of preparation.
It will be evident from Dawson's account that the operation of the
memory is inseparable from and continuous with the opening
composition or proposal; for the role of memory is to set forth the
subject with all its necessary "persons, wordes, and workes."
The understanding then proceeds to analyze ("discourse" upon)
the meaning of the topic, in relation to the individual self, until
gradually the will takes fire and the appropriate personal affections
arise. It is clear too from Dawson's account that these affections of
the will inevitably lead into the colloquy, where the speaker utters
his fears and hopes, his sorrows and joys, in "affectionate speach"
before God. The full process of meditation always ends with such a
colloquy, but, as Dawson points out, "We may make such manner
of speaches in other places of our meditation, and it will be best,
and almost needfull so to do."

At the same time, the interior drama will tend to have a firm construction, for the process of meditation, in treatiing each "point," will tend to display a threefold movement, according with the action of that interior trinity, memory, understanding, and will. Now and then we may find this threefold process echoed or epitomized within the borders of a short poem; or we may find the process suggested at length in a long poem such as Southwell's *Saint Peters Complaint* or Crashaw's *On the name of Jesus*. But what one should expect to find, more often, is some part of the whole meditative action, set down as particularly memorable, perhaps in accordance with the kind of self-examination adviscd by Dawson under the heading: "What is to be done after Meditation." One is urged here to scrutinize carefully the manner in which one has performed every part of the meditative process, from preparation through colloquy; to examine closely the distractions, consolations, or desolations that one may have experienced; and finally, to "note in some little booke those thinges which have passed in our Meditation, or some part of them, if we think them worth the paynes." Most of the poems in this volume, I believe, are the result of such retrospective examination of the practice of meditation: memorable moments of self-knowledge, affections of sorrow and love, colloquies with the divine presence, recollected and preserved through the aid of the kindred art of poetry.

Meditation points toward poetry, in its use of images, in its technique of arousing the passionate affections of the will, in its suggestion that the ultimate reach of meditation is found in the advice of Paul to the Ephesians: "Be filled with the Spirit; speaking to yourselves in psalms and hymns and spiritual songs, singing and making melody in your heart to the Lord." A meditative poem, then, represents the convergence of two arts upon a single object: in English poetry of the late Renaissance the art of meditation entered into and transformed its kindred art of poetry. To express its highest reaches, the art of meditation drew upon all the poetical resources available in the culture of its day. Southwell, writing in an era dominated by the uninspired verse of the poetical miscellanies – with their heavy-footed, alliterative style and their doggerel ballad-stanzas – could use his meditative techniques, along with his knowledge of Italian poetry, to impart a new and startling vigor even to a moribund poetical mode. Alabaster, writing near the end of the 1590s, at the close of the great era of English sonneteering, could use his meditative art to transform the Elizabethan sonnet. Donne, knowing all the devices of current poetry – whether in satire, love song, sonnet, Ovidian elegy, funeral elegy, courtly compliment, or religious hymn – attained his greatest creations in those poems where his mastery of the meditative art could deepen and strengthen these popular modes of poetic art. Herbert, master of music, adept in every form of Elizabethan song or sonnet, could turn all these varied forms into a temple of praise for his Master's presence. And Crashaw, drawn to the extravagant modes of the Continental Baroque, could nevertheless, at his best, tame and control his extravaganzas by the firm structure of a meditation.

What shall we do, then, with the term "metaphysical" traditionally applied to most of the poets in this volume? For critical and historical purposes we should, I believe, attempt to distinguish between the "metaphysical" and the "meditative" qualities in this poetry. Familiarity with Grierson's pioneer anthology, *Metaphysical Lyrics and Poems* (1921), or with Miss Helen Gardner's superb Penguin selection, *The Metaphysical Poets* (1957), or with Frank Warnke's recent illuminating study and selection, *European Metaphysical Poetry* (1961) will be sufficient to demonstrate that there was a pervasive poetical style in England as well as on the Continent, a style that we have come to call "metaphysical." That style of writing gradually arose, it seems, in response to a widespread reaction against the efflorescent, expansive, highly melodious mode of the earlier Renaissance, as found in Edmund Spenser; it arose also, I believe, in response to a widespread feeling that the manifold expansions of human outlook were rapidly moving out of control: expansions through recovery of the classics, through a new emphasis upon the early fathers of the Church, through the advance of science in all areas, and through the vigorous exploration of the earth by seamen, traders, and conquistadors. As a result, in the latter part of the sixteenth century, poetry showed a tendency to coalesce and concentrate its powers toward the sharp illumination and control of carefully selected moments in experience.

Poems tend to begin abruptly, in the midst of an occasion; and the meaning of the occasion is explored and grasped through a peculiar use of metaphor. The old Renaissance "conceit," the ingenious comparison, is developed into a device by which the extremes of abstraction and concreteness, the extremes of unlikeness, may be woven together into a fabric of argument unified by the prevailing force of "wit." *Wit*, in all the rich and varied senses that the word held in this era: intellect, reason, powerful mental capacity, cleverness, ingenuity, intellectual quickness, inventive and constructive ability, a talent for uttering brilliant things, the power of amusing surprise.

The norm of this "metaphysical" style may be suggested by one of Thomas Carew's poems, *To my inconstant Mistris*, a poem that shows the strong influence of Donne:

> When thou, poore excommunicate
> From all the Joyes of love, shalt see
> The full reward, and glorious fate,
> Which my strong faith shall purchase me,
> Then curse thine owne inconstancy.
>
> A fayrer hand than thine, shall cure
> That heart, which thy false oathes did wound;
> And to my soul, a soul more pure
> Than thine, shall by Loves hand be bound,
> And both with equall glory crown'd.
>
> Then shalt thou weepe, entreat, complain
> To Love, as I did once to thee;
> When all thy teares shall be as vain
> As mine were then, for thou shalt bee
> Damn'ed for thy false Apostasie.

The poem is built upon an original use of the familiar conceit by which the experience of human love is rendered in religious terms. Here the faithless lady is excommunicated as a false apostate from the religion of love, while her lover will receive the reward of his "strong faith" by being crowned in glory, like the saints in heaven. But, paradoxically, his faith will be demonstrated, his constancy in love rewarded, by the act of turning to another lady, with a "fayrer hand" and "a soul more pure." Inconstancy is thus met with the threat of counter-inconstancy; and all the rich religious terms take on in the end a swagger of bravado. The poem thus presents a brief episode in erotic frustration, a vignette in which the backlash of the lover's bitterness is conveyed by the immediacy of his language, by the conversational flexibility of actual speech working within a strict stanza-form. Here we may see a representative poem in the metaphysical style, composed by a man whose life and works give no evidence of any significant concern with religious meditation.

Now, to see how the interior discipline of meditation could work within this "witty" mode of writing, it may be helpful to select one of the lesser poems of this volume, written by a man whose poetical skill is far less than Thomas Carew's: I choose one of Alabaster's sonnets, dealing with "the ensignes of Christes Crucifyinge." The sonnet begins with a direct address to the symbols of the Crucifixion, which the speaker appears to have directly before his eyes; crying out to them, fully aware of the paradoxes that they represent, he proposes the question of his own proper response:

> O sweete, and bitter monuments of paine
> bitter to Christ who all the paine endured
> butt sweete to mee, whose Death my life procured
> how shall I full express, such loss, such gaine?

Turning to consider the powers that lie within himself, his tongue, his eyes, his soul, he proceeds to explain to himself how these may be led toward their proper end, by writing in the book of his soul the record of his sin:

> My tonge shall bee my penne, mine eyes shall raine,
> teares for my Inke, the place where I was cured
> shall bee my booke, where haveing all abjured
> and calling heavens to record in that plaine
> thus plainely will I write, noe sinne like mine;

And finally, holding fast with tenacious logic to his previous images, he closes in a plea of colloquy with the Lord, whose presence has been implicit throughout:

> when I have done, doe thou Jesue divine
> take upp the tarte spunge of thy passione
> and blott itt forth: then bee thy spirit the Quill
> thy bloode the Inke, and with compassione
> write thus uppon my soule: thy Jesue still.

Abrupt opening, condensed and compact phrasing, with touches of colloquial speech, witty development of central conceits, coalescing the abstract and the concrete, logic, paradox – all the essential qualities of the European metaphysical style are there – yet something more creates the poem's modest success. Essentially the poem depends upon the speaker's mastery of the introspective art of meditation. He has learned how to make himself present before the "monuments" of the Passion, how to concentrate memory, understanding, and will upon these symbols of Christ's suffering, how to develop the personal meaning of the Passion through the use of appropriate similitudes, how to drive home the meaning for the self in affectionate colloquy with God. The art of meditation has provided the techniques by which Alabaster could create a brief interior drama. It is, I believe, in these techniques of self-dramatization that we find the peculiar contribution of the art of meditation to poetry. They are techniques that may combine with a great variety of poetical styles: early Elizabethan, metaphysical, Jonsonian, baroque, or Miltonic.

Thus in Alabaster's sonnet we have a rudimentary example of the convergence of the two arts, the meditative and the poetic, in a poem written, it seems, about ten years before John Donne's Holy Sonnets, and over thirty years before the completion of Herbert's *Temple*. In a much more complex way, the same coalescence of the two arts may be found in the poems of Donne: in his finest satire, in several of his best love poems, in the greatest of his funeral elegies, as well as in his Holy Sonnets and the last hymns. That is not to say that all of Donne's poetry is touched by this convergence of the meditative art upon the metaphysical mode; it is only to say that the meditative art is evident, in varying degrees, in many of the poems upon which Donne's reputation primarily rests, even in some poems where the art of meditation is turned, with wit, to secular ends.

An effort to distinguish between the "meditative" and the "metaphysical" may help to solve the problem of Donne's relation to later poets of the seventeenth century. Though the explicit indebtedness to Donne is obvious in some of the secular poetry of the period (such as Carew's), the specific debts to Donne in the religious poetry of Herbert, Crashaw, or Vaughan – where one somehow feels a more essential kinship – are much more elusive, or indeed almost nonexistent. The problem cannot be resolved by arguing that Herbert's poetry centrally descends from Donne, and that since Herbert influenced Crashaw and Vaughan, the two latter poets are thus at least the grandsons of Donne. Several recent studies have shown Herbert's deep-rooted independence of Donne: his use of medieval forms and symbols, his mastery of all varieties of Elizabethan poetry and song, his mastery of the meditative techniques. What Herbert passed on to Vaughan was his own great and original creation, which

Vaughan himself proceeded to use in his own highly original way, combining Herbert's example with the example of the "Sons" of Ben Jonson, to whose line he displays his allegiance in his early secular poems. The few echoes of Donne that we meet in Vaughan's first volume (1646) are overwhelmed by his dominant experiments in the Jonsonian mode of the couplet-rhetoric, as the opening poem of the volume clearly testifies, a poem addressed to a certain friend, R. W.:

> When we are dead, and now, no more
> Our harmles mirth, our wit, and score
> Distracts the Towne; when all is spent
> That the base niggard world hath lent
> Thy purse, or mine; when the loath'd noise
> Of Drawers, Prentises, and boyes
> Hath left us, and the clam'rous barre
> Items no pints i' th' Moone, or Starre . . .
> When all these Mulcts are paid, and I
> From thee, deare wit, must part, and dye;
> Wee'le beg the world would be so kinde,
> To give's one grave, as wee'de one minde;
> There (as the wiser few suspect,
> That spirits after death affect)
> Our soules shall meet, and thence will they
> (Freed from the tyranny of clay)
> With equall wings, and ancient love
> Into the Elysian fields remove,
> Where in those blessed walkes they'le find,
> More of thy Genius, and my mind:
>   First, in the shade of his owne bayes,
> Great *BEN* they'le see, whose sacred Layes,
> The learned Ghosts admire, and throng,
> To catch the subject of his Song.
> Then *Randolph* in those holy Meades,
> His Lovers, and *Amyntas* reads,
> Whilst his Nightingall close by,
> Sings his, and her owne Elegie;
> From thence dismiss'd by subtill roades,
> Through airie paths, and sad aboads;
> They'le come into the drowsie fields
> Of Lethe, which such vertue yeelds,
> That (if what Poets sing be true)
> The streames all sorrow can subdue.

This steady, terse, and easy handling of the tetrameter couplet is a hallmark of the Jonsonian mode, and it is a form into which many of Vaughan's finest poems in *Silex Scintillans* are cast. Yet poems in the tetrameter couplet are not at all characteristic of Donne or Herbert. It is worth noting, too, in passing, that this Jonsonian use of the tetrameter couplet is found in Crashaw's poems on St. Teresa (along with variations into the pentameter); and it is also one of Andrew Marvell's favorite forms. This does not mean that we should substitute Jonson for Donne as the prime poetical model for these writers; in fact, the influence of Jonson and that of Donne are almost inseparably intermingled throughout the seventeenth century, and particularly in Marvell, the most eclectic of poets. But the appearance of a Jonsonian style in these poets will provide striking evidence of the way in which the art of meditation could and did combine with any available mode in poetry.

To his early practice in the Jonsonian mode, and to the great example of Herbert, Vaughan added the indispensable element: his own powerful mode of Augustinian meditation, probing the memory for glimmerings of the divine light of Eden, never quite lost in man. Thus too with Traherne, who carries to an optimistic extreme the Augustinian conviction that the divine image lies within man's memory, to be uncovered and restored by meditation. Traherne's *Third Century*, with its intermingled prose and poetry, provides a particularly clear example of the convergence of the two arts.

Crashaw, though resembling Herbert and Jonson in places, finds his central poetic allegiance in the Continental Baroque. The kinship that he truly holds with Donne and Herbert does not lie within poetical traditions, strictly so called; it lies rather in Crashaw's own underlying mastery of the art of meditation, by which he often gives the firm and subtle structure of his "wit of Love" to violent sensory effects that may on the surface seem to escape all reasonable control.

Finally, faraway from England, and even farther away, in every respect, from the Italy where Richard Crashaw found his final refuge, the meditative line of the seventeenth century ends with the Puritan Edward Taylor, writing his *Preparatory Meditations* in the wilderness of Massachusetts, before offering the Lord's Supper to his company of the Elect. Taylor's chief poetical models appear to have been Herbert and Quarles, but the rude power of his poetry seems to derive from his command of the traditional method of meditation, adapted to his Puritan beliefs. It is an appropriate tribute to the deep and varied appeal of the art of meditation in this era that its first significant English poet should have been the young Jesuit, Robert Southwell, who returned secretly to his native land after ten years of training by the Counter Reformation, and that the last should have been the Calvinist Taylor, who left England to seek the freedom of his faith in the New World.

In the end, no definition can hope to hold the adventurous vitality of the meditative art, as changing, resourceful, and elusive as the mind in which the meditation is enacted. But perhaps it is enough to say that the central meditative action consists of an interior drama, in which a man projects a self upon a mental stage, and there comes to understand that self in the light of a divine presence.

NOTE

1. See St. Francis de Sales, *Introduction to the Devout Life* [1609], tr. and ed. by John K. Ryan (Image Books, 1955), pp. 83–84. The whole treatise, especially the second part, is of the utmost interest to anyone concerned with studying the details of meditative practice.

9

RELIGIOUS POETRY IN THE UNITED STATES

Richard P. Blackmur

Richard P. Blackmur was for many years Professor of English at Princeton University. Some of his many books of criticism include The Double Agent *(1935),* The Expense of Greatness *(1940),* Form and Value in Modern Poetry *(1952),* Language as Gesture *(1952),* The Lion and the Honeycomb *(1955), and* Anni Mirabiles, 1921-1925 *(1956). "Religious Poetry in the United States," by Richard P. Blackmur was originally written for Vol. 2,* Religious Perspectives in American Culture. *From* Religion in American Life, *eds. J. W. Smith and A. L. Jamison (Copyright © 1961 by Princeton University Press), pp. 273–87. Reprinted by permission of Princeton University Press.*

After meditating off and on for three years about American religious verse, I find that it seems to reach in different directions and by different routes than those taken by what is called English or French or Italian religious verse; and it appears to have used, or cultivated, different forces in the Psyche than those within the specific familiar limits of traditional Christian feeling and dogma. It is as if religion itself had reached, or is in the process of reaching, another and different stage in its history than our regular historical sense would have predicted. Some of our Protestant theologians – as Reinhold

Niebuhr – say this in their own way when they refer to present times as post-Christian; and they shall have all the rest of the words on this aspect of the subject, which is American religious verse and especially the small amount of it which is also poetry; but I want to keep in mind that unexpected forces of the Psyche are at work in it.

Which is also poetry. Anyone has enough talent to write verse within a body of recognized conventions, but very few have enough talent to make their verse poetry. We are all poets in little, else we could not read it when large; it is a matter, as Croce insisted, of quantity not quality of talent. Most verses written out of love are drivel, and most versifications of the psalms take the poetry out of them and substitute mnemonic rehearsals of doctrine and archetypal images. Hence the morals, like the love, are flagrant, and all the substance of the writer's faith and passion which he would have made public is missing forever. He is not there in front of us, and he has not put his presence into his verse. It is the presence of the human Psyche in words that makes the scandal of poetry as its presence in action makes the scandal of religion.

The distinction is worth insisting on, and I can think of no better language for it than a short passage from George Santayana's preface to *Interpretations of Poetry and Religion* where he outlines the single idea to which his whole book leads. "This idea is that religion and poetry are identical in essence, and differ merely in the way in which they are attached to practical affairs. Poetry is called religion when it intervenes in life, and religion, when it merely supervenes upon life, is seen to be nothing but poetry."[1] It is a matter of choice, chance, and tact or grace, which is which; and religious poetry, I take it, is when the two are taken together. As religion takes new forms and changes the nature and scope of its interventions, so the poetry associated with religion supervenes differently upon our reading lives in manifest presence. There is an area in us where religious poetry at one and the same time both comes among our actions and overcomes them, an ordering together with a ravishing.

The second of the Homeric Hymns to Aphrodite is like that, and the *Pervigilium Veneris*, and perhaps the invocation to Venus in *De Rerum Natura*. They intervene and supervene at once as they persuade us of our occupation. Though the first is a narrative of events. the second an incantation, and the third a part of a philoso- phical discourse, in each the intervention is religious, the supervention poetic: they touch on behavior fused with aspiration. Reading, we act and breathe and lose the action in our breath. It is the same thing, I think, when we come to the *Cantico delle Creature* of St. Francis where the gap between God and nature is annihilated through the salutation of both in single breath and all our occupation is gone and come at once. Reading St. Francis' Canticle our substance is ravished with all weathers – *omne tempo* – and all the weathers have their own meaning in the being of God. The first three poems we know are not Christian; of the Canticle we know that it is a Christian who wrote it, and one who changed Christianity through the forces that led him to write it. Here are two lines of Iacopone da Todi (of whom it is said that he wrote the *Stabat Mater*) taken from the beginning of his poem on the incarnation of the divine word:

> *Fiorito è Cristo nella carne pura:*
> *or se ralegri l'umana natura*

> Christ has flowered in pure flesh:
> Now let human nature rejoice

and three from the beginning of his poem "That it is the highest wisdom to be thought mad for love of Christ":

> *Senno me pare è cortesia . empazir per lo bel Messia. . . .*
> *Ello me sa sì gran sapere . a chi per Dio vol empazire,*
> *en Parige non se vidde . ancor si gran diloso fia.*[2]

Sense and nobleness it seems to me to go mad for the fair Messiah. . . . It seems to me great wisdom in a man if he wish to go mad for God; no philosophy so great as this has yet been seen in Paris.

Iacopone was a Franciscan, too, of the second generation, and a splendid Christian struggle had begun in his poetry, of which St Francis was free in his simplicity of salutation – the struggle, the wrestling of spirit, to join himself to God. It is a man we know who speaks, as it was in the others a voice we discovered. We hear a voice like this in Donne (in *Batter my Heart*), in Crashaw (*Hymn to St. Teresa*), in George Herbert (*The Pulley*), even in Milton (*Samson Agonistes*). In them all there is a spiritual sensuality behaving like a prodigal mathematics. Religious poetry was for them, as it is somewhat today, a natural technique for the speculative framing and the dramatic solution of the problem of the troubles that beset us when we would play the role of God in our own way.

Those who care for the word may say that this was the Baroque spirit at work, and this might be apt from St. John of the Cross to Milton; but it does not help with Iacopone, and helps very little with later poets in the nineteenth and twentieth centuries, like Crane and Eliot and Auden, nor with all those who have read too much St. Augustine and Gerard Manley Hopkins. I would say rather that it is the great wrestling tradition which has inhabited the great majority of religious poets since the Council of Trent, and it makes no difference whether they were Catholic or Protestant or non-juring or simple abstainers. The Reformation and the Counter-Reformation alike put upon us the compulsion to a wrestling (and to an irregular metaphysic to account for the wrestling): a wrestling with God, with the self, with the conscience, and above all in our latter day with our behavior. Pascal stands as a natural monument of one form of this wrestling, Baudelaire as another, and Henry James and James Joyce as a kind of composite for our day. But the mind roams and needs a point of return which is in Genesis (xxxii, 22–32);

And Jacob was left alone; and there wrestled a man with him until the breaking of the day.

And when he saw that he prevailed not against him, he touched the hollow of his thigh; and the hollow of Jacob's thigh was out of joint, as he wrestled with him.

And he said, Let me go, for the day breaketh. And he said, I will not let thee go, except thou bless me.

And he said unto him, What is thy name? And he said, Jacob.

And he said, Thy name shall be called no more Jacob, but Israel: for as a prince hast thou power with God and with man, and hast prevailed.

And Jacob asked him, and said, Tell me, I pray thee, thy name. And he said, Wherefore is it that thou dost ask after my name? And he blessed him there.

And Jacob called the name of the place Peniel: for I have seen God face to face, and my life is preserved.

And as he passed over Penuel the sun rose upon him, and he halted upon his thigh.

Therefore the children of Israel eat not of the sinew which shrank, which is upon the hollow of the thigh, unto this day: because he touched the hollow of Jacob's thigh in the sinew that shrank.

It is astonishing that we do not have poems called *The Place Peniel* and *The Sinew that Shrank;* for there is in this adventure of Jacob half the subject-matter of modern poetry – which is why we can fill in so well the bareness of this original account with the muscle and nerve of our own wrestling with God, man, or angel, as it may turn out – at any rate a damaging *and* saving confrontation of the self and the "other" self. What seem to be the beginnings of American religious poetry – Anne Bradstreet and Edward Taylor – illustrate the theme in its simple form as the versification of typical experiences and enthusiasms, of doctrine and behavior, where versification is a kind of rehearsal for an act or a role yet to be undertaken. Mrs. Bradstreet, for example, has a dialogue between Flesh and Spirit which precisely fits this description. Her much lovelier, and more sensuous, poem beginning "As weary pilgrim, now at rest" has a feeling in it of a longing, a wooing, of confrontation; but we do not feel either instance or instant. There is no architecture, and the last line ("Then Come, deare bridgrome, Come away!") seems merely pious where it had struggled to be an act of piety. This, at the furthest imaginable reach, I should like to compare to Henry Adams' *A Prayer to the Virgin of Chartres,* a poem which he carried for many year was a kind of amulet in his wallet, and in which there is present both all the architecture of the cathedral at Chartres and all the space in the Hall of Dynamos at the Paris World's Fair. This is, I think, one of those poems in which the poetry ceases to matter – in which, as in Mrs. Bradstreet, the verse does some damage to the moving thought under the words; but there is a great struggle for the confrontation of a vision gone: the vastation in which one still lives. Here is the last stanza:

> Help me to bear! not my own baby load,
>   But yours; who bore the failure of the light,
> The strength, the knowledge and the thought of God, –
>   The futile folly of the Infinite.[3]

One thinks of a Pascal of our days. *Le silence éternel de ces espaces infinis . . .* and there is a regret only for the *words* of the last line. Under them there is a full act of piety to the numinous power, and Jacob's adventure is very near.

It is near perhaps because, not very good poetry itself, it is in the mode of poetry rather than the mode of religion. Herman Melville left a manuscript poem (which is said to have been much rewritten) that may be taken as evidence as to how these modes may cross – how two prayers may be said at the same time – in the special self-consciousness of American imagination. The poem is called "Art" but it deals also with Jacob. Since it is short it is quoted entire.

In placid hours well-pleased we dream
Of many a brave unbodied scheme.
But form to lend, pulsed life create,
What unlike things must meet and mate:
A flame to melt – a wind to freeze;
Sad patience – joyous energies;
Humility – yet pride and scorn;
Instinct and study; love and hate;
Audacity – reverence. These must mate,
And fuse with Jacob's mystic heart,
To wrestle with the angel – Art.[4]

The poetry – the art, the Angel Art – at which these lines are aimed, is, it seems to me, one excellent way to describe what has happened to religious poetry in America, and it is possible to religion herself, too. To keep to the poetry, it has simultaneously insisted on the value of what it can itself create and on the pressure (who knows its value) of the numinous power within us, and the relationship between the two is mutinous; as for God – the intervening power – there is discontent, distrust, and dismay for what he has created, but with a lingering addiction of first and last resort. It is Melville again who put this in the final quatrain of an otherwise undistinguished poem about a picture called "The Coming Storm" by Sandford Gifford. For Melville it was the storm in the lull of which we live.

No utter surprise can come to him
    Who reaches Shakespeare's core;
That which we seek and shun is there –
    Man's final lore.[5]

Of these lines F. O. Matthiessen observed that they "constitute one of the most profound recognitions of the value of tragedy ever to have been made." I think tragedy an accidental word here, which might have been any other whole word, and especially the word religion; and Shakespeare is another accident. Melville fought the archetypes he sought, and he sought the God he fought. The lines represent many confrontations and many visions, and are therefore always ready to exact from us the details with which to fill them out in what we have done with our own behavior, or in the qualms it has left in us. If it were not so long there is a poem of Melville's called *After the Pleasure Party* which I would quote in illustration at full length; but I content myself with a few lines plus its subtitle, "Lines traced under an Image of Armor Threatening":

> 'Tis Vesta struck with Sappho's smart.
> No fable her delirious leap:
> With more of cause in desperate heart,
> Myself could take it – but to sleep! . . .
>
> Could I remake me! or set free
> This sexless bound in sex, then plunge
> Deeper than Sappho, in a lunge
> Piercing Pan's paramount mystery![6]

These are matters which had been exorcised by Christianity, but they are none the less the very earth of religious concern, and they have been creeping back into the articulations as well as the bloodstream of Christians. Though the argument (since it is the argument of our actual motion) would be worth pursuing for its interest and vitality, for present purposes we can get about as far ahead by thinking of Edward Taylor and Robert Lowell in single context. Both are characteristic New England wrestlers with the spirit. Each has the ghastly sophistication of the Christian Puritan Protestant – a hangnail may be taken as excruciation – and each is aware of the bottomless resources of Enthusiasm and Antinomianism generally. (I remember that T. S. Eliot once in a hot moment reprehended certain addicts of the Inner Voice by saying that it was the eternal voice of Vanity, Fear, and Lust; and he was right.) Lowell wrestles – or behavior wrestles – against the conscience of his faith as revealed to him at the moment. Taylor wrestles against his private conscience. Taylor is full of the *strong lines* of the late metaphysicals, and Lowell writes in strong lines of his own making; each – and I mean the words literally – is obstinate in the spontaneity of his corruption, arrogant in his inadequacy: each is fiercely humble. The chasm between them is like the chasm each saw in himself: upon no razor's edge can this be crossed, and yet one's feet are upon razors. One of Taylor's poems is called *The Souls Groan to Christ for Succour* and it is of such groans that the majority of Lowell's poems are made. Another pair of Taylor's poems make grating accusations of the inner and the outer man where each, so to speak, is stripped into a reversal of role. In each the "other" self confronts the self; and, again, so it is with Lowell, the devil in him wrestles with the man, the angel with the god, in such poems as *To Delmore Schwartz* and *To Speak of Woe that is in Marriage*. The difference is that Taylor pushes his sensibility into conceit (almost into formal allegory) and the conceit is the meaning of the sensibility, while Lowell drenches his conceit (the position he has been forced into) with his sensibility and the sensibility, like a road-barrier, is the meaning we are stopped by. Taylor cultivates the numinous or religious force for a purpose already anticipated. Lowell makes the force the purpose itself. For Taylor unity already existed and had to be acknowledged as a mystery that enlightens; for Lowell what unity there is you make yourself and it darkens you forever.

One can imagine Lowell repeating the remark in Gide: God woos us by his calamities, and that is how he shows his love for us; but we cannot imagine Lowell repeating what Taylor heard as *Christ's Reply* to *The Souls Groan to Christ for Succour*, for it would have done this latter-day or post-Christian Christian no good. Taylor can write at the end of *Upon a Wasp Chilled with Cold*:

> Till I enravisht climb into
> The Godhead on this ladder doe:
> Where all my pipes inspir'de upraise
> An Heavenly musick, furr'd with praise.[7]

Lowell writes at the end of his *Memories of West Street and Lepke*:

> Flabby, bald, lobotomized,
> He drifted in a sheepish calm,
> where no agonizing reappraisal
> jarred his concentration on the electric chair –
> hanging like an oasis in his air
> of lost connections . . .[8]

The difference is absolute, and we have come again full circle to Iacopone:

> *Fiorito è Cristo nella carne pura:*
> *or se ralegri l'umana natura.*

That is, we can speak of Whitman, for he could have written the Italian lines with only the substitution, to him simple and natural, of himself for Christ: All of me has flowered in my flesh, so let us rejoice in human nature. Indeed it is not in his naïve barbarism (in which the artists and intellectuals of the last century found such companionship) but in his direct and deeply civilized piety, which is precisely where he resembles Iacopone, that his poetry endures. Since it is more familiar to more people than most of his poems, we can let *When Lilacs Last in the Dooryard Bloom'd* stand for the rest, the more especially because in this poem it is very clear how he met his archetypes – his governing and vitalizing images – the symbols that made him fruitful in words – both in the open road and in the thicket of the Psyche: in what man does and in what he finds doing in himself, in which is included what man has in the past done with his poetry. Whitman, says Northrup Frye in his *Anatomy of Criticism*, was "perfectly right in feeling that the *content* of poetry is normally an immediate and contemporary environment. He was right, being the kind of poet he was, in making the content of his own *When Lilacs Last in the Dooryard Bloom'd* an elegy on Lincoln and not a conventional Adonis lament. Yet his elegy is, in its *form*, as conventional as *Lycidas*, complete with purple flowers thrown on coffins, a great star drooping in the west, imagery of 'ever-returning spring' and all the rest of it. Poetry organizes the content of the world as it passes before the poet, but the forms in which that content is organized come out of the structure of poetry itself."[9]

This is very fine; but I should like to add for present purposes that this is how *religious* poetry operates – when poetry comes nearest to positive intervention in the actions of the soul. As Mr. Frye says, it is not only the Adonis material; there is also the sprig of lilac with its mastering odor, the hidden bird and the secluded swamp, and the "tallying chant" in which all come together: "Lilac and star and bird twined with the chant of my soul." There are two progresses in the poem, of Lincoln's body and of the images, which join in the sacred knowledge of death. Lincoln, Lilac, and Thrush are merged in a full act of piety.

It is a difference of half a century as much as a difference of sensibility in the particular poets that strikes us when we look into the thicket of Robert Frost: in which there are obstinate possibilities and obstinate forces, not human themselves, that yet – as they are cultivated into the sensibility – change the human dimension and alter, a little, the reticulation of the elements of the human Psyche. To acknowledge this is a religious action: a momentary conversion. The consuming or purifying fire is always at hand in such acknowledgments, and the more so if, as in Frost, the individual is held on to, nevertheless and because. But one does not wish to exaggerate. Here is an example in the poem *Come In*.

> As I came to the edge of the woods,
> Thrush music – hark!
> Now if it was dusk outside,
> Inside it was dark.
>
> Too dark in the woods for a bird
> By sleight of wing
> To better its perch for the night,
> Though it still could sing.
>
> The last of the light of the sun
> That had died in the west
> Still lived for one song more
> In a thrush's breast.
>
> Far in the pillared dark
> Thrush music went –
> Almost like a call to come in
> To the dark and lament.
>
> But no, I was out for stars:
> I would not come in.
> I meant not even if asked;
> And I hadn't been.[10]

Frost exposed himself to the thrush in the wood – the *selva oscura* – the thicket where perceptions not one's own become a part of one, and found himself confronted with himself. There is no doctrine here and no dogma, but there is the perception out of which many doctrines have sprung and the kind of grasping imagination which has made dogma vital. Those who have need of doctrine and dogma first, before they risk perception, may bring what they will and it will work. Let us say only that there are two remotenesses here: of what is dark and at hand and of what is light (the little that is known of it) and afar; and there is a double invitation to loneliness. Intimations spring from one to the other through the man between, changing and remaining in the graininess of his voice. This is Frost's way, I hazard it, of recording the light in the dark and the dark in the light and the coiling movement between them of the self confronting the self.

It is perhaps unfair to make a foil for Frost's poem of Edwin

Markham's *The Man with the Hoe* – once so famous for its perception of man's lot and man's need; but I can think of nothing that
shows so well the difference between poetry and good will as to
think of the two poems together. Let us put it baldly. Millet's
painting was in natural piety to the land and the man with the hoe
was very close to being a part of the land which was his life, which it
takes deep knowledge to perceive. To my mind Frost's poem and
Millet's painting are two versions of the same perception of the
human condition, which it is damnation to ignore and a strange
redemption to accept. Markham made of the painting a poem of
social protest and flagrantly righteous indignation. Out of a false
naïveté he saw a false arhetype and constructed a faulty icono-
graphy. It is the condition in which every perception disappears and
hope is thereby hollow. In Frost's poem, not Markham's, the dumb
Terror replies to God.

For the other type of foil to Frost, the type that sustains and
protects, there is the poetry of Emily Dickinson, which puts the
hand upon the quick within her and sings hymns to the actuality of
every illusion, and every crowding hope, that struck her. In her,
religion supervenes and poetry intervenes upon her secular life
without discrimination. Faith, she thought, was the experiment of
our Lord.

> The auctioneer of parting,
> His "Going, going, gone,"
> Shouts even from the crucifix
> And brings the hammer down.
>
> He only sells the wilderness.
> The prices of despair
> Range from a single human heart
> To two – not any more.[11]

The variety is sufficient, but I should not like to stop lest it be
thought I would set up categories into which religious poetry should,
or must, fall. I think of Hart Crane's *Voyages*, of Wallace Stevens'
Sunday Morning, of Archibald MacLeish's play about Job, and of
the new Catholic poets such as Daniel Berrigan, Thomas Merton,
and Ned O'Gorman. All of these poets, and no doubt many more,
write poetry which can be understood only if it is taken as religious;
and yet the variety varies more than the winds. To repeat, since
there is no seal upon us in this post-Christian time, our religious

like our other emotions come out of Pandora's box; or, to repeat
more precisely, as religion takes new forms and changes the nature
and scope of its interventions, so the poetry associated with religion
supervenes differently upon our reading lives. If there is anything
in common not only with itself but with the past, aside from its
impulse, I do not know what it is, but it is possible to make a few
unaligned suggestions. We are likely to be concerned with the
excruciation (as Jacob was not); with Jacob's wrestling with Angel,
Man or God; with the dark night of the soul that never ends since
it was a darkness we ourselves made; with the nightmares of the
numen or the night-life of the spirit rather than its waking wide
safety; and altogether with the great sweep of rival creation since,
like Ivan in *The Brothers Karamazov*, we can accept God but not
his Creation. We are lost, as Eliot seems to suggest (in his essay on
Dante), in our new immersion in our lower dreams, with the higher
dreams gone by the board or unavailing; and indeed only Eliot
seems to see the place where the two dreams cross, and it may be
only his language that sees that, for he himself calls it "The unread
vision in the higher dream" and "the brief transit where the dreams
cross." These are the hardships we come by in our daily life, and our
poetry reflects them since they are actual.

What is actual, when we would be religious, invades us like a
nightmare of our own behavior suddenly seen, and it is our own
monsters that keep us from God, and no mere scholarship of the
dark will save us, only acknowledgment. We must remove the
obstacles, as Pascal saw, that keep us from falling into the abyss;
and the obstacles are of our own invention. I think of Allen Tate
and his poem *The Wolves*, of W. H. Auden and his poem *Petition*,
and of Eliot's *Little Gidding*. Each of these poems, by way of those
intrusive monsters anthropology, psychology, and behavior, finds
it time for human nature to rejoice, each tries to construct something, as Eliot says, upon which to rejoice, but each is left impaled
upon the nature of man. Each therefore is the prayer of what is
terrible in human nature (which is nature herself) addressed to the
"honor of man," to "a change of heart," and to the "refining fire."

What then are they doing? As one reorganizes one's life one sees
that one has been religious all along in the poetry one has made of
it. Religious poetry has to do with the modes of power and power-
lessness, of glory and misery. These it asserts. With these it wrestles

and argues; to them submits; on them rises; in them dies. These are the terms of the poem's relation with the numinous force; the force within the self, other than the self, greater than the self, which, as one cultivates it, moves one beyond the self. Poetry is one of the ways of cultivation; and the harvest is vision. One would see God and die – so Petrarch put it. In any case there is a confrontation, and in the confrontation a flowing of force ending in an access or filling of being, else in a vastation or desolation; and the two are much the same: in calm of mind all passion spent, or *In la sua voluntade è nostra pace*. Who can say which is which?

> And courage never to submit or yield
> And what is else not to be overcome . . .

> O dark, dark, dark, amid the blaze of noon . . .

> *Sunt lacrimae rerum et mentem mortalia tangunt* . . .

> Myself, my Sepulcher, a moving Grave . . .

> *or se ralegri l'umana natura.*

NOTES

1. *Interpretations of Poetry and Religion* (New York, 1922), p. v.

2. *The Penguin Book of Italian Verse*, George Kay, ed. (New York and Harmondsworth, 1958), pp. 13, 17.

3. *Prayer to the Virgin of Chartres*, in *Letters to a Niece* (Boston and New York, 1920), p. 134.

4. *Collected Poems of Herman Melville*, Howard P. Vincent, ed. (Chicago, 1947), p. 231.

5. *Ibid.*, p. 94.

6. *Poets of the English Language*, W. H. Auden and Norman H. Pearson, eds. (New York, 1950), V, 310, 312.

7. T. H. Johnson, "Edward Taylor Gleanings," *NEQ*, XVI, June 1943, p. 283.

8. *Life Studies* (New York, 1959), p. 86.

9. *Anatomy of Criticism* (Princeton, 1957), p. 102.

10. *A Witness Tree* (New York, 1942), p. 16.

11. *Poets of the English Language*, W. H. Auden and Norman H. Pearson, eds. (New York, 1950), V, 396.

THE HAZARD OF MODERN POETRY

Erich Heller

Erich Heller immigrated to England from his native Bohemia in 1939 and taught at the London School of Economics, Cambridge University, and the University of Wales before finally settling in the United States where he is now Avalon Professor of the Humanities at Northwestern University. He is the author of The Disinherited Mind *(1952),* The Ironic German, A Study of Thomas Mann *(1958), and* The Artist's Journey Into the Interior, And Other Essays *(1965). The following selection is a portion of "The Hazard of Modern Poetry" which was first delivered as a series of talks on the B.B.C. Third Programme and printed in* The Listener *and then published by Bowes & Bowes (Cambridge, England, 1953). Reprinted by kind permission of the author and Bowes & Bowes.*

It is on an Easter Sunday that Goethe's Faust comes back to his study from one of the most lyrical walks of German literature. He is accompanied by a strange black poodle that, out in the fields, insisted on joining him. Faust opens the Gospel according to St. John, determined to translate it into his "beloved German". He is defeated by the very first line. What is it that was in the beginning? *Logos* – the Word. No, it seems impossible to rate the word so high. "Meaning" might be better. Yet it sounds too feeble to be placed at the source of everything that is. And Faust tries "Force"; but having moved away so far from the original text, why should the translator not go further in his freedom? "In the beginning was the Deed." This satisfies Faust – and excites the poodle. The translation comes to nothing because at this point the dog grows restive. He will not listen even to Faust's most potent demon-soothing magic. For he comes from Hell and is a devil.

Easter Sunday and a magician; *Logos* into Word, Word into Deed, dog into devil – the scene is set for the hazard of modern poetry.

But perhaps we ought to be more scholarly. Let us therefore turn to the *History of the Royal Society, its Institution, Design and Progress in the Advancement of Experimental Philosophy*. It was written in the second half of the seventeenth century by Thomas Sprat, Bishop of Rochester. The poet Cowley prefaced it poetically, stating the book's polemical and apologetic themes with that greater verve and vigour which, in mundane matters, the poet can more easily afford than the bishop. The poem celebrates Philosophy or Reason, referred to as He, for – so we are told – it is a "Male Virtue". Even before the foundation of the Royal Society he was a promising youngster:

> But, oh! the Guardians and the Tutors then,
> (Some negligent, and some ambitious Men)
>   Would ne'er consent to set him free,
> Or his own natural Powers to let him see,
> Lest that should put an end to their Authoritie.
> That his own Business he might quite forget,
> They amus'd him with the sports of wanton wit,
> With the Desserts of Poetry they fed him,
> Instead of solid Meats t'encrease his Force , , ,

Luckily, the importer of solid meats was close at hand:

> Bacon at last, a mighty Man arose,
>   Whom a wise King and Nature chose
>   Lord Chancellor of both their Laws,
> And boldly undertook the injur'd Pupil's Cause.

And how, according to this vision of an early scientific enthusiast, did the Lord Chancellor set about his bold business? Thus:

> From Words, which are but Pictures of the Thought,
> (Though we our Thoughts from them perversely drew)

To Things, the Mind's right Object, he it brought:
Like foolish Birds to painted Grapes we flew;
He sought and gather'd for our Use the true;
And when on Heaps the chosen Bunches lay,
He pressed them wisely the mechanic Way,
Till all their Juice did in one Vessel join,
Ferment into a Nourishment Divine,
    The thirsty Soul's refreshing Wine.

Maybe this is the first significantly ludicrous poem ever written. It not only reads like an anticipated parody of Faust's "Word into Deed", but also states with naive earnestness a theme that for three centuries to come was to pursue the lives and works of poets and artists with a persistent curse, whispering into their ears now the sinister threats of unreality, and now again the subtle temptation of transcendent glory. Can we trace the flight of the foolish birds back to the nest where they were fledged; where on the wings of words, which are but pictures of the thought, they left behind the things, the mind's right object? The bird's-eye view of an immensely complex landscape of time may choose for closer inspection a scene in Marburg. There a theological dispute is in progress. The disputants are two powerful theologian-reformers of the sixteenth century: Martin Luther and Ulrich Zwingli. To the modern lay-mind their debate may seem like mere scholastic hair-splitting, but history would suggest that it was more like Samson's hair-cut. Its consequences most certainly unsteadied the pillars upon which a great house stood.

The dispute is about the nature of the eucharist, the sacrament of the Lord's Supper. The bread and the wine – are they the body and blood of Christ, or are they "mere symbols"? Luther, with all his deviations from the traditional dogma, is the man of the Middle Ages. The word and the sign are for him not merely "pictures of the thought", but the thing itself. Yet for Zwingli, steeped in the enlightened thought of the Italian Renaissance, this is a barbarous absurdity. The sacrament is "merely" a symbol, that is, it symbolically represents what in itself it is not.

This is indeed a very particular occasion. It is a unique and uniquely sacred symbol that is being discussed. The issue is clearly defined and specified. It is not even new. There are precedents for it throughout the history of Christian theology. All this should warn us against facile generalizations. Yet there remains the fact that

never before had this question raised so much dust and generated
so much heat. For now it is merely the theological climax of a deep
revolution in the thoughts and feelings with which men respond to
the world they inhabit; the Miltonian opportunity for a "Truth
who, when she gets a free and willing hand, opens herself faster
than the pace of method and discourse can overtake her". It is now
that thirty years of war lie ahead, and the slow emergence of an age
in which not only the sacraments but the holiness of all that is holy
will cease to be "literally true". There will be a world which must
find it more and more difficult even to grasp, let alone accept, what
was in Luther's mind when he fought Zwingli's "demythologizing"
(an activity as hazardous as the word that expresses it, tongue-twister
for angels and bedevilling the minds of men.) Lost will be that unity
of word and deed, of picture and thing, of the bread and the glorified body. Body will become merely body, and symbol merely
symbol. And as for the refreshing wine, it will be drunk by thirsty
souls only when in the very depths of their thirst they are quite sure
that it was pressed from real grapes in the mechanic way.

What, then, is the nature of the revolution signalled by a theological
dispute that seems concerned merely with degrees of symbolic
"literalness"? And what, above all, has it to do with our subject,
which is the fortunes of modern poetry? Perhaps we can answer
both questions at once by saying that Zwingli's argument did to the
status of religion, poetry, and art what some time later Copernicus
did to the status of the earth. As the earth was to become merely a
planet in the company of planets, so now the spirit of poetry became
merely a spirit in the society of spirits. Of course, I do not confuse a
theological controversy with an exercise in aesthetic theory. But I
do suggest that at the end of a period that we rather vaguely call
the Middle Ages there occurred a radical change in man's idea of
reality, in that complex fabric of unconsciously held convictions
about what is real and what is not. This was a revolution comparable
to that earlier one which Nietzsche called the victory of the Socratic
mind over the spirit of Dionysian tragedy. And indeed both victories
saddled us with the unending bother of aesthetic philosophy. Plato
was the first great man of Greece who charged poetry with the
offence of confounding man's soberly useful notions about reality,
an indictment that led to Aristotle's theory about the "use" of tragedy. And ever since Zwingli the most common response to the

reality of symbols has been a shrugging of shoulders, or an edified raising of eyes and brows, or an apologia for poetry, or an aesthetic theory.

It would, of course, be absurd to believe that before the triumph of that reason which Cowley celebrated, men were less able than we are (and are we really so able?) to distinguish between illusion and reality, between lunacy and common sense. This would be putting the question in terms that do not apply, because these are the terms of modernity. It is even possible that on the level of an *élite* the ability to discriminate was more assured than is ours. For only when the spiritual is known and felt to be real, can there be realistic discrimination between things that claim to be things of the spirit. These men held in their hands, touching and weighing it, the reality of the infinite; we have merely its taste. And it is wiser, or so they say, not to judge in a conflict of tastes – *de gustibus non disputandum*. They knew the symbol when they saw it; we only see it, and are left in the dark. For it is merely a symbol, and may mean this or that or nothing on earth.

One way of speaking of the revolution I have in mind is to say that it reduced the stature of the symbol to the *merely* symbolic. Thus it deprived the language of religion as well as of art of an essential degree of reality. At the beginning the separation proved most beneficial to both partners. Reality, freed from its commitments to the symbol, became more really real than before. The hand of man, reaching out for his reality, was no longer unsteadied by the awe and fear of the symbolic mystery. He acquired the surgeon's hygienic dexterity. And reality, pressed the mechanic way, yielded ample nourishment, real if not divine. As reality became more real, so the symbol became more symbolic and art more artistic. The artist ceased to be a humble craftsman, supplying goods for the common trade between Heaven and earth. He set himself up as a dealer in very special specialties, with a Heaven all to himself and an earth to look down upon.

But there were also signs of uneasiness. They mounted to a climax of tension in the seventeenth century. What was first felt to be a liberation appeared more and more as a robbery. Robbed of its real significance, what did the symbol signify? Robbed of its symbolic meaning, what did reality mean? What was the State on earth? A Leviathan. What was God? More and more a *deus absconditus*, an infinitely remote and impenetrably veiled God. This was not only the century of Newton, the century of cosmic tidiness and calculable pulls and pushes. This it was indeed in the sphere of "reality", that obedient patient under the fingers of man's mind. But in the sphere of the soul, disobedient sufferer of God's anger and grace, it was the century of Pascal and Hobbes, of the desperate and once more triumphant convolutions of the baroque, and of the metaphysical poets. Commerce between the separated spheres, felt to be urgent again, moved uneasily, intensely, and anxiously along disrupted lines of communication. Strategical points had to be gained by cunning, break-throughs to be dared with the passion of spiritual violence. The baroque was the architectural style of such manoeuvres of the soul. And as for spiritual cunning, it was in the conceits of metaphysical poetry, in the self-conscious ambiguities of poetical language (there are, we are told, as many types of it as deadly sins), and in the paradoxes of Pascal's religious thought. For ambiguity and paradox are the manner of speaking when reality and symbol, man's mind and his soul, are at cross-purposes.

The estrangement was to continue. The symbol was made homeless in the real world, and the real world made itself a stranger to the symbol. Architecture, the most "real" of all the arts, steadily declined. After the seventeenth century Europe no longer dwelt or worshipped or ruled in buildings created in the image of authentic spiritual vision. For all that was real was an encumbrance to the spirit who, in his turn, only occasionally called on the real, and even then with the embarrassment of an uninvited guest. He was most at home where there was least "reality" – in music. The music of modern Europe is the one and only art in which it surpassed the achievement of former ages. This is no accident of history: it is the speechless triumph of the spirit in a world of words without deeds and deeds without words.

The great revolutions in human history do not change the face of the earth. They change the face of man, the image in which he beholds himself and the world around him. The earth merely follows suit. It is the truly pathetic fallacy of empiricism that it offers as safe harbour what is the ocean itself, the storms, the waves and the shipwrecks, namely man's experience of himself and the "objective" world. The history of human kind is a repository of scuttled objective truths, and a museum of irrefutable facts – refuted not by empirical discoveries, but by man's mysterious decisions to experience differently from time to time. All relevant objective truths are born and die as absurdities. They come into being as the monstrous claim of an inspired rebel and pass away with the eccentricity of a superstitious crank. Only between these extremities of the mind is "objective truth" truly true, alive at the centre of everything. Then this truth inspires the deeds of men and helps them to form the images of faith. Thus "objective truth" is equally at work in the totems and taboos of savages, the pyramids of Egypt, the gods and centaurs of the Olympian friezes, the cosmology of Dante and the theory of the expanding universe. And who, I wonder, could journey from Delphi to the Byzantine monastery of Hosios Lucas, leaving the Charioteer in the morning, and in the evening gazing at the mosaic Madonna in the apse of the monastery's church, without being followed into his dreams by echoes from the abyss that divides throughout the ages truth from truth, and the image of man from the image of man?

The ostrich is said to bury his head in the sand at the approach of inescapable danger. Experience is to the empiricist what the sand is to the ostrich's head. Truth, however, does not reside in that which is both blinding and shifting. Only the inescapable danger that there may be no Truth is inescapably true. Hence it is not empirical knowledge that is the organ of Truth. What is empirically true and real now is largely what has escaped the attention of the past, and will escape from the future as a boring anachronism. Uncertainty alone is ineluctably real. It is through despair that man escapes from even this inescapable reality. But he meets it in faith, recognizing it without losing hope and suffering it not without love.

The elusiveness of this faith and the persistent closeness of that despair make modern poetry the hazardous enterprise that it is. True, the poet is at all times more easily afflicted than others by despair and the waning of faith. But these are more than individual perils in our age, for at its very centre is an amorphous indecision. The physicists, always busy empirically to vindicate metaphysical notions about the nature of the world, seem today more directly preoccupied with the metaphysical beliefs insensibly accepted by the community. With the precision of mathematical reasoning they explore the terrible imprecision of our faith. For both our faith and our physics are fascinated by the vast voids inside and outside everything that exists, by empty fields of tension, and by the indeterminate motion of particles senselessly speeding around one another in order to hide from themselves the nothingness at the core of all things.

This, it seems, is the consummation of that revolution of which I have spoken. Before it began, the world, with its bread and its wine, was in all its sinfulness the centre of divine attention. From this obstinate supervision man struggled into a new freedom. He exercised it gloriously within the vast symbolic space that lies between divine presence and divine remoteness. He learned to speak his own language. But the more freely he spoke, the less the word counted. For it became the sport of wanton wit. And thought's more reliable objects were therefore things, the true outcome of the deed that was at the beginning. At the end there may be neither words nor deeds, but merely, for all we know, a slight disease, a rash of matter that matters little to so robust a body of nothingness.

Against this background I invite you to ponder the problems of modern poetry – problems that poetry shares with all the other arts. Therefore, in speaking about poetry we always mean more than poetry, just as poetry always means more than itself. What is it, then, that poetry, means? Its meaning is the vindication of the worth and value of the world, of life and of human experience. At heart all poetry is praise and celebration. Its joy is not mere pleasure, its lamentation not mere weeping, and its despair not mere despondency. Whatever it does, it cannot but confirm the existence of a meaningful world – even when it denounces its meaninglessness. Poetry means order, even with the indictment of chaos; it means hope, even with the outcry of despair. It is concerned with the true stature of things. And being concerned with the true stature of things, all great poetry is realistic.

But what is to happen if doubt about the true stature of things invades the very sphere of experience and intuitive insight in which poetry is formed? If suspicion attacks the value of the real world? Then the poetic impulse will seek refuge in a sphere all its own, a little cosmos of inwardness salvaged from the devaluation of the world. "The Discovery and Colonization of Inwardness" – this might be a fitting title for the story of poetry from the Renaissance to our day. It begins with the vitality of adventurers, driven from their homeland by the impoverishment of its soil, and culminates in a display of unexpected treasures. Will it end with the home-sickness of a defeated race? Or with the father's return to the prodigal son?

THE POETRY OF REALITY

J. Hillis Miller

J. Hillis Miller is Professor of English and Chairman of the Department at The Johns Hopkins University. He is the author of Charles Dickens: The World of his Novels *(1958),* The Disappearance of God *(1963), and* The Form of Victorian Fiction *(1968), as well as editor of several volumes of critical essays. The following essay is reprinted by permission of the publishers from J. Hillis Miller,* Poets of Reality: Six Twentieth-Century Writers, *Cambridge, Massachusetts, The Belknap Press of Harvard University Press, Copyright, 1965, by the President and Fellows of Harvard College.*

Reality is not that external scene but the life that is lived in it. Reality is things as they are. The general sense of the word proliferates its special senses. It is a jungle in itself.[1]

A change in literature as dramatic as the appearance of romanticism in the late eighteenth century has been taking place during the last fifty years. This book tries to explore the change through a study of six writers who have participated in it. Each of the chapters which follow attempts to show the configuration of themes which permeates one writer's work and unifies it. This chapter describes the historical milieu within which the particular worlds of the six writers may be followed in their planetary trajectories.

My interpretation of these writers questions the assumption that twentieth-century poetry is merely an extension of romanticism. A new kind of poetry has appeared in our day, a poetry which grows out of romanticism, but goes beyond it. Many twentieth-century poets begin with an experience of the nihilism which is one of the possible consequences of romanticism. My chapter on Conrad attempts to identify this nihilism by analysis of a writer who follows it into its darkness and so prepares the way beyond it. Each succeeding chapter describes one version of the journey beyond nihilism toward a poetry of reality. The new art which gradually emerges in the work of Yeats, Eliot, Thomas and Stevens reaches full development in the poetry of William Carlos Williams.

Much romantic literature presupposes a double bifurcation. Existence is divided into two realms, heaven and earth, supernatural and natural, the "real" world and the derived world. It is also divided into subjective and objective realms. Man as subjective ego opposes himself to everything else. This "everything else" is set against the mind as object of its knowledge. Though some pre-romantic and romantic writers (Smart, Macpherson, Blake) speak from the perspective of a visionary or apocalyptic union of subject and object, earth and heaven, many romantic poets start with both forms of dualism. They must try through the act of poetry to reach the supersensible world by bringing together subject and object. To reach God through the object presupposes the presence of God within the object, and the romantic poets usually believe in one way or another that there is a supernatural power deeply interfused in nature.

Writers of the middle nineteenth century, as I tried to show in *The Disappearance of God*,[2] tend to accept the romantic dichotomy of subject and object, but are no longer able to experience God as both immanent and transcendent. God seems to Tennyson, to Arnold, or to the early Hopkins to have withdrawn beyond the physical world. For such poets God still exists, but he is no longer present in nature. What once was a unity, gathering all together, has exploded into fragments. The isolated ego faces the other dimensions of existence across an empty space. Subject, objects, words, other minds, the supernatural – each of these realms is divorced from the others, and man finds himself one of the "poor fragments of a broken world."[3] Accepting this situation as a necessary beginning, the Victorian poets try to reunite the fragments, to bring God back to earth as a "fusing flame" present in man's heart, in nature, in society, and in language, binding them together in "one common wave of thought and joy."[4]

Another way of thinking grows up side by side with that of the mid-nineteenth-century poets. A God who has disappeared from nature and from the human heart can come to be seen not as invisible but as nonexistent. The unseen God of Arnold or Tennyson becomes the dead God of Nietzsche. If the disappearance of God is presupposed by much Victorian poetry, the death of God is the starting point for many twentieth-century writers.

What does it mean to say that God is dead? Nietzsche's "madman" in *The Joyful Wisdom* announces the death of God, and explains it:

"Where is God gone?" he called out. "I mean to tell you! *We have killed him,* – you and I! We are all his murderers! But how have we done it? How were we able to drink up the sea? Who gave us the sponge to wipe away the whole horizon? What did we do when we loosened this earth from its sun? Whither does it now move? Whither do we move? Away from all suns? Do we not dash on unceasingly? Backwards, sideways, forewards, in all directions? Is there still an above and below? Do we not stray, as through infinite nothingness? Does not empty space breathe upon us? Has it not become colder? Does not night come on continually, darker and darker? Shall we not have to light lanterns in the morning? Do we not hear the noise of the grave-diggers who are burying God? Do we not smell the divine putrefaction? – for even Gods putrefy! God is dead! God remains dead! And we have killed him!"[5]

Man has killed God by separating his subjectivity from everything but itself. The ego has put everything in doubt, and has defined all outside itself as the object of its thinking power. *Cogito ergo sum:* the absolute certainty about the self reached by Descartes' hyperbolic doubt leads to the assumption that things exist, for me at least, only because I think them. When everything exists only as reflected in the ego, then man has drunk up the sea. If man is defined as subject, everything else turns into object. This includes God, who now becomes merely the highest object of man's knowledge. God, once the creative sun, the power establishing the horizon where heaven and earth come together, becomes an object of thought like any other. When man drinks up the sea he also drinks up God, the creator of the sea. In this way man is the murderer of God. Man once was a created being among other created beings, existing in an objective world sustained by its creator, and oriented by that creator as to high and low, right and wrong. Now, to borrow the passage from Bradley which Eliot quotes in the notes to *The Waste Land,* "regarded as an existence which appears in a soul, the whole world for each is peculiar and private to that soul."

When God and the creation become objects of consciousness, man becomes a nihilist. Nihilism is the nothingness of consciousness when consciousness becomes the foundation of everything. Man the murderer of God and drinker of the sea of creation wanders through the infinite nothingness of his own ego. Nothing now has any worth except the arbitrary value he sets on things as he assimilates them into his consciousness. Nietzsche's transvaluation of values is the expunging of God as the absolute value and source of the valuation of everything else. In the emptiness left after the death of God, man becomes the sovereign valuer, the measure of all things.

Many qualities of modern culture are consonant with the definition of man as a hollow sphere within which everything must appear in order to exist. The devouring nothingness of consciousness is the will to power over things. The will wants to assimilate everything to itself, to make everything a reflection within its mirror. Seen from this perspective, romanticism and technology appear to be similar rather than antithetical.

Romanticism attempts to marry subject and object through the image. The romantic image may be the representation of object within the sphere of the subject, as in Wordsworth, or the carrying of subject into the object, as in Keats, or the wedding of subject and object, as in Coleridge, but in most of its varieties an initial dualism, apparent or real, is assumed. Romanticism develops naturally into the various forms of perspectivism, whether in the poetry of the dramatic monologue or in the novel, which, in its concern for point of view, is perfectly consonant with romanticism. The development of fiction from Jane Austen to Conrad and James is a gradual exploration of the fact that for modern man nothing exists except as it is seen by someone viewing the world from his own perspective. If romantic poetry most often shows the mind assimilating natural objects – urns, nightingales, daffodils, or wind-hovers – the novel turns its attention to the relations between several minds, but both poetry and fiction usually presuppose the isolation of each mind.

Science and technology, like romanticism, take all things as objects for man's representation. This may appear in a theoretical form, as in the numbers and calculations which transform into mathematical formulas everything from subatomic particles to the farthest and largest galaxies. Or it may appear in a physical form, the humanization of nature, as earths and ores are turned into automobiles, refrigerators, skyscrapers, and rockets, so that no corner of the earth or sky has not been conquered by man and made over in his image.

Romantic literature and modern technology are aspects of a world-embracing evolution of culture. As this development proceeds, man comes even to forget that he has been the murderer of God. The presence of God within the object, as it existed for the early romantics, is forgotten, and forgotten is the pathos of the Victorians' reaching out for a God disappearing over the horizon of an objectified world. The triumph of technology is the forgetting of the death of God. In the silence of this forgetting the process of universal calculation and reduction to order can go on peacefully extending its dominion. The world no longer offers any resistance to man's limitless hunger for conquest. This process has continued through the first two-thirds of the twentieth century, and is the chief determinant of man's sensibility in many parts of the world today. Many people have forgotten that they have forgotten the death of God, the living God of Abraham and Isaac, Dante and Pascal. Many who believe that they believe in God believe in him only as the highest value, that is, as a creation of man the inventor of values.

Only if the nihilism latent in our culture would appear as nihilism would it be possible to go beyond it by understanding it. In spite of two world wars, and the shadow of world annihilation, this is a course which our civilization has not yet chosen, or had chosen for it. Nevertheless, a central tradition of modern literature has been a countercurrent moving against the direction of history. In this literature, if not in our culture as a whole, nihilism has gradually been exposed, experienced in its implications, and, in some cases, transcended.

The special place of Joseph Conrad in English literature lies in the fact that in him the nihilism covertly dominant in modern culture is brought to the surface and shown for what it is. Conrad can best be understood as the culmination of a development within the novel, a development particularly well-marked in England, though of course it also exists on the continent and in America. After the attempt to recover an absent God in nineteenth-century poetry, a subsequent stage in man's spiritual history is expressed more fully in fiction than in poetry. The novel shows man attempting to establish a human world based on interpersonal relations. In the novel man comes more and more to be defined in terms of the strength of his will, and the secret nihilism resulting from his new place as the source of all value is slowly revealed.

Conrad is part of European literature and takes his place with Dostoevsky, Mann, Gide, Proust, and Camus as an explorer of modern perspectivism and nihilism. Within the narrower limits of the English novel, however, he comes at the end of a native tradition. From Dickens and George Eliot through Trollope, Meredith, and Hardy the negative implications of subjectivism become more and more apparent. It remained for Conrad to explore nihilism to its depths, and, in doing so, to point the way toward the transcendence of nihilism by the poets of the twentieth century.

In Conrad's fiction the focus of the novel turns outward from its concentration on relations between man and man within civilized society to a concern for the world-wide expansion of Western man's will to power. Conrad is the novelist not of the city but of imperialism. Several consequences follow from this. He is able to show that society is an arbitrary set of rules and judgments, a house of cards built over an abyss. It was relatively easy for characters in Victorian fiction to be shown taking English society for granted as permanent and right. The fact that Western culture has the fragility of an edifice which might have been constructed differently is brought to light when Conrad sets the "masquerade" of imperialism against the alien jungle. With this revelation, the nature of man's will to power begins to emerge, and at the same time there is a glimpse of an escape from nihilism.

The will to power seemed a subjective thing, a private possession of each separate ego. Though the struggle for dominance of mind against mind might lead to an impasse, non-human nature seemed to yield passively to man's sovereign will. Everything, it seemed, could be turned into an object of man's calculation, control, or evaluation. In *Heart of Darkness* (1899) Conrad shows how imperialism becomes the expansion of the will toward unlimited dominion over existence. What begins as greed, the desire for ivory, and as altruism, the desire to carry the torch of civilization to the jungle, becomes the longing to "wring the heart" of the wilderness and "exterminate all the brutes." The benign project of civilizing the dark places of the world becomes the conscious desire to annihilate everything which opposes man's absolute will. Kurtz's megalomania finally becomes limitless. There is "nothing either above or below him." He has "kicked himself loose of the earth," and in doing so has "kicked the very earth to pieces."

It is just here, in the moment of its triumph, that nihilism reverses itself, as, in Mann's *Doktor Faustus*, Leverkühn's last and most diabolical composition leads through the abyss to the sound of children's voices singing. Conrad's work does not yet turn the malign into the benign, but it leads to a reversal which prepares for the daylight of later literature. When Kurtz's will has expanded to boundless dimensions, it reveals itself to be what it has secretly been all along: nothing. Kurtz is "hollow at the core." Into his emptiness comes the darkness. The darkness is in the heart of each man, but it is in the heart of nature too, and transcends both man and nature as their hidden substance and foundation.

When the wilderness finds Kurtz out and takes "a terrible vengeance for the fantastic invasion,"[6] then the dawn of an escape from nihilism appears, an escape through the darkness. By following the path of nihilism to the end, man confronts once again a spiritual power external to himself. Though this power appears as an inexpressibly threatening horror, still it is something beyond the self. It offers the possibility of an escape from subjectivism.

The strategy of this escape will appear from the point of view of the tradition it reverses the most dangerous of choices, a leap into the abyss. It will mean giving up the most cherished certainties. The act by which man turns the world inside-out into his mind leads to nihilism. This can be escaped only by a counter-revolution in which man turns himself inside-out and steps, as Wallace Stevens puts it, "barefoot into reality."[7] This leap into the world characterizes the reversal enacted in one way or another by the five poets studied here.

To walk barefoot into reality means abandoning the independence of the ego. Instead of making everything an object for the self, the mind must efface itself before reality, or plunge into the density of an exterior world, dispersing itself in a milieu which exceeds it and which it has not made. The effacement of the ego before reality means abandoning the will to power over things. This is the most difficult of acts for a modern man to perform. It goes counter to all the penchants of our culture. To abandon its project of dominion the will must will not to will. Only through an abnegation of the will can objects begin to manifest themselves as they are, in the integrity of their presence. When man is willing to let things be then they appear in a space which is no longer that of an objective world opposed to the mind. In this new space the mind is dispersed everywhere in things and forms one with them.

This new space is the realm of the twentieth-century poem. It is a space in which things, the mind, and words coincide in closest intimacy. In this space flower the chicory and Queen Anne's lace of William Carlos Williams' poems. In this space his wheelbarrow and his broken bits of green bottle glass appear. In a similar poetic space appear "the pans above the stove, the pots on the table, the tulips among them" of Stevens' "poem of life." The "ghosts" who "return to earth" in Stevens' poems are those who have been alienated in the false angelism of subjectivity. They return from the emptiness of "the wilderness of stars" to step into a tangible reality of things as they are. There they can "run fingers over leaves/And against the most coiled thorn."[8]

The return to earth making twentieth-century poetry possible is accompanied by the abandonment of still another quality of the old world. This is the dimension of depth. In a number of ways the world of nineteenth-century poetry is often characterized by extension and exclusion. The mind is separated from its objects, and those objects are placed in a predominantly visual space. In this space each object is detached from the others. To be in one place is to be excluded from other places, and space stretches out infinitely in all directions. Beyond those infinite distances is the God who has absented himself from his creation. The pathos of the disappearance of God is the pathos of infinite space.

Along with spatial and theological depth go other distances: the distance of mind from mind, the distance within each self separating the self from itself. If each subject is separated from all objects, it is no less divided from other subjects and can encounter them only across a gap generated by its tendency to turn everything into an image. From the assumption of the isolation of the ego develops that conflict of subjectivities which is a central theme of fiction. For Matthew Arnold and other inheritors of romanticism the self is also separated from its own depths, the gulf within the mind which hides the deep buried self. To reach that self is as difficult as to reach God beyond the silence of infinite spaces.

In the new art these depths tend to disappear. The space of separation is turned inside-out, so that elements once dispersed are gathered together in a new region of co-presence. This space is often more auditory, tactile, or kinesthetic than visual. To be within it is to possess all of it, and there is no longer a sense of endless distances extending in all directions. The mind, its objects, other minds, and the ground of both mind and things are present in a single realm of proximity.

The disappearance of dimensions of depth in twentieth century art provides special difficulties for someone trained in the habits of romanticism. An abstract expressionist painting does not "mean" anything in the sense of referring beyond itself in any version of traditional symbolism. It is what it is, paint on canvas, just as Williams' wheelbarrow is what it is. In the space of the new poetry the world is contracted to a point – the wheelbarrow, the chicory flower, the bits of green glass. The poem is "not ideas about the thing but the thing itself,"[9] part of the world and not about it. In the same way the characters of Williams' fiction, like those of the French "new novel," have little psychological depth. They exist as their thoughts, their gestures, their speech, and these have the same objective existence as the wheelbarrow or the flower. In such a world "anywhere is everywhere,"[10] and the romantic dialectic of movement through stages to attain a goal disappears. In place of advance in steps toward an end there is the continuous present of a poetry which matches in its speed the constant flight of time. Each moment appears out of nothing in the words of the poem and in that instant things emerge anew and move and are dissolved.[11]

If any spiritual power can exist for the new poetry it must be an immanent presence. There can be for many writers no return to the traditional conception of God as the highest existence, creator of all other existences, transcending his creation as well as dwelling within it. If there is to be a God in the new world it must be a presence within things and not beyond them. The new poets have at the farthest limit of their experience caught a glimpse of a fugitive presence, something shared by all things in the fact that they are. This presence flows everywhere, like the light which makes things visible, and yet can never be seen as a thing in itself. It is the presence of things present, what Stevens calls "the swarthy water/That flows round the earth and through the skies,/Twisting among the universal spaces."[12] In the same poem he gives this power its simplest name: "It is being." The most familiar object, in coming into the light, reveals being, and poetry brings being into the open by naming things as they are, in their glistening immediacy, the wheelbarrow glazed with rain water, the steeple at Farmington shining and swaying. The new poetry is therefore "the outlines of being and its expressings, the syllables of its law."[13] These outlines are glimpsed as the words of the poem vanish with the moment which brought them into existence. The space of such a poem is the space of the present in its evanescence. This present holds men closely with discovery as, "in the instant of speech,/The breadth of an accelerando moves,/Captives the being, widens – and was there."[14] The instant's motion is a space grown wide, and within that brief space of time all existence is named, captured, and revealed.

These are the characteristics of the domain which twentieth-century literature has come to inhabit. The entry into the new world is not easy to make and has not everywhere been made. Our culture still moves along the track laid out for it by science and dualistic thinking, and many writers remain enclosed within the old world. Moreover, every artist who crosses the frontier does so in his own way, a way to some degree unlike any other. I do not wish to minimize the differences between twentieth-century writers, but to suggest a context in which those differences may be fruitfully explored.

Examples of the new immediacy may be found in widely divergent areas of contemporary thought and art: in the flatness of the paintings of Mark Rothko and Franz Kline, as opposed to the romantic depth in the work of Paul Klee; in the "superficiality," as of a mystery which is all on the surface, of the novels of Ivy Compton-Burnett or Alain Robbe-Grillet; in the philosophy of Martin Heidegger or the German and French phenomenologists; in the descriptive linguistic analysis of Ludwig Wittgenstein and the British common language philosophers; in the poetry of Jorge

Guillén, René Char, or Charles Olson; in the literary criticism of
Gaston Bachelard, Jean-Pierre Richard, or Marcel Raymond. All
these writers and artists have in one way or another entered a new
realm, and, for all of them, if there is a fugitive spiritual power it
will be within things and people, not altogether beyond them.

Yeats, Eliot, Thomas, Stevens, and Williams have played important roles in this twentieth-century revolution in man's experience of existence. Each begins with an experience of nihilism
or its concomitants, and each in his own way enters the new reality:
Yeats by his affirmation of the infinite richness of the finite moment;
Eliot by his discovery that the Incarnation is here and now; Thomas
by an acceptance of death which makes the poet an ark rescuing all
things; Stevens by his identification of imagination and reality in
the poetry of being; Williams by his plunge into the "filthy Passaic."
This book traces the itineraries leading these writers to goals which
are different and yet have a family resemblance. The unity of twentieth-century poetry is suggested by the fact that these authors are
in the end poets not of absence but of proximity. In their work
reality comes to be present to the senses, present to the mind which
possesses it through the senses, and present in the words of the
poems which ratify this possession. Such poetry is often open-ended
in form. It follows in its motion the flowing of time and reveals,
through this mobility, the reality of things as they are. Wallace
Stevens speaks for all these poets when he affirms the union of inner
and outer, natural and supernatural, in the transcience and nearness
of the real:

> We seek
> Nothing beyond reality, Within it,
> Everything, the spirit's alchemicana
> Included, the spirit that goes roundabout
> And through included, not merely the visible,
> The solid, but the movable, the moment,
> The coming on of feasts and the habits of saints,
> The pattern of the heavens and high, night air.[15]

NOTES

1. Wallace Stevens, *The Necessary Angel: Essays on Reality and the Imagina-tion* (New York: Alfred A. Knopf, 1951), pp. 25, 26.
2. The Belknap Press of Harvard University Press, 1963.

188   LITERATURE AND RELIGION

3. Matthew Arnold's phrase, *Obermann Once More*, in from *Poetical Works*, ed. C. B. Tinker and H. F. Lowry (London: Oxford University Press, 1950), p. 320.

4. *Obermann Once More*, pp. 320, 323.

5. Book III, Section 125, trans. Thomas Common (New York: Frederick Ungar, 1960), pp. 167, 168.

6. Quotations from *Heart of Darkness* are cited from *Youth and Two Other Stories* (Garden City, N.Y.: Doubleday, Page, 1925), pp. 118, 131, 144, 148.

7. Wallace Stevens, *Large Red Man Reading* in *The Collected Poems* (New York: Alfred A. Knopf, 1954), p. 423.

8. *Large Red Man Reading*, pp. 423, 424.

9. Stevens, *The Collected Poems*, p. 534.

10. William Carlos Williams, *Paterson* (New York: New Directions, 1963), p. 273.

11. See Wallace Stevens, *Opus Posthumous* (New York: Alfred A. Knopf, 1957), p. 110.

12. *Metaphor as Degeneration* in *The Collected Poems*, p. 444.

13. *Large Red Man Reading*, p. 424.

14. Wallace Stevens, *A Primitive Like an Orb*, in *The Collected Poems*, p. 440.

15. *An Ordinary Evening in New Haven* in *The Collected Poems*, pp. 471, 472.

PART THREE: RELIGION AND THE
APPROPRIATION OF LITERATURE

12

POETRY AND PRAYER

Nathan A. Scott, Jr.

Nathan A. Scott, Jr. is Professor of Theology and Literature in The Divinity School and the Department of English of the University of Chicago. He is the author of Modern Literature and the Religious Frontier *(1958),* Albert Camus *(1962),* Samuel Beckett *(1965),* The Broken Center: Studies in the Theological Horizon of Modern Literature *(1966), and* Craters of the Spirit *(1968), and has edited several collections of essays both on modern literature and on theology and literary criticism. The following essay originally appeared in* Thought *(Vol. XLI, no. 160, Spring, 1966), and was later published in* Negative Capability: Studies in the New Literature and the Religious Situation, *by Nathan A. Scott, Jr. Copyright © 1969 by Yale University. Reprinted by permission of the author,* Thought, *and Yale University Press.*

Though most of the students who are working with me in the University of Chicago are engaged in interdisciplinary doctoral studies in theology and literature and are winning a fairly sophisticated awareness of the theoretical materials they need to be canvassing, I cannot recall having discovered any one of their number in recent years who, without having been told to do so, had felt the need to read the Abbé Henri Bremond's *Prière et Poésie,* or who indeed even evinced any sense of what still deserves to be considered impressive in this famous book. In this, I suppose these young people present a reflection of a generally prevalent attitude today of suspicion and indifference toward what is often referred to, in a tone of denigration, as "mystical aesthetic." However much in certain respects the Romantic dispensation may have persisted on into the age of Eliot, its cult of inspiration, its doctrine of transport, the whole machinery of what is popularly considered to be its characteristic *frisson*, has lost its appeal for contemporary taste. The line of thinking about poetry anciently expressed in the *Ion* and the *Peri Hupsous* and reiterated in the modern period by the English and German Romantics is regarded as making for a kind of inflationary effusiveness that brings genuine reflection to a halt. Thus whatever is to be found trenching on a poetics of Elevation and the Sublime is given a very hard time by the reigning schools of our period.

As Jacques Maritain was at pains to remind us, however, in his Mellon Lectures in the early '50s, this strain of vigorous anti-Romanticism in modern theory of literature has in fact entailed a mystique of its own. For the eagerness of an earlier generation to regard poetry as an affair of transport and exaltation has in our time simply been replaced by an equally great eagerness to regard it as merely an affair of *operation* in which artists function only as "engineers in the manufacturing of an artifact of words or sounds."[1] And this antiseptic reduction is not without its own obscurantism.

Yet, for all of our great inclination today toward austerity in the conception of the poem and the poet's vocation, when I do succeed in persuading my own graduate students (or – as they might prefer to have it put – in gently coercing them) to read Henri Bremond, the experience that I occasionally have is that of feeling that they, on putting down *Prière et Poésie*, have felt that at least the Abbé was perhaps the most distinguished of Longinus' modern epigones and that *something* important is at least being adumbrated in this book. It will, of course, be remembered that the line taken is one which insists on the essentially mystical character of poetic apprehension: it is argued that the inherent dynamism of the poetic mind necessarily drives it toward a state of prayer from which the poet turns away only in order to complete the labor of composition itself. The excitement to which poetic art conduces is the excitement of a mystical experience that has not discovered itself to be what in point of fact it really is and that does not, therefore, go on to allow the contemplative impulse to complete itself in an act of mergence with the Divine Ground. The poetic transaction, in other words, belongs to a secondary order of mystical experience – secondary, that is, because it does not, characteristically, culminate in the Beatific Vision. Yet, even so, the Abbé contended, this is an order of experience whose nature it is to afford a kind of radically intuitive penetration of reality that is essentially akin to mystical apprehension and that would indeed, if given full play, develop into a truly mystical sentiency. In short, the inherent thrust of the poetic experience propels it toward Transcendence, and its end is prayer and the soul's enjoyment of the Divine Presence.

This is, in general, the contour belonging to the argument of this famous book. But the argument, in its detail, is not, of course, itself any longer felt to carry a cogency that is altogether compelling and persuasive (though, of its sort, it is perhaps, in Bremond's exposition, the major modern instance). In the first place, simply at the level of what is implied for theory of literature, what is most troubling about the doctrine of *Prière et Poésie* is its tendency to dissolve the objective reality of works of literary art into a particular kind of eidetic consequence to which, presumably, they conduce. What is being promoted, in effect, is a basic shift of the center of poetic theory from the poem to its results, and the error here is that which W. K. Wimsatt and Monroe Beardsley have taught us to understand as exemplifying the Affective Fallacy – which is fallacious because it refocuses aesthetic discussion away from those norms of corrigibility resident in the work of art itself and attempts to base it on various unadjudicable subjective meanings.[2] The essential logic of Bremond's position, in other words, is not calculated to accord due recognition to those values in literature that are inherent and terminal; it sanctions our paying serious attention to literature only in so far as it can be determined to have certain non-literary consequences. Which is to say that, finally, the Abbé shows himself (in paraphrase of T. S. Eliot's famous dictum) to have been interested in considering poetry not as poetry but as another thing, or as the occasion or stimulus for another thing.

Nor can one feel that anything at all is gained in clarity by thinking of the poet as characterized primarily by a certain expertness in *vision*; for surely he is, first of all, a certain kind of maker. The Abbé liked to suppose that "the more of a poet any particular poet is, the more he is tormented by the need of communicating his experience" – which provoked T. S. Eliot's delightfully tart rejoinder that, on the contrary, "the poet is tormented primarily by the need to write a poem"[3] (as indeed "are a legion of people who are not poets"[4]).

Finally, it would also seem that the issue involving the relation of *poiesis* to religious experience requires definition in terms of an infinitely greater tact than Henri Bremond managed to summon. For, as Rosalind Murray has reminded us, the poet "is in fact never saying: 'Speak, Lord, for Thy servant heareth,' but always 'Tell me something that I can make use of!' "[5] Which is to say that art is a productive activity, a virtue of the practical intellect – and, as such, it is concerned to fashion (and to discover) an order amidst the rich and enigmatic heterogeneity of the created world. Whereas, that more final quest of

knowledge through connaturality which is peculiar to mystical experience comes about either, in natural mystical experience, by means of merely intellectual concentration producing a void through which the Self is ineffably touched or, in grace-given mystical experience, by means of charity, which connatures the soul with God, and which transcends both emotion and the human recesses of the subjectivity. Poetic experience is from the very start oriented toward expression, and terminates in a word uttered, or a work produced; while mystical experience tends toward silence, and terminates in an immanent fruition of the absolute.[6]

Yet, however much the Abbé Henri Bremond's formulation may need to be corrected and revised, he has by no means stood alone in supposing that there is a periphery of experience on which poetry does crucially touch the life of prayer. And we ought not to be dissuaded from freshly attempting to think the issue through by the almost habitual tendency of those who have previously contemplated it to become entangled in something like the Abbé's confusions.

It ought, of course, first of all to be understood that, most especially if the materials of modern literature are in view, it will not be profitable for us to restrict the scope of poetry to those forms of verbal art which employ the techniques of verse. In his book *The Arts of the Beautiful*, M. Gilson offers, somewhat confusedly, a recent statement of the conventional notion that there is some uniquely close connection between verse and "beauty" in the arts of the word and that metered expression is the natural medium of poetry.[7] But, as Edmund Wilson reminded us many years ago in an extraordinarily perceptive essay in *The Triple Thinkers,* the plain fact of the matter is that the time has come "to discard the word 'poetry' or to define it in such a way as to take account of the fact that the most intense, the most profound, the most beautifully composed and the most comprehensive of the great works of literary art . . . have been written sometimes in verse technique, sometimes in prose technique, depending partly on the taste of the author, partly on the mere current fashion."[8] And, as he said, "If, in writing about 'poetry,' one limits oneself to 'poets' who compose in verse, one excludes too much of modern literature"[9] – as, for example, that crucial river scene in *The Ambassadors* in which Strether suddenly discerns the true relationship between Chad and Mme de Vionnet, or the *Anna Livia Plurabelle* "canto" of *Finnegans Wake,* or the account of the last desperate winter, amid the icy wastes of Yuriatin, that Yurii Andreievich and Larisa have together in *Zhivago,* or the colloquies between Gogo and Didi in *Godot,* or the climactic scene in *Mutter Courage,* in which the Mother sits humped over the dead Kattrin, and so on and on and on. It seems sensible, therefore, when one uses the term "poetry," to mean simply all the high forms of literature that make fictions in such a way as to invite the mind to gaze, with radical amazement, into the depth of the human mystery.

When the poetic enterprise is understood, then, to have this kind of spaciousness of scope and possibility, in what respects may it be considered to represent a singular employment of the imagination? This is a question that has, I think, been most cogently answered in that tradition of late Kantian thought which, in recent speculation, is perhaps most impressively represented by such thinkers as Ernst Cassirer, Wilbur Marshall Urban, Susanne Langer, and Philip Wheelwright. In this line of modern aesthetic, poetry, and the arts generally, are regarded as one of the great ways whereby the imagination reaches "intentively" beyond the immediate givens of experience (as it also does in scientific pursuits), and does so by way of contemplating what these givens may symbolize or mean. Man, as Cassirer liked to say, is the *animal symbolicum.*[10] He does not merely receive various kinds of challenge and inducement from his external environment and then react to them; his experience is not wholly, or even most basically, contained within the functional circle of stimulus-and-response; he lives in the new dimension of what Mrs. Langer calls "symbolic transformation."[11] He does not live simply in "a world of hard facts, or according to his immediate needs and desires,"[12] but always in the midst of the sciences, arts, myths, and religions whereby the data of immediate experience are wrought into the significant forms that the mind requires for its sanity and peace.

It is the mistaken tendency, however, of the reigning school in Anglo-American philosophy today to suppose that reality is handled with genuine precision and seriousness only by those modes of symbolization that are susceptible of being authenticated by controlled experiments of an empirical order. Discursive symbolism alone is considered to be capable of providing vehicles for thought, and truth is not regarded as a possible property of those nondiscursive types of symbolic form that are so much of the essence of all artistic and religious expression. The common supposition is that, in regard to what is "really" the case, a pointer reading of some sort represents a kind of symbolic form that has a truly referential capacity; whereas a work of poetic art or a prayer, however fascinating it may be to study the special "language game" involved, need not be expected to afford insight into anything other than the particular style of imagination of which it is an expression.

The denial of any ontological intention to those forms of symbolic action characteristic of poetic art has doubtless in part been encouraged by that modern apologetic for poetry which descends from the Symbolists and which so radically asserts the autonomousness of the poetic universe as in effect to close off all avenues leading from it to the outside world. But this doctrine is itself an exacerbated response to the more fundamental and the more pervasive modern attitude of skepticism about the dignity of any cognitive pretension that may be made by the various nonscientific types of symbolic discourse. For, in a culture so riddled as our own with the disease of positivism, the most natural assumption is that the order which science seeks in the world is that in terms of which alone it is possible to harmonize the significant realities of human existence.

Yet, the satisfaction which we continue to derive from the highly complicated systems of utterance and discourse that comprise the various forms of literary art is surely a persisting attestation to the possibility of our taking hold of What Is[13] by methods other than those of empirical science. And what is, of course, decisive is the great need that we have to pay attention to, even to revel in, the raw concreteness of things – and the unavailability for this purpose of any other symbolic stratagems except those which art employs. The fact of the matter is that the human spirit simply cannot dwell habitually in that "system of all-inclusive relations" which is what the universe was declared to be by the distinguished British Hegelian of the last century, T. H. Green. One of man's deepest yearnings is to savor, in the full flavor of their richly existential particularity, the immediate givens that constitute the furniture and environment of his living. And it is only by way of a living confrontation with the full-fledged otherness of the things of this world – its people, its events, its natural realities and processes that there can ever be borne in upon us that awareness apart from which we are not fully human, of being placed in a universe whose ontological amplitude does not already lie within the depths of man himself but entails, rather, dimensions of Transcendence that hint at "unknown modes of Being."

Both science and art bring into play activities of the mind that involve its mingling with the circumambient world, but the scientific employments of reason entail a certain principled impatience with the raggedly concrete and individual aspects of reality. What matters, in the perspective of science, is not the radical singularity of particular things and events but the logical relations and the general laws that are instanced in particular cases. Aristotle puts the matter in this way in the *Posterior Analytics* (87b, 28): "Perception must be of a particular, whereas scientific knowledge involves the recognition of the commensurate universal." Thus he very nicely expresses the ineradicable bias of scientific mentality – which does not linger upon singulars and which is always baffled until it finds universals. This is of the very essence of its peculiar asceticism. Scientific mentality assumes that no significantly veridical information about the world can be derived from a contemplation of the particular event, the unrepeatable experience, the unique reality; so it is always withdrawing from particular realities in order to get to the universal rules which they may be taken to exhibit or confirm; and it is happy only when it reaches that region of unresisting generalities which can, completely and without remainder, be subdued by the abstractive intellect.

Indeed, it is this rigorous asceticism of scientific mentality that doubtless accounts for the suspiciousness with which it has perennially viewed the arts, and most especially the poetic arts. For poetry is a virtue of that "intransitive attention"[14] which is bestowed on the quiddity and what Scotus called the "hecceity" (i.e., the sheer "thisness") of things. The catharsis which it brings is simply the profound relief that is enjoyed by the mind when, in being offered a chance to luxuriate in the contemplation of the intractable givenness and particularity of individual existents, it wins some surety that its scope is larger than its own brainpan. The poet – that is, the artist in language, whatever may be his particular genre – does not, characteristically, bring the abstractive passion of science, and its universalizing perspectives, to his dealings with the world; he consents to allow what is irregular and nonconformist and unique to have a very sharp impact upon him, and he does not spirit it away into any "system of all-inclusive relations." He wants to apprehend that irreducible particularity of a thing whereby it is what it is instead of being a thousand other possible things.

Poetry is, in short, forever fascinated with what is radically specific and individual – with the brooding, eerie gloom of *this* lonely heath (as in Hardy's *The Return of the Native*), with the unhinging fright of *this* young soldier before the advance to the front (as in Crane's *The Red Badge of Courage*), with the "dooms of love" through which *my* father moved (as in E. E. Cummings' great elegy). Richard Wilbur, for example, sees "a landscapeful of small black birds . . . convene at some command . . . in the middle of the air"; and, then, they are gone, rolling "like a drunken fingerprint across the sky" – shattering and maddening ". . . space/With their divergences." And, as he says,

> Delighted with myself and with the birds,
> I set them down and give them leave to be.
> It is by words and the defeat of words,
> Down sudden vistas of the vain attempt,
> That for a flying moment one may see
> By what cross-purposes the world is dreamt.[15]

His poem is called *An Event* – and it is precisely in terms of such singularity as this that the poet normally finds his "glass of vision" where with to "see/By what cross-purposes the world is dreamt."

It is Gerard Manley Hopkins who gives us one of the great renderings in modern theory of this unshakeable commitment which poetry has to the rich unicity of the concrete singular. In the period following his years at Oxford, as he was working out his basic understanding of what is distinctively characteristic of the *via poetica*, he found his thought more and more to be centralized in two concepts which, in terms of his own coinage, are designated as "inscape" and "instress." Even after the most careful rummaging through his *Papers*, it is difficult to be certain that one has altogether got right his exact intention in regard to the meaning of these terms. "Inscape" naturally implies a contrast between itself and "land-scape," and one supposes that Hopkins meant it to suggest not an outer reality, not something necessarily and unevadably present, but something that is discoverable only by the most tactful pene-tration into the inwardness of the things of earth – that essential design which constitutes intrinsic form. By "instress" he seems to have meant that energy of being whereby a thing manages to be what it is. He assumed, as he said, that "mere possibility, passive power, is not power proper and has no activity": "it cannot of itself come to stress, cannot instress itself."[16] In order for a thing to be "upheld,"[17] it must be imbued with a perfection of being sufficient to enable it to maintain its actuality. The instress of a given reality, in other words, is that power by which its inscape is held together: as one sees into a thing, it is that ontological potency which one feels to be the essential ground of the basic design, that principle of enablement whereby it is what it is, rather than another thing. Instress might, indeed, be said to be the "cause" of inscape. As Hopkins said in his letter of February 15, 1879, to Robert Bridges, "as air, melody, is what strikes me most of all in music and design in painting, so design, pattern or what I am in the habit of calling 'inscape' is what I above all aim at in poetry."[18]

The Roman statesman and monk of the sixth century, Cassiodorus, declared, "God is really wonderful and extremely wise in having distinguished every one of his creatures by a unique dispensation lest unseemly confusion overwhelm them."[19] And it is indeed this unique dispensation, this inscape, in things to which it is the prin-cipal responsibility of poetry to pay attention. Its love affair, as

Hopkins said, is with "the particularity of each unique thing as observed," and it wants to notice and to look at all the "hecceities" that come our way.

Though poetry addresses itself to the radically singular, concrete, individual aspects of reality, it has perennially been the wisdom of those who have reflected upon it most deeply (ever since Aristotle) to discern that, though it begins with the singular rather than the universal, it ends by somehow presenting both, by treating the singular in such a way that it becomes a glass of vision through which the universal may be seen. This is doubtless what Whitehead meant when he remarked somewhere that "Art at its highest exemplifies the metaphysical doctrine of the interweaving of absoluteness upon relativitly." The compelling power of "things" to command the poet's attention flows from the relationships that the things exemplify and bespeak. Indeed, the things which poetry handles, though separate and distinct, are (as Father McCarron was reminding us many years ago in his fine little book *Realization*) "interacting as in a story or fragment of a story. Such action upon one another is the evidence of their interrelationship."[20] And, were it not for this interrelationship amongst things, poetry would be impossible. Nothing that exists is an island unto itself; or, to change the metaphor, everything that holds membership in the world is an element of a seamless garment – the "ragged edges" of every individual reality splay off onto those of another, and "the world is a wedding." Day Lewis reminds us that "if we shoot a bird, we wound ourselves,"[21] and Wordsworth was often wanting us to remember that

>   dark
> Inscrutable workmanship that reconciles
> Discordant elements, makes them cling together
> In one society.

So, since any point which, from a certain angle of vision, may be seen to be a center is likely, from another perspective, to be found to be on the periphery of still another center, the poet is bound to find – and does in fact always find – that his concrete singular, when faced with great intensity, "without losing any of its bright actuality, tends also to be, or at least to suggest overtones of, something more."[22] It becomes what Hegel called a "concrete universal." And it is the habit that poetic art has of dwelling upon the interrelationships, the clusters of analogy among things, that makes it essentially symbolic. It wants to show how deeply resemblance and analogy are characteristic of reality itself; it wants to show how miraculously the concrete individual, when steadily contemplated, opens out into a kind of infinite depth and extension, so that its ultimate significance is discerned to flow from relations in which it stands to still other things consubstantial with itself. Thus, as Coleridge was insisting in the *Biographia Literaria*, the poet does not see reality as "essentially fixed and dead" but as "essentially vital." His great commitment, to be sure, is to the individual fact; yet it is not the mere fact that captivates him, but the concrete singular as it is itself ignited by such a power of reciprocity as permits it to trench upon still other realities, so that it takes on the lustre of a "something more." This is why indeed synecdoche and metaphor – whether in verse, drama, or fiction – are so much of the essence of poetic art, for the poet's final intention is to produce such a "coalescence"[23] of the heterogeneities of experience as will evoke in us some awareness of the vitally fluid unity of the world and thus offer a kind of attestation to an infinitude beyond "the light of sense."

The ontological dimension, in other words, to which poetic experience belongs is the dimension of depth. For the strange greatness of the poet's task – of a Shakespeare, a Melville, a Tolstoi, an Eliot – involves his effort, through all the marvellous cunning of his craft, to arrange for another visitation being paid us by the concrete realities of our world (many of them long since familiar) – and one that will stir us into fresh apprehension of how really inexhaustible in fact they are. Is it not the case, for example, that Shakespeare's Lear, Melville's Ahab, Tolstoi's Anna, and the dramatic actions of which they are a part testify, as it were, to the infinite depth and the radical mysteriousness of the human reality in the very disclosures that they bring to us of what is recalcitrantly finite in the world of the human creature? Or, to think of what is quite a different sort of case, it ought not to be any great occasion of astonishment that his early admiration of the poet of *Une Saison en Enfer* should have been found by Paul Claudel to be a kind of *preparatio* in his own life for a deeper entrance into the Christian faith; for, despite all the violence of spirit and all the blasphemy that are expressed in Rimbaud's poetry, here at least one encounters a sense of the abysses encircling human life that might indeed well lead to a deeper seizure of a Gospel of Grace. Or, again, to move from the vertiginous *Inferno* of Rimbaud to the arcadian countryside of Robert Frost's *New England*, one feels even in something so apparently simple and earthbound as Frost's *Stopping By Woods on a Snowy Evening* that curious metaphysical vastness and resonance which are so much the hallmarks of great poetry. Even when the frame of reference is of so limited a sort as in Frost's brief lyric, the poet, in the degree to which he has entered into a real engagement with his medium and the world that presses in upon him, is attempting to intensify our experiential encounter with whatever segment of reality it may be that has laid hold of his imagination. And the miracle that is so much of the essence of the poetic process grows out of the fact that the more profoundly the poet realizes and renders his "inscape" the more it tends to "point beyond itself, or rather, points to unplumbed and unplumbable depths within itself."[24] It becomes vocal, it attains the power of "speaking" to us, and thus we are introduced into the order of what Gabriel Marcel calls Presence, there where reality is encountered in its dimension of depth, of inexhaustibility, of radical mystery. Here it is that we feel ourselves "spoken" to by the deep things of ourselves and our world, as though they were but a taproot uniting the human reality with the ultimate Ground of all reality.

It is, I believe, in some such way as this that poetic experience is suffused, in its intensest modes, with an awareness of the world, in its concrete phenomenality, as a sacrament of the divine immanence. And, of course, to be in the situation of beholding the world in its dimension of depth and to know ourselves searched and "spoken" to by that depth is very nearly to be in the situation of prayer; for prayer is nothing but the most cruelly delusive auto-suggestion, if it be not a heedless exposure of ourselves to what is ultimately Deep in the common, ordinary, concrete realities of our experience. Catholic Christianity, in its Roman, Orthodox, and Anglican forms has produced a literature of manuals on "the spiritual life" that is now so large as doubtless to be a cause of catalogic despair to the curators of theological libraries. And surely most of this literature, in our late stage of things, ought to begin to receive a very stringent reassessment, if for no other reason than that the very concept of "the spiritual life" – in the sense of a space apart from our normal daily habitat, a "religious quarter" – is, as Bishop

Robinson has reminded us, most profoundly unbiblical.[25] As that good Scotsman of the Iona Community, George Macleod, bids us to realize,

> What debilitates our prayer life . . . is our presupposition that the pressures of life are on one side while God is on some other side: interested and concerned but on some other side. With this supposition, when evening comes with an ending to our pressures, we are apt to go eagerly to God – disconcertingly to find a vacuum. We seek to fill the vacuum with "spiritual thoughts." The more we try the more desperate does the situation become: till in effect we say that we are not really the praying type. Thus we begin to lean perilously to one side of the knife-edge.
>
> There are, of course, evenings when our prayer-life is refreshing; but, analysed, they turn out to be the times when the pressures have been so weighty that you have simply had to go with them to God. But this precisely is the recovery of the knife-edge.[26]

Dr. Macleod's intention is to assert what any robust Christianity must surely need to assert, that the place of prayer is, most essentially, not what traditional spirituality calls "the interior life" but the Emmaus Road, not at the edges of life but in the midst of it, where all the pressures of the human reality are felt with greatest intensity. As that remarkable young German Protestant theologian, Dietrich Bonhoeffer, was declaring so movingly just before his martyrdom on a Nazi scaffold at the close of World War II, the life of the Christian man is a "worldly" life.[27] And this, I am proposing, is where it is the special concern of great literature to take us – back into the world, and into those deeper places of it, where the existential reality takes on the character of a threshold, becoming "the borderland of a something more."[28]

It ought not to be supposed, however, most especially where the characteristic literature of the modern period is in view, that there is any *scala sacra* affording a simple and direct ascent from poetry to prayer – and, in so far as the Abbé Henri Bremond's formulations tend to encourage this expectation, it may be just in this respect that they lead to the greatest confusion. Ours is, of course, a literature that has deeply involved itself in all those questions with which it has traditionally been the office of religious faith to deal; but it has done so generally in a spirit of resistance and even of competition, so far as the great traditions of Christian belief are concerned. When we put ourselves in mind of such artists as Kafka, Rilke, Lawrence, Gide, and Brecht, it does indeed seem that the modern writer has been taking "a swarm of spears into his breast" and fighting through all the issues of the age without any adventitious aids or supports at all.[29] When you are dealing with *Death in Venice*, *The Castle*, the *Duino Elegies*, and the late poems of Yeats, you are dealing with a literature that manifests a most intense concern with the whole issue of what in the language of religion is called salvation. "Its purpose," as remarked by one commentator, "is to trouble and upset us, to make us doubt the value of those things which our parents, and all of respectable society, taught us we were to be most sure of. More than the secular literature of any other time . . . modern literature reaches into our most private selves,"[30] in its effort to discover what it means to be human in this late, bad time. Thus one cannot but be struck by the absurdity of the judgment expressed many years ago by Ortega in his famous essay *The Dehumanization of Art*, in which he declared that modern literature was progressively moving away from the human; for this, surely, as a basic thesis about the poetry, fiction, and drama of the twentieth century, is quite indefensible. Indeed, it may well be that no other body of literature has been so extreme and so explicit in its concern with the human situation. It is in fact a literature that, in the most decisive way, asks us to deal with doctrine, and with the hardest kind of doctrine – that which has to do with the nature of ourselves. And what in part makes its doctrine about the human story so notable is the very radical kind of independence that it exhibits vis-à-vis the established traditions of Christian belief.

It is natural in our time, though, to take for granted a kind of tension between Christianity and the poetic imagination not only because of the extreme autonomy that, morally and religiously, the modern writer has often laid claim to. What is also at issue here is the sharp divergence from traditional Christian perspectives of the very negative vision of the human prospect that has been generally characteristic of our literature. In the representative expressions of our period-style – in the poetry of Ezra Pound and Gottfried Benn; in the theatre of Brecht, Beckett, and Ionesco; in the fiction of Kafka, Sartre, Robbe-Grillet, and John Hawkes – the human image that is projected is something like those doomed ghosts in the pictures of the contemporary English painter Francis Bacon, who look out at the world heart-stricken and aghast; or it is like a face described by the English writer Alex Comfort in his novel *On This Side*

Nothing: "I saw the same fear in her face that I should have felt if a stranger called at night, the worldwide twentieth-century fear which one sees wherever one knocks unexpectedly at any door."

Indeed, all those writers who are today rendering experience in the classic modern idioms are forging an image of the human creature as one ousted from the precincts of security and grace – as one who has no place of safety and whose being is therefore "porous . . . like those cryptic human figures in modern sculpture that are full of holes or gaps."[31] The German philosopher, Helmut Kuhn, several years ago entitled his study of Existentialism *Encounter With Nothingness*, and it would be difficult to come by any other phrase that so concisely renders the spiritual drama that is enacted in much of the representative literature of our period. The protagonists in these records of modern sensibility are creatures "full of holes and gaps, faceless, riddled with doubts and negations, starkly finite"[32] – and, in their porousness, they are at the point of being invaded by the surrounding Nothingness. Perhaps the ideogram most perfectly depicting the human presence which this literature portrays is the cipher.

This sense of man's impoverishment and indigence that so deeply informs a widely prevalent mood today does not, of course, spring from any merely willful inclination toward Manichaean styles of imagination. It is rather doubtless in part a consequence of our feeling overwhelmed by the ambiguous results of our own creativity. By virtue of the political and scientific instrumentalities that we have fashioned, we find ourselves living in a world whose potential explosiveness infinitely surpasses any of the dangers that in one period or another have figured in man's recorded past. And, in this perilous time, there has arisen – and naturally so – a crisis of confidence in our ability to manage the arena of history. In the presence of a scientific establishment that has ushered in the nuclear age and in the presence of a political establishment that generates so much frightening tension in the world community, we feel that – like Mary Shelley's Frankenstein – we may have created a "second nature" which is beyond our capacity to control. Far more profoundly even, the sense of human life as totally contingent and as therefore exposed to the invading pressures of Nothingness is today a result of that general collapse of confidence in the cogency of traditional religious faith which undoubtedly constitutes the basic loss that underlies all the other losses that are felt by the men and women of our age.

However one accounts, though, for what is presently negative in the human image that drifts throughout the literature of our time, its bleakness cannot be gainsaid and does in fact bespeak a vision of man which is very sharply divergent from that which is proposed by the Christian Gospel. For, far from being any kind of faceless cipher, man is disclosed in the Christian story about reality to be a creature "trailing clouds of glory." In the perspectives of biblical thought, the "glory" of God is that power, that creative energy, by which whatever exists is called into existence; and man is declared to be made in the image of this glory. Which is to say that he is a radically theological being; he is "open" to the ineffable mystery of the Ground of Being; the light of his being is (as it is so beautifully said by Hans Urs von Balthasar)[33] "a dialogical light," for, in the basic constitution of his nature, he is turned toward God, and – in Christian experience – the God whom he meets is turned toward him. But, though "trailing clouds of glory," man is yet, in the Christian sense of things, known to be essentially a creature. He must have air to breathe; he needs space in which to abide; if he cannot find warmth and nourishment, he will perish; yet, even with plentifulness of what are called "creature comforts," his life is but of short duration – and though we sing in our chains like the sea, said Dylan Thomas, Time holds us green and dying.[34] Our lives are embedded not only in the contingencies of nature but also in the relativities of history, since our perspectives are always partial and conditioned by the particular time and place that we happen to occupy. Yet, though man is a creature, "the fact that, through reason and memory and imagination, he can surmount himself and his world indeterminately means that his life cannot find its true ground in any of the proximate norms that emerge out of historical experience, and that he is therefore driven by the inner dynamism of his nature toward a transcendent norm."[35] He is, in short, open to God, or, as it is said in the very drastic language of the Bible, he is made "in the image of God" (Gen 1:26). Which is to say that we do indeed (as St. Paul puts it) "reflect as in a mirror the splendour of the Lord; [and] thus we are transfigured into his likeness, from splendour to splendour" (II Cor 3:18; NEB trans.) – "from glory to glory." To be human is, in short, in the Christian sense of reality, to be stamped by and to bear the imprint in oneself of the glory of God.

This is, however, a way of thinking about human existence that differs most sharply from the sense of things that tends generally to be expressed in the literature of our time. Thus, from one standpoint, it might well be expected that those representing Christian perspectives would face this literature with a good deal of suspiciousness and hostility. Yet this need not be the case, and, indeed, in my judgment, it ought not to be the case; for the Christian man cannot reasonably expect the artist to do impossibles. The plain fact of the matter is that for perhaps the great majority of men today in the Western world there has occurred a profound erosion of the terrain of religious faith. Nor is this something which the Christian man confronts externally, for, in so far as he breathes the atmosphere of our age, he is himself in some sort a secular man. Thus it is that many of the most sensitive theologians of our period – Protestants like the late Paul Tillich and the late Dietrich Bonhoeffer, Roman Catholics like Karl Rahner and Hans Urs von Balthasar, Anglicans like John Robinson and Paul Van Buren – thus it is that they, in one way or another, are brooding upon the "eclipse" of God, or the "absence" of God. It is indeed something like this that constitutes a primary datum for the religious imagination in our time, since men whose standards of intelligibility derive from a world of electric lights and telephones and nuclear fission are not certain now as to how it is that we may continue any longer to speak of God and of Transcendence. Where is the "place," to speak metaphorically – where is the place in which God may be said to be? This will, increasingly, for contemporary theology be the central question to be anxiously wrestled with.

We have, all of us, so the speak, "fallen" into the Profane, and the historian of religion Mircea Eliade suggests that "desacralization" is the category that most comprehensively describes the spiritual situation of modern man.[36] So our literature, if it is to be an authentically contemporary literature, will inevitably be secular, and the world which it describes will be a world in which God appears in some way to have disappeared. And not only will ours be a secular literature, but I would myself hope that it would be radically secular, since skepticism and negation and denial may, if they are profound enough, by reason of their very radicalism, begin to quicken sensibilities of another order that are now either being put aside or declining into atrophy. In the degree to which it deepens the sense of religious deprivation, a radically secular literature may, in other words, by a dialectical route bring us once again into proximity to the Presence that we had thought to be absent – and thus it may become itself a kind of witness to the Indestructible.

The late C. S. Lewis was on one occasion recalling the impact that George Macdonald's *Phantastes* had upon him, when he first chanced to read it in his youth: "It did nothing to my intellect nor (at that time) to my conscience. Their turn came far later and with the help of many other books and men. . . . What it actually did to me was to convert, even to baptize . . . my imagination."[37] Now it may be something like this – namely, baptism of the imagination – that is deeply needed by every genuinely modern man, whether he recognizes it or not and whatever may be the creeds to which he formally gives his suffrage. To read the prayer with which the 90th Psalm begins –

> Lord, thou hast been our dwelling-place in all generations.
> Before the mountains were brought forth,
> Or ever thou hadst formed the earth and the world,
> Even from everlasting to everlasting, thou art God.

– to read such language as this is for all of us to know, however we may stand in regard to the things of religion, that here is a kind of capacity for naked encounter with the Sacred which few of us any longer possess. And what I am proposing is that, toward the end of a new baptism for the modern imagination, a radically secular literature may have a profoundly fruitful religious function to perform. For, by the very resoluteness with which it may plunge us into the Dark, it may precipitate us out of our forgetfulness, so that, in a way, our deprivation of the Transcendent may itself bring us into proximity to its Mystery.

> They that wait upon the Lord shall renew their strength; they shall mount up with wings as eagles; they shall run and not be weary; they shall walk and not faint (Isa. 40:31).

It is, I suspect, in some such circuitous and dialectical way as this that poetic experience in our time may become a *preparatio* for prayer.

NOTES

1. Jacques Maritain, *Creative Intuition in Art and Poetry*, p. 62.
2. See W. K. Wimstatt, Jr., and Monroe C. Beardsley, "The Affective Fallacy," *The Sewanee Review*, 57 (Winter 1949). This essay is reprinted in Professor Wimstatt's *The Verbal Icon: Studies in the Meaning of Poetry* (Lexington: University of Kentucky Press, 1954).
3. T. S. Eliot, *The Use of Poetry and the Use of Criticism* (London: Faber and Faber, 1934), p. 138.
4. *Ibid.*
5. Rosalind Murray, *The Forsaken Fountain* (London: Hollis and Carter, 1948), p. 91.
6. Jacques Maritain, pp. 234–35.
7. See Etienne Gilson, *The Arts of the Beautiful* (New York: Charles Scribner's Sons, 1965), chap. 4.
8. Edmund Wilson, "Is Verse a Dying Technique?" *The Triple Thinkers* (New York: Oxford University Press, 1948), p. 21.
9. *Ibid.*, p. 25.
10. Ernst Cassirer, *An Essay on Man* (Garden City: Doubleday [Anchor Books], 1953), p. 44.
11. See Susanne K. Langer, *Philosophy in a New Key* (New York: Penguin Books, 1948), chap. 2.
12. Ernst Cassirer, p. 43.
13. This usage is Philip Wheelwright's; see his *Metaphor and Reality* (Bloomington: Indiana University Press, 1962), p. 30 and passim.
14. The term "intransitive attention" is used by Eliseo Vivas to define the chief differentia of the aesthetic experience. It is, he says, an experience of "intransitive attention"; see his "A Definition of the Aesthetic Experience," *Creation and Discovery: Essays in Criticism and Aesthetics* (New York: Noonday Press, 1955), pp. 93–99.
15. Richard Wilbur, *An Event in Things of This World* (New York: Harcourt Brace, 1956), p. 46.
16. *The Note-Books and Papers of Gerard Manley Hopkins*, ed. Humphrey House (London and New York: Oxford University Press, 1937), p. 310.
17. *Ibid.*, p. 98.
18. *The Letters of Gerard Manley Hopkins to Robert Bridges*, ed. C. C. Abbott (London and New York: Oxford University Press, 1935), p. 66.
19. Quoted in Philip Wheelright, *The Burning Fountain: A Study in the Language of Symbolism* (Bloomington: Indiana University Press, 1954), pp. 78–79.
20. Hugh McCarron, *Realization: A Philosophy of Poetry* (London: Sheed and Ward, 1937), p. 73.
21. C. Day Lewis, *The Poetic Image* (London: Jonathan Cape, 1947), p. 33.
22. Philip Wheelwright, *Metaphor and Reality*, p. 167.

23. *Ibid.*, pp. 164–69; "coalescence," as a feature of the world when beheld in the terms of poetic vision, is analyzed by Professor Wheelwright in these pages with a marvelous sensitiveness and tact.

24. Theodore M. Greene, "The Ontological Dimension of Experience," *Thought*, 29, no. 114 (Autumn 1954), 374.

25. John A. T. Robinson, *Honest to God* (Philadelphia: Westminster Press and London: SCM Press, 1963), p. 102.

26. George Macleod, *Only One Way Left* (Glasgow: Iona Community, 1956), p. 160.

27. See Dietrich Bonhoeffer, *Letters and Papers from Prison*, ed. Eberhard Bethge (London: SCM Press, and New York: Macmillan Co., Revised Edition 1967).

28. Philip Wheelwright, *The Burning Fountain*, p. 8.

29. See Amos N. Wilder, *Modern Poetry and the Christian Tradition* (New York: Charles Scribners Sons, 1952), p. 196.

30. Lionel Trilling, "Commitment to the Modern," *Teachers College Record*, 64, no. 5 (February 1963), 405–06.

31. William Barrett, *Irrational Man: A Study in Existential Philosophy* (Garden City: Doubleday, 1958), p. 54.

32. *Ibid.*, p. 57.

33. Hans Urs von Balthasar, *Science, Religion and Christianity*, trans. Hilda Graef (Westminster, Md.: Newman Press, 1958), p. 49.

34. I have paraphrased the last two lines of Thomas' *Fern Hill*; see *The Collected Poems of Dylan Thomas* (New York, New Directions, 1953), p. 180.

35. Nathan A. Scott, Jr., *Reinhold Niebuhr* (Minneapolis: University of Minnesota Press, 1963), p. 22.

36. See Mircea Eliade, *Birth and Rebirth*, trans. Willard Trask (New York: Harper & Row, 1958), p. 9.

37. C. S. Lewis, *George Macdonald: An Anthology* (New York: Macmillan, 1947), p. 21. My attention has been called to this passage by my student, Gunnar Urang, who in a dissertation in progress at the University of Chicago, finds the fiction of C. S. Lewis, Charles Williams, and J. R. R. Tolkien to represent an attempt to "baptize" the modern imagination.

13

THE SYMBOL GIVES RISE TO THOUGHT

Paul Ricoeur

Paul Ricoeur is Professor of Philosophy at the University of Paris and John Nuveen Professor of Theology at the Divinity School of the University of Chicago. His works translated into English include Fallible Man (*1965*), History and Truth (*1965*), Freedom and Nature: The Voluntary and the Involuntary (*1966*), *and* Freud and Philosophy: An Essay on Interpretation (*1970*). *This is a slightly abbreviated version of "Conclusion: The Symbol Gives Rise to Thought," from* The Symbolism of Evil *by Paul Ricoeur, translated by Emerson Buchanan. Copyright © 1967 by Paul Ricoeur. Reprinted by permission of Harper & Row, Publishers, Inc.*

That sentence,* which enchants me, says two things: the symbol gives; but what it gives is occasion for thought, something to think about.

The symbol gives: a philosophy instructed by myths arises at a certain moment in reflection, and, beyond philosophical reflection, it wishes to answer to a certain situation of modern culture.

Recourse to the archaic, the nocturnal, the oneiric, which is also, as Bachelard says in his *Poétique de l'Espace*, a way of approaching the birthplace of language, represents an attempt to escape the

---

* The reference is to the aphorism which constitutes the title of the essay.

difficulties of a radical beginning in philosophy. The beginning is not what one finds first; the point of departure must be reached, it must be won. Understanding of symbols can play a part in the movement towards the point of departure; for, if the beginning is to be reached, it is first necessary for thought to inhabit the fullness of language. We know the harassing backward flight of thought in search of the first truth and, more radically still, in search of a point of departure that might well not be a first truth. The illusion is not in looking for a point of departure, but in looking for it without presuppositions. There is no philosophy without presuppositions. A meditation on symbols starts from speech that has already taken place, and in which everything has already been said in some fashion; it wishes to be thought with its presuppositions. For it, the first task is not to begin but, from the midst of speech, to remember; to remember with a view to beginning.

Moreover, this task has a precise meaning *now*, at a certain stage in philosophical discussion, and, more broadly, in connection with certain traits of our "modernity." The historical moment of the philosophy of symbols is that of forgetfulness and restoration. Forgetfulness of hierophanies, forgetfulness of the signs of the sacred loss of man himself insofar as he belongs to the sacred. The forgetfulness, we know, is the counterpart of the great task of nourishing men, of satisfying their needs by mastering nature through a planetary technique. It is in the age when our language has become more precise, more univocal, more technical in a word, more suited to those integral formalizations which are called precisely symbolic logic, it is in this very age of discourse that we want to recharge our language, that we want to start again from the fullness of language.

That also is a gift of our "modernity," for we moderns are the heirs of philology, of exegesis, of the phenomenology of religion, of the psychoanalysis of language. The same epoch holds in reserve both the possibility of emptying language by radically formalizing it and the possibility of filling it anew by reminding itself of the fullest meanings, the most pregnant ones, the ones which are most bound by the presence of the sacred to man.

It is not regret for the sunken Atlantides that animates us, but hope for a re-creation of language. Beyond the desert of criticism, we wish to be called again.

But what the symbol gives rise to is thinking. After the gift, positing. The aphorism suggests at the same time that everything has already been said enigmatically and yet that it is always necessary to begin everything and to begin it again in the dimension of thinking. It is this articulation of thought given to itself in the realm of symbols and of thought positing and thinking that constitutes the critical point of our whole enterprise.

How can we make the symbol the starting-point of our thinking, if it is not an allegory? How shall we disengage from the symbol an "other," if it is, as Schelling says, *tauté*-gorical? What we need is an interpretation that respects the original enigma of the symbols, that lets itself be taught by them, but that, beginning from there, promotes the meaning, forms the meaning in the full responsibility of autonomous thought.

Such is the problem: how can thought be bound and free at the same time? How can the immediacy of the symbol and the mediation of thought be held together?

The enterprise would be a hopeless one if symbols were radically alien to philosophical discourse. But symbols are already in the element of speech. We have said sufficiently that they rescue feeling and even fear from silence and confusion; they provide a language for avowal, for confession; in virtue of them, man remains language through and through. That is not the most important thing: there exists nowhere a symbolic language without hermeneutics; wherever a man dreams or raves, another man arises to give an interpretation; what was already discourse, even if incoherent, is brought into coherent discourse by hermeneutics. In this respect, the hermeneutics of modern men is continuous with the spontaneous interpretations that have never been lacking to symbols. On the other hand, what is peculiar to the modern hermeneutics is that it remains in the line of critical thought. But its critical function does not turn it away from its appropriative function; I should say, rather, that it makes it more authentic and more perfect. The dissolution of the myth as explanation is the necessary way to the restoration of the myth as symbol. Thus, the time of restoration is not a different time from that of criticism; we are in every way children of criticism, and we seek to go beyond criticism by means of criticism, by a criticism that is no longer reductive but restorative. That is the purpose which animated Schelling, Schleiermacher, Dilthey, and today, in various

ways, Leenhardt, van der Leeuw, Eliade, Jung, Bultmann. Today
we have a more acute awareness of the immensity of the wager of
this hermeneutics. On the one hand, it represents the advanced
point of criticism, as an awareness of the myth as myth. By that
awareness it hastens the movement of demythologization, which is
only the counterpart of an ever more rigorous decision about what
is history according to the historical method; demythologization
is the irreversible gain of truthfulness, intellectual honesty, objectivity. On the other hand, modern hermeneutics entertains the
project of a revivification of philosophy through contact with the
fundamental symbols of consciousness.

Does that mean that we could go back to a primitive naïveté?
Not at all. In every way, something has been lost, irremediably lost:
immediacy of belief. But if we can no longer live the great symbolisms
of the sacred in accordance with the original belief in them, we can,
we modern men, aim at a second naïveté in and through criticism.
In short, it is by *interpreting* that we can hear again. Thus it is
in hermeneutics that the symbol's gift of meaning and the endeavor
to understand by deciphering are knotted together.

How does hermeneutics meet the problem?

What we have just called a knot – the knot where the symbol
gives and criticism interprets – appears in hermeneutics as a circle.
The circle can be stated bluntly: "We must understand in order to
believe, but we must believe in order to understand." The circle is
not a vicious circle, still less a mortal one; it is a living and stimulating
circle. We must believe in order to understand: never, in fact, does
the interpreter get near to what his text says unless he lives in the
aura of the meaning he is inquiring after. As Bultmann very well
says in his famous article on "the problem of hermeneutics" in
Glauben und Verstehen: "All understanding, like all interpretation,
is . . . continually oriented by the manner of posing the question
and by what it aims at [by its *Woraufhin*]. Consequently, it is never
without presuppositions; that is to say, it is always directed by a
prior understanding of the thing about which it interrogates the
text. It is only on the basis of that prior understanding that it can,
in general, interrogate and interpret." And again: "The presupposi-
tion of all understanding is the vital relation of the interpreter to
the thing about which the text speaks directly or indirectly." In
insisting on this coincidence with the *Woraufhin*, with the thing about

which the text speaks, Bultmann warns against a confusion which would consist in identifying this participation in the meaning with some psychological coincidence between the interpreter and the "particular expressions of life," according to Dilthey's expression. It is not a kinship of one life with another that hermeneutics requires, but a kinship of thought with what the life aims at – in short, of thought with the thing which is in question. It is in this sense that we must believe in order to understand. And yet, it is only by understanding that we can believe.

For the second immediacy that we seek and the second naïveté that we await are no longer accessible to us anywhere else than in a hermeneutics; we can believe only by interpreting. It is the "modern" mode of belief in symbols, an expression of the distress of modernity and a remedy for that distress.

Such is the circle: hermeneutics proceeds from a prior understanding of the very thing that it tries to understand by interpreting it. But thanks to that circle in hermeneutics, I can still today communicate with the sacred by making explicit the prior understanding that gives life to the interpretation. Thus hermeneutics, an acquisition of "modernity," is one of the modes by which that "modernity" transcends itself, insofar as it is forgetfulness of the sacred. I believe that being can still speak to me – no longer, of course, under the precritical form of immediate belief, but as the second immediacy aimed at by hermeneutics. This second naïveté aims to be the postcritical equivalent of the precritcal hierophany.

The conjunction of belief and criticism furnishes, as a consequence, the second interpretation of the sentence we are meditating on: "The symbol gives rise to thought." And this conjunction is a circular relation between a believing and an understanding. We see, then, with what prudence one can speak of "demythologization"; it is legitimate to speak of "demythologizing" if demythologizing is distinguished carefully from "demythicizing." All criticism "demythologizes" insofar as it is criticism; that is to say, it always adds to the separation of the historical (according to the rules of the critical method) and the pseudo-historical. What criticism continually endeavors to exorcize is the *logos* of the *mythos* (for example, the representation of the universe as a series of places, one above the other, with the earth in the middle, the heavens above, and hell below). As an advance post of "modernity," criticism cannot help being a "demythologization"; that is an irreversible gain of truth-fulness, of intellectual honesty, and therefore of objectivity. But it is precisely because it accelerates the movement of "demytholo-gization" that modern hermeneutics brings to light the dimension of the symbol, as a primordial sign of the sacred; it is thus that it participates in the revivification of philosophy through contact with symbols; it is one of the ways of rejuvenating philosophy. This paradox, in accordance with which "demythologization" is also a recharging of thought with the aid of symbols, is only a corollary of what we have called the circle of believing and under-standing in hermeneutics.

These reflections on the "circle" in hermeneutics put us on the road to a *philosophical* hermeneutics, but they do not take its place. The awareness of that "circle" is only a necessary stage by which we pass from a simple "re-enactment" without belief to autonomous "thought."

There is, indeed, a way of understanding symbols which, in a sense, remains within the symbolic mode. This is the case of all purely comparative phenomenology that limits itself to understand-ing symbols through symbols. Such an understanding, within the symbols, is necessary for the purpose of breaking with explicative and reductive thinking, and indeed it is sufficient for a descriptive phenomenology, for it is already a way of understanding, insofar as it examines, retains, connects; for it, there is a "world" of symbols. To understand, for it, is to display the multiple and inexhaustible intentions of each symbol, to discover intentional analogies between myths and rites, to run through the levels of experience and repre-sentation that are unified by the symbol.

This mode of understanding, of which Éliade's works provide very good examples, tends to place the symbols in a whole which is homogeneous with the symbols, but vaster, and which forms a system on the plane of the symbols themselves. Our analysis of the symbols and myths of human evil belongs to that sort of under-standing, insofar as it is a life of thought devoted to its symbols.

But it has not been possible to limit ourselves to such understand-ing of symbols in symbols. There the question of truth is unceasingly eluded. Although the phenomenologist may give the name of truth to the internal coherence, the systematicity, of the world of symbols, such truth is truth without belief, truth at a distance, reduced, from which one has expelled the question: do *I* believe that? what do *I* make of these symbolic meanings, these hierophanics? That question cannot be raised as long as one remains at the level of comparativism, running from one symbol to another, without oneself being anywhere. That level can only be an intermediate stage, the stage of understanding in extension, panoramic understanding, curious but not concerned. It has been necessary to enter into a passionate, though critical, relation with the truth-value of each symbol.

Thus, the transition to philosophical hermeneutics was begun when we passed from the statics to the dynamics of the mythical symbols. The world of symbols is not a tranquil and reconciled world; every symbol is iconoclastic in comparison with some other symbol, just as every symbol, left to itself, tends to thicken, to become solidified in an idolatry. It is necessary, then, to participate in the struggle, in the dynamics, in which the symbolism itself becomes a prey to a spontaneous hermeneutics that seeks to transcend it. It is only by participating in this dynamics that comprehension can reach the strictly critical dimension of exegesis and become a hermeneutic; but then one must abandon the position – or rather, the exile – of the remote and disinterested spectator, in order to appropriate in each case a particular symbolism.

Well, then, we have left the plane of truth without belief and come to the circle of hermeneutics, to the believing for the sake of understanding which is also understanding for the sake of believing. I entered that circle as soon as I admitted that I read the ensemble of the myths from a certain point of view, that the mythical space was for me an oriented space, and that my perspective angle was the pre-eminence of the Jewish confession of sins, its symbolism, and its mythology. By that adoption of one myth, the appropriation of all of them became possible, at least up to a certain point.

But that appropriation, in revealing its circular character, requires in its turn to be transcended. The exegete, as exegete, can live indefinitely within the circle, as the comparativist can practice endlessly the *epoché* of truth and live in neutralized belief. But the philosopher, who elsewhere practices rigorous consistency in reflection, cannot stop at this stage; awareness of the hermeneutic circle has torn him away from the conveniences of neutralized belief.

But this is to instigate him to think with the symbols as a *starting-point*, and no longer *in* the symbols.

How shall we get beyond the "circle of hermeneutics"? By transforming it into a *wager*.

I wager that I shall have a better understanding of man and of the bond between the being of man and the being of all beings if I follow the *indication* of symbolic thought. That wager then becomes the task of *verifying* my wager and saturating it, so to speak, with intelligibility. In return, the task transforms my wager: in betting *on* the significance of the symbolic world, I bet at the same time *that* my wager will be restored to me in power of reflection, in the element of coherent discourse.

Then there opens before me the field of philosophical hermeneutics properly so called: no longer an allegorizing interpretation that pretends to find a disguised philosophy under the imaginative garments of the myth, but a philosophy that starts from the symbols and endeavors to promote the meaning, to form it, by a creative interpretation. I shall venture to call that endeavor, at least provisionally, a "transcendental deduction" of symbols. Transcendental deduction, in the Kantian sense, consists in justifying a concept by showing that it makes possible the construction of a domain of objectivity. Now, if I use the symbols of deviation, wandering, and captivity as a detector of reality, if I decipher man on the basis of the mythical symbols of chaos, mixture, and fall, in short, if I elaborate an empirics of the servile will under the guidance of a mythology of evil existence, then I can say that in return I have "deduced" – in the transcendental meaning of the word – the symbolism of human evil. In fact, the symbol, used as a means of detecting and deciphering human reality, will have been verified by its power to raise up, to illuminate, to give order to that region of human experience, that region of confession, which we were too ready to reduce to error, habit, emotion, passivity – in short, to one or another of the dimensions of finitude that have no need of the symbols of evil to open them up and discover them. But the expression, "transcendental deduction of symbols," is not absolutely satisfactory; it orients us toward the idea that the justification of the symbol by its power to reveal constitutes a simple argumentation of *self-awareness*, a simple extension of reflexive circumscription, whereas a philosophy instructed by the symbols has for its task a qualitative transformation of reflexive consciousness. Every symbol is finally a hierophany, a manifestation of the bond between man and the sacred. Now in treating the symbol as a simple revealer of self-awareness, we cut it off from its ontological function; we pretend to believe that "know thyself" is purely reflexive, whereas it is first of all an appeal by which each man is invited to situate himself better in being – in Greek terms, to "be wise." As the *Charmides* of Plato says: "The God [at Delphi], by way of salutation, says to them, in reality: Be *wise;* but, as a soothsayer, he says it in enigmatic form. *Be wise* and *Know thyself* are fundamentally the same thing, as appears from the text and as I maintain. But one may be deceived about it; and that is what happened to the authors of the following inscriptions: *Nothing too much* and *To stand surety for someone invites misfortune.* Regarding *Know thyself* as advice and not as a salutation of the god, they wished to contribute their share of good advice and so they made those dedicatory inscriptions" (165*a*).

Finally, then, it is as an index of the situation of man at the heart of the being in which he moves, exists, and wills, that the symbol speaks to us. Consequently, the task of the philosopher guided by symbols would be to break out of the enchanted enclosure of consciousness of oneself, to end the prerogative of self-reflection. The symbol gives reason to think that the *Cogito* is within being, and not vice versa. Thus the second naïveté would be a second Copernican revolution: the being which posits itself in the *Cogito* has still to discover that the very act by which it abstracts itself from the whole does not cease to share in the being that challenges it in every symbol. All the symbols of guilt – deviation, wandering, captivity, – all the myths – chaos, blinding, mixture, fall – speak of the situation of the being of man in the being of the world. The task, then, is, starting from the symbols, to elaborate existential concepts – that is to say, not only structures of reflection but structures of existence, insofar as existence is the being of man. Then the problem will arise, how the quasi-being and the quasi-nothingness of human evil are articulated upon the being of man and upon the nothingness of his finitude.

If, then, we call the elaboration of an empirics of the servile will a transcendental deduction, the transcendental deduction itself must be inscribed in an ontology of finitude and evil that elevates the symbols to the rank of existential concepts.

Such is the *wager*. Only he can object to this mode of thought who thinks that philosophy, to begin from itself, must be a philosophy without presuppositions. A philosophy that starts from the fullness of language is a philosophy with presuppositions. To be honest, it must make its presuppositions explicit, state them as beliefs, wager on the beliefs, and try to make the wager pay off in understanding.

Such a wager is the contrary of an apologetics that pretends to lead reflection, without a break, from knowledge toward belief. A philosophy that begins with symbols proceeds in the opposite direction, in accordance with an essentially Anselmian schema. It finds man already settled, with a preliminary title, within its foundation. His being there may appear contingent and restricted. Why symbols? Why these symbols? But, beginning from this contingency and restrictedness of a culture that has hit upon these symbols rather than others, philosophy endeavors, through reflection and speculation, to disclose the rationality of its foundation.

Only a philosophy first nourished on the fullness of language can subsequently be indifferent to the modes of approach to its problems and to the conditions of its activity, and remain constantly concerned with thematizing the universal and rational structure of its adherence.

14

THE POETRY OF MEANING

Stanley Romaine Hopper

Stanley Romaine Hopper is the Bishop W. Earl Ledden Professor of Religion at Syracuse University. He is the author of The Crisis of Faith (*1944*), *and editor of several volumes of essays on modern literature and religion. The following essay, with only slight revisions, was originally published as the "Introduction" to* Interpretation: The Poetry of Meaning, *edited by Stanley Romaine Hopper and David L. Miller (New York: Harcourt, Brace & World, Inc., 1967). Copyright © 1967 by Drew University. Reprinted by permission of the author and Drew University.*

We have been experiencing for some decades now the breaking up of the conceptual mirror in which, for two millenniums or more, the Western consciousness has grown accustomed to seeing itself. The psychical discomforts and social traumas that accompany radical change are by this time evident. From politics to philosophy, from science to the arts, from world upheaval to religion – everything bears witness to it. Our classical world-picture, together with its conceptual mirror, has shattered. In his *Tiger at the Gates*, Giraudoux put it bluntly:

HELEN: If you break the mirror, will what is reflected in it cease to exist?
HECTOR: That is the whole question.[1]

It is not, perhaps, the whole question, but it is the first and necessary

one: and it is the question underneath the questions of meaning
and interpretation so pervasive of serious discussion in the several
disciplines today.

I. THE SETTING OF THE PROBLEM

The negative features of this breakup have been rehearsed now
many times, particularly in our literature and in our arts, where the
imagination can lay hold of our distresses obliquely and achieve
through fictive candor what the culture's collective psyche may not
yet be able to tolerate. Theology and philosophy, more deeply
inured in the thought forms of the tradition, and hedged in by protective sophistication, do not give, as the poem may, "a candid
kind to everything."[2] Philosophy (by way of positivism, pragmatism,
existentialism, phenomenology, linguistic analysis, and the questions
of symbolic form) has been moving through a radical revision of
its methods and its aims. Despite what has always seemed to me
the charismatic dead weight of the scholastic, supranaturalistic
literalism of language and method in the early work and influence
of Barth, theology, too, has been edging its way into what Auerbach
has called "figural interpretation," in which "history," "event," the
"Word," and the like, are permitted to *function* symbolically, thus
retaining within their figural complex the meanings that their
propositional formulations have lost.

It is this development which, at bottom, has made for the enormous and crucial importance of hermeneutics in current theological
discussion, superseding the debates concerning myth and kerygma.
The problem of interpretation is prior, just as the questions it
raises are more radical and more basic.[3] The radical ambiguity of
much contemporary theology resides in the attempt to retain within
figural interpretation the literalistic reminiscences of the unbroken
conceptual mirror.

Nevertheless, with the letting go of the classical conceptual mirror,
contemporary theology has boldly raised the question as to whether
what was reflected in it will cease to exist – including theology itself.[4]
Indeed, it might appear (in propositional terms) that what was
reflected in it is already lost, and that theology, along with traditional
linguistic modes and presuppositions, is no longer possible. This
may mean simply that theology, in its classical modes, has explored

the full arc of its tautological possibilities, and in its latter day adjustments, where these are less than radical, it only repeats or linguistically reinstates its emptied and exhausted forms, becoming thus the clownish cliché of itself. "A picture held us captive," wrote Wittgenstein. "And we could not get outside it, for it lay in our language and language seemed to repeat it to us inexorably."[5]

A more charitable view, however, and perhaps a more accurate one, must concede to theology itself a courageous confrontation of its own dilemma, and a persistent probing, by way of post-Barthian revisions, into the deeper questions of its message and its meaning. I should not venture to review this history in a few brief paragraphs, for it obviously demands analyses in depth of the work of Barth, Brunner, Gogarten, Bultmann, Fuchs, Ebeling, and others, together with some account of the American response to these somewhat intricate and Protean developments.

It may be useful to note, however, one quick attempt to "place" these voices in the current theological scene. It was proposed by my distinguished colleague, the late Professor Carl Michalson,[6] that the several positions of Europe's celebrated theologians were clearly exposed by the "turn" (sometimes called "reversal") in the thought of Martin Heidegger. The emergence of the "later Heidegger" (as contrasted with the "earlier Heidegger") *placed* almost automatically the persons in the drama of European religious thinking. Barth "lay to the right and Bultmann to the left," with Otto Weber and Hermann Diem still further to the right of Barth, and Ernst Fuchs and Gerhard Ebeling to the left of Bultmann; but the important thing, Michalson argued, was not that these positions were suddenly exposed, but that "a corridor (was disclosed) between them." There was, in short, a third possibility, perceived by Heinrich Ott of Basel, who proposed the doing of theology on the basis of the work of the later Heidegger.[7]

This proposal has represented for theology a challenge of central significance. It permits Ott to say, "Theology is really hermeneutic . . ."[8] Professor Michalson characterizes Ott's view more sharply: it is "systematic theology as the hermeneutical analysis of being"; while that of Bultmann (building on the work of the "early Heidegger" is 'hermeneutic as the analysis of human existence."[9] Barth's theology is a theology based upon "the *being* of God," a phrase obviously in need of considerable "unpacking." These classifications permitted Professor Michalson to align himself with Barth and the Bultmann-early Heidegger-Ebeling line as against the later Heidegger-Ott line and to oppose the "historical" to the "ontological": "ontological hermeneutic is unsuited to a radically historical faith; . . . in theology the question of the historical form of God's word will be given priority over the question of its being."[10]

But then, that is just the question that is at issue here: are we not already speaking metaphorically when terms such as "historical *form*" and "God's *word*" are employed, and are we not already speaking mythologically or poetically in order, hopefully, to disclose an unveiling of (God's) being? Otherwise, are we not still thinking scholastically, literalistically, or metaphysically, and throwing ourselves open to the suspicion of latent fideism?

From these and other questions of a like character, three perspectives on the hermeneutic problem appear:

1. The question of religious meaning and interpretation, raised from the side of theology as hermeneutic.

2. The relevance and implications of the work of the "later Heidegger" with its appeal to poetry and the art work as the model for the thinking and saying of primary truth.

3. The place of metaphor (and symbol, image, myth, etc.) in the thinking and saying of primary truth: the metaphorical character, that is, of our language about truth and the gods.

II. THE RELEVANCE OF HEIDEGGER

It has always seemed to me that the almost imperious presence of Heidegger can best be grasped by seeing, as he sees, that "we come too late for gods and too early for Being."[12] Our times experience the "lack" or absence of God. The term "God" can no longer be translated into any actual experience of our daily lives. This is what Nietzsche meant by his formula, repeated so stridently in these days, that "God is dead." This is to be taken metaphorically. It meant for Nietzsche the decline of official Christianity as built up against the background of Platonic idealism and the tradition of Western metaphysics. Heidegger concurs, being persuaded that Western metaphysics is bankrupt and has come to its end. Metaphysics became, through Plato and Aristotle, idealistic and substantive, concerned with the question of reality; thinking became propositional, its *logos* logical, its criterion the *adequatio rei ad intellectum*. Hence the Western consciousness committed its "forgetfulness" of being. Truth became a function of a subjectivized and intellectualized mode of "knowing," placing the subject intellectualistically over against the object (whether in Plato or Descartes), and (even in Plato) truth became a question of the "correctness" of one's views. We were thus led by inadvertence into the supposition that truth is at our disposal: we stand over against it, confer value upon it, and manipulate it technically. Its Aristotelian grammar lay in our language, and our language has repeated it to us inexorably. Poetry, by the same token, became an adornment accompanying existence, just as (for Aristotle) metaphor remained an ornament upon the trees of propositional discourse. Theology too, speaking itself through this metaphysical stance, became a theo-*logic*, propositionally intact but unable to evoke the god or to let the truth be unconcealed.

Suddenly today, the "lack of God helps," as the poet Hölderlin saw. The failure of our formulae releases us unexpectedly from their tyranny: we are again in a position to retrieve Being. Theologically this is awkward. Gerhard Ebeling has noted that "a doctrine of God is today abstract speculation if the phenomenon of modern atheism is not present in it from the very beginning."[13] And again, in speaking of Heidegger's thought, he insists that theology must speak of God nonmetaphysically, which "means, according to the dominant theological tradition, godlessly."[14] Philosophically it is necessary, in Heidegger's view, to prepare an overcoming of metaphysics, so understood; and, theologically, he has remarked that "the door remains open for a nonmetaphysical God."[15] We must abide, therefore, within the "lack" of God's presence, and emulate the poet: "without fear of the appearance of godlessness he must remain near the failure ('lack') of the god, and wait long enough in the prepared proximity of the failure, until out of the proximity of the failing god the initial word is granted, which names the High One."[16]

It is the merit of Heinrich Ott to have proposed an understanding of systematic theology that would correspond to the Heideggerian perspective of thinking and speaking. This means a translation of theological discourse from the classical grammar of Western metaphysics to a mode of speaking and thinking that is commensurate with the poet's response to primary being (Heidegger's "fundamental ontology"). Truth is no longer to be found in the agreement of the intellect with the subject matter, but is to be understood in terms of the Greek notion of *a-letheia*, an unveiling or unconcealing, an occurrence. Such truth must be experienced. It is "the essential act of man": it is an encounter; it is a response. It overcomes the objectivizing characteristic of our subjectivist-objectivist style of thinking.

Two additional questions emerge. The first, and immediate one, is the question as to whether there can be a non-objectivizing thinking about Being, or about God. The second question is the question as to what kind of language, or thinking, is appropriate to a fundamental ontology, to a language that does not commit objectification, or reification, upon its subject matter in the very mode of its utterance.

Heidegger expressed his interest in these questions through a series of "suggestions" on the problem of a non-objectifying thinking and speaking in contemporary theology.[17] There were, he thought, three themes which needed to be thought through. First, it is essential to determine *what* theology as a mode of thinking and speaking has to discuss. "That '*what*' is the Christian faith and what is believed." Second, it is necessary to determine what is meant by *objectifying* thinking and speaking *prior* to a discussion of non-objectifying thinking and speaking. Is *all* thinking already objectifying, or is it not? If not, then it is necessary, third, to consider to what extent the problem of a non-objectifying thinking and speaking is a genuine problem at all, or whether, indeed, something is here inquired after, the interrogation of which only thinks past the subject matter, distracts from the theme of theology and unnecessarily complicates it. What is important is that theology should understand its task: namely, to speak in accordance with its subject matter "out of faith for faith." It "becomes clear that thinking and speaking are not exhausted in theoretical-scientific representation (*Vorstellen*) and assertion. Thinking in every instance is a letting-be-said of that which shows itself, and is accordingly a cor-responding (*Entsprechen*, saying) to that which shows itself. . . ."

It will be conceded that there is a place and function for "thought" of the objectifying or scientific kind, that there is a certain objectivization implicit in every use of words; but it does not follow that all speech must reify its subject or that language may not perform an entirely different function, namely, that of bringing Being to appearance, of letting that which is appear *as* that which it is. But what is the nature of the language that brings Being to appearance?

III. THE PRIMACY OF METAPHOR

"Everything is only a metaphor; there is only poetry," according to Norman O. Brown.[18] This implies that from the propositional and "metaphysical" point of view, the nature of reality is intrinsically hidden. Within the limits of our finite perceiving it must be "grasped" in perspectival and contextual modes – that is to say mythically, metaphorically, symbolically. Even the formal analytical "system" is a representation, a symbolic net thrown upon the stars. There is always "Something More" beyond the formal inclusions of our closely threaded premises. Nevertheless we say of God, the symbol for that ungrasped Ultimacy, that "God speaks," "God acts"; or we say with Heraclitus that "the Lord whose oracle is at Delphi neither speaks nor conceals, but gives signs." These signs are the ciphers that we read, whether religiously with Pascal, or philosophically with Karl Jaspers. The reading is in either case "poetic" – "Poetry is quick as tigers, clever as cats, vivid as oranges"[19] – and we discover that it is through our imaginative grasp that we *form*ulate our significant worlds. Heidegger found the adequate expression for this recognition in the lines from Hölderlin:

> ... *dichterisch wohnet*
> *Der Mensch auf dieser Erde.*[20]

Poetically man dwells upon the earth! Poetry, for Heidegger, is the fundamental naming of the gods, but it is the gods themselves who bring us to language. It is through this fundamental reciprocity that the essence of language is disclosed, as well as the fact that "the foundation of human existence is conversation."[21]

From one point of view it may be urged that this is nothing more nor less than the famous *hermeneutical circle* described by Dilthey, in which every part of a literary work requires the whole to make it intelligible; yet the whole by which we manage the interpretation of the parts must itself be built up by careful scrutiny of the parts. Heidegger acknowledges this: "As the disclosedness of the 'there,' understanding always pertains to the whole of Being-in-the-world.

In every understanding of the world, existence is understood with it, and *vice versa.* . . ."

This implies a pugnacious paradox: "Any interpretation which is to contribute understanding, must already have understood what is to be interpreted."[22] But it is not necessary to regard this logical circularity as a *vicious* circle. "What is decisive is not to get out of the circle but to come into it in the right way" . . . for "in the circle is hidden a positive possibility of the most primordial kind of knowing."[23] The dimension of understanding that is hidden here is much like the "Unconscious" in the verses of the poet:

> The centre that I cannot find
> Is known to my Unconscious Mind;
> I have no reason to despair
> Because I am already there.[24]

The truth that is already there, but that must be unconcealed, is structurally rooted "in the existential constitution of Dasein – that is, in the understanding which interprets. An entity for which, as Being-in-the-world, its Being is itself an issue, has, ontologically, a circular structure."[25] What is needed, then, is some insight into the strategies of uncovering that which already lies within the information and data that are ready to hand. It is one thing, Heidegger says, to "give a report" in which we talk about things, but it is quite another to "grasp entities in their *Being.*" "For the latter task we lack not only most of the words but, above all, the 'grammar.' "[26]

Three clues to such a "grammar" may be specified in Heidegger's work.

The first has to do with what he terms the *as*-structure of our seeing. It is the *as* factor that makes up the structure of explicitness of anything that is "understood." The structure is implicit in our seeing, even when suppressed, passed over or "ontically unexpressed." Which means that our understanding-seeing is essentially metaphorical, whether the metaphorical likeness (the acknowledged *as* structure) is recognized or unexpressed. But "if the 'as' is ontically unexpressed, this must not seduce us into overlooking it as a *constitutive state for understanding, existential* and *a priori.*"[27]

The second has to do with his analysis of the term "truth," signifying that which shows itself. It is the *logos as a-letheia*, an understanding that is pre-Socratic, going back at least as far as

Heraclitus. As Julián Marías has pointed out, this is a concept of truth that is itself metaphorical.[28] To define "truth" conceptually in theoretical ways is precisely, for Heidegger, to cover up the meaning that early Greek thought gave to it.

Both of these clues to meaning are developed in the early Heidegger, but it is not difficult to move to the third clue, which belongs to the later period of his work, namely, his bringing forward of the poem and the art work as the model for that kind of unconcealing of Being that is central to his notion of *a-letheia*. The basis for it is certainly laid already in *Being and Time* in his definition of phenomenology. It means, he says, "to let that which shows itself be seen from itself in the very way in which it shows itself from itself."[29] It is through the art work that we are enabled to see what a thing is as it is in itself. The art work "assembles" things into "world."

This can be illustrated quite simply by way of a poem of Wallace Stevens, which he calls *Anecdote of the Jar*.

> I placed a jar in Tennessee,
> And round it was, upon a hill.
> It made the slovenly wilderness
> Surround that hill.
>
> The wilderness rose up to it,
> And sprawled around, no longer wild.
> The jar was round upon the ground
> And tall and of a port in air.
>
> It took dominion everywhere.
> The jar was gray and bare.
> It did not give of bird or bush,
> Like nothing else in Tennessee.[30]

This is, quite simply, the anecdote of the art work. The placing of the art work in the sprawling wilderness of things has the effect of suddenly *assembling* everything within its purview. The wilderness "rose up to it" as it "took dominion everywhere," and suddenly the wilderness was no longer wild. Earth becomes world. The art work lets the earth and the world appear in their tension (Heraclitean "strife"): men, now suddenly *ek*-sisting in the tension thus opened up, become released toward things as they are assembled into world. At the same time nothing in itself is altered; everything remains what it is. Similarly, in art works of a more complex kind, the assemblage also is more complex: it is assemblage in what Heidegger calls the "foursome" – earth, world, (mortal) men, and gods. In such an assemblage the entire drama of Dasein is unconcealed. Here too we become true (in response to that which is unconcealed) as we learn to *dwell* with freedom toward the foursome – learning how "to spare the earth, receive the sky, expect the gods, and have a capacity for death."[31] Only where language is, is there world. But language is what it is by virtue of the *logos*, which, understood after the aesthetic modes of *a-letheia*, is the "articulated openness within which everything is assembled" into world;[32] but this, in its turn, is that place of dwelling articulated by and through what others have called root metaphors. When a root metaphor dies, a world is lost, and we are too if we cannot release ourselves from idolatrous fixations upon the *forms* of our knowing.

"I believe," Kenneth Burke has said, and most felicitously, "in the right of every man to worship God in his own metaphor." There may, of course, be no alternative, save in the fact that we seek, in our metaphysical passion, for a Metaphor of metaphors; but this also must appear within the assemblages of the foursome – at the *crux*, that is, of the strife between *a-letheia* and the drama of the existential situation.

IV. THE DISCLOSURE OF THE UNDISCLOSED

We suggested at the beginning that the breaking up of the conceptual mirror of the "Western consciousness" carries with it radical implications both for our notions of "ultimacy" and for our ways of understanding it, and that both of these questions are central to contemporary dealings with the "hermeneutic quest" in religious thinking and with Heidegger's plea for an understanding of truth as *a-letheia*. What is surprising is the way in which the *movement* of these questions *through* contemporary interpretations (in all fields having to do with "meaning" and "communication") at once remains the same and brings about its own reversal, as though this too might be an "anecdote" of the modes and limits of finite understanding.

For example, in works so different as those of Norman O. Brown, in *Love's Body*,[33] and Heinrich Ott, in his essay on "Hermeneutics and Personhood,"[34] aphorism and dialogue, respectively, are proposed as models for poetic knowing. Other interpreters, such as Julian Marias and Owen Barfield, though equally concerned with the modes of poetic knowing, do not wish to restrict poetic form to aphorism; and Barfield, in observing that poetry implies a "crossing the threshold between two dimensions of consciousness" implicitly regards the dialogic model, in its personalistic form, as too *rationalistic* to be fully open to the mystery of Being-in-ourselves. Again, Kenneth Burke and Beda Allemann, employing models of drama and antimetaphor respectively, come up with symbols without meaning – if meaning implies a world behind the world to which our metaphoric bridging could significantly be anchored. Yet the centrality of the poetic is in each case affirmed, and each investigation buttresses the other. What are we to make of these seeming contradictions and agreements?

Perhaps it is enough to point to the problem. But perhaps it is necessary also to point to that to which the problem points. When Brown asserts the need for a Dionysian Christianity, the mythos of drama, with its chthonic descent, is appealed to quite as firmly as in Burke, where poetic language, when complete, will take us "into-and-out-of [the complete play with its exhilaration as the close]." This movement will enter also into the dialogic drama once it is seen that the *persona* of "I" and "Thou" are masks through which the "soul may leap to what it then suddenly recognizes beyond the mask. *Finis tragoedia: incipit comoedia,*"[35] as Joseph Campbell has said.

This was, for Nicholas of Cusa, a movement through the opposites to a recognition of the faceless Face behind all faces – not to be beheld through the forming of concepts, but rather through rapture: "In all faces is seen the Face of faces, veiled, and in a riddle, howbeit unveiled it is not seen, until above all faces a man enter into a certain secret and mystic silence where there is no knowledge or concept of a face. . . ."[36]

Heidegger also knows this silence and observes its presence behind and within our language. Allemann notes its presence between our words. Drama also is not wholly lacking in this silence between our words, as the works of Ionesco, Beckett and Pinter, for example, make clear. The metaphors of unconcealment, of assemblage in the foursome are not without dramatic implications. What Christian *theo-poiesis* does is to effect disclosure through the crucial nexus of event, thereby making the crux of knowing, both morally and aesthetically, radically decisive in time. The drama of the Cross is implicit in our language whenever we cease to dwell poetically in the world: that is, whenever "meaning" is not disclosed, whenever the clichés of everydayness or abstraction fixate words. Fixation crucifies. The Cross occurs whenever Primordial Being is unheard, elided, or refused. This would imply that Christianity, in its historical forms, has progressively destroyed its own meanings through fixation of its language, brought about by reason of its capitulation to a grammar not its own. Therefore its metaphors no longer function, and its central symbol elicits no response. Allemann's analysis of metaphor discloses this. Contemporary works, without benefit of another world beyond or behind "this world" as given, must set up metaphorical relations within their own chosen frames of reference. A text becomes "the metaphor of itself." The attempt to dispense with metaphor altogether – as in the *nouveau roman* and the novels of Kafka – tends to convert the particular work into an "absolute" metaphor. Or, as Paul Celan suggests, symbolic figurations tend to suffer their own *reductio ad absurdum*. Metaphor in its Aristotelian mode is suddenly artificial; there is no extrinsic Other to which a metaphor may appeal; but the *form* of this appealing remains fixated in our language where we repeat its modes inexorably. The anti-metaphor works against this, and, *mirabile dictu*, exacts surprise and unconcealments from our finite particulars by letting things be what they are. Whereat fresh wonders shine and mystery appears precisely where we thought no *logos* lay concealed. From "the infinite qualitative distinction between time and eternity, God and man" of thirty years ago, we have suddenly come upon reversal into radical immanence.

This is a vision of reality that begins with Heraclitus, for whom *logos* not only meant *a-letheia*, as Heidegger reminds us, but for whom it also meant utterance – as though the whole of things were essentially the speech of Being. It knows that "*phusis* loves to hide." Its symbols are the fire, the bow, the lyre. Its *logos* is a presence that "steers all things through all things." Like Pascal's cosmos, its center is everywhere and its circumference is nowhere. But also it is like Augustine's discovery of God: He was nearer to Augustine than Augustine was to himself. "Thou wert with me, but I was not with Thee." It is out of this discrepancy, where the Presence is not recognized, that the aboriginal crime is born. This is the cleavage that we then inflict on all the world.

Rilke's sonnet comes to mind:

> *A god can do it. But how, tell me, shall*
> *a man follow him through the narrow lyre?*
> *His mind is cleavage. At the crossing of two*
> *heartways stands no temple for Apollo.*[37]

"At the crossing of two heartways stands no temple. . . ." But, as Norman Brown remarked, it is precisely there, at the crossing of our heartways, that all our temples stand. Quite so. But Rilke's point is that there is no temple *for Apollo*. Apollo is the sun-god, and, as the sun-god, Apollo symbolizes the excessive rationalization of life. The overemphasis of the *ratio* deletes the temple. We must go down now, as Rilke sees, with *Orpheus* to reconcile the opposite of "above" and "below" in all their manifold expressions. Orpheus can go down and Orpheus can return by the power of his song. But:

> *Song, as you teach it, is not desire,*
> *not suing for something yet in the end attained;*
> *song is existence. Easy for the god.*
> *But when do we exist? And when does he*
> *spend upon our being the earth and the stars?*[38]

Gesang ist Dasein! Not song, which is a pressing for returns; not the coercing of the givenness of things.

> *Real singing is a different breath.*
> *A breath for nothing. A wafting in the god. A wind.*[39]

Rilke seems to be saying that we must learn, with trust, to be one with, a breathing with the inhale and exhale of Being, in order that "the god" may breathe through us, and we, through the translation of its breath into song, may be (as I have ventured to remark elsewhere)[40] the eyes of becoming and a tongue for Being's utterance.

NOTES

1. Jean Giraudoux, *Tiger at the Gates*. Trans. Christopher Fry (New York: Oxford University Press, 1955), p. 32.

2. Wallace Stevens, "Notes Toward a Supreme Fiction," III, in *The Collected Poems of Wallace Stevens* (New York: Alfred A. Knopf, 1954), p. 382.

3. For a résumé of the Continental and American discussion of the hermeneutic question in theology today, the reader is referred to the excellent introductory chapters of James M. Robinson in Volumes I and II of the "New Frontiers in Theology" series: Vol. I, *The Later Heidegger and Theology*, pp. 48–56, and Vol. II, *The New Hermeneutic*, pp. 1–77. This second volume contains papers presented at the First Consultation on Hermeneutics convened at Drew University in 1962. (Both volumes are edited by James M. Robinson and John B. Cobb, Jr., and are published by Harper & Row, New York, 1963 and 1964 respectively.)

4. *Ibid.*, I, 6; cf. also the essay by Heinrich Ott, "What Is Systematic Theology?", pp. 77ff.

5. Ludwig Wittgenstein: *Philosophical Investigations*, trans. G. E. M. Anscombe (Oxford: Basil Blackwell, 1958), p. 48e (# 115).

6. In "Theology as Ontology and History," in *New Frontiers*, I, 139f.

7. *Vide* Heinrich Ott: *Denken und Sein. Der Weg Martin Heideggers und der Weg der Theologie* (Zürich: EVZ-Verlag, 1959).

8. *Op. cit.*, p. 78.

9. *Ibid.*, p. 156.

10. *Ibid.*, p. 156.

11. *Vide New Frontiers*, II, on "The New Hermeneutic," which contains the papers presented at that Consultation.

12. *Einführung in die Metaphysic* (Tübingen: Niemeyer, 1953), p. 7.

13. *Wort und Glaube* (Tübingen: J. C. F. Mohr, 1960), p. 359; cited in *New Frontiers*, I, 74n.

14. "Zeitschrift für Theologie und Kirche," Beiheft 2, 1961, p. 124; cited in *New Frontiers*, I, 74n.

15. *New Frontiers*, I, 5.

16. "Remembrance of the Poet," in Martin Heidegger: *Existence and Being*, with an introduction by Werner Brock (London: Vision Press Ltd., 1949), pp. 285–86.

17. These suggestions were addressed to me for use in the Second Consultation on Hermeneutics convened at Drew University in 1964. I include a brief summary here.

18. Norman O. Brown, *Love's Body* (New York: Random House, 1966), p. 266.

19. Delmore Schwartz, "The Kingdom of Poetry," in *Summer Knowledge* (New York: Doubleday, 1959), p. 189. Schwartz, in his later poetry, shows the influence of Heidegger, Rilke, and Hölderlin.

20. "In Lieblicher Bläue . . .," in Hölderlin, *His Poems*, trans., with a critical study, by Michael Hamberger (New York: Pantheon, 1952), p. 263.

21. "Hölderlin and the Essence of Poetry," *Existence and Being*, p. 307.

22. Martin Heidegger, *Being and Time*, trans. John Macquarrie and Edward Robinson (London: SCM Press and New York: Harper & Row, 1962), p. 194 (H. 152).

23. *Ibid.*, p. 195 (H. 153).

24. W. H. Auden, *The Labyrinth*, in *The Collected Poetry of W. H. Auden* (New York: Random House, 1945), p. 10.

25. Heidegger, *Being and Time*, p. 195.

26. *Ibid.*, p. 63 (H. 39).

27. *Ibid.*, p. 190 (H. 149).

28. Hopper and Miller, eds.: *Interpretation: The Poetry of Meaning*, p. 43.

29. *Ibid.*, p. 58 (H. 34).

30. *The Collected Poems of Wallace Stevens*, p. 76.

31. Vincent Vycinas, *Earth and Gods, An Introduction to the Philosophy of Martin Heidegger* (The Hague: Martinus Nijhoff, 1961), p. 15.

32. *Ibid.*, p. 83.

33. Norman O. Brown, *Love's Body*.

34. Hopper and Miller, eds.: *Interpretation: The Poetry of Meaning*, pp. 2–33.

35. Joseph Campbell: *The Masks of God*, Vol. I, *Primitive Mythology* (New York: Viking, 1959), p. 51; cited from Nicholas of Cusa, *De Visione*, trans. Emma Gurney Salter (London: J. M. Dent; New York, E. P. Dutton, 1928), pp. 25–27.

36. *Ibid.*

37. Rainer Maria Rilke, *Sonnets to Orpheus*, I, 3, trans. by M. D. Herter Norton (New York: W. W. Norton, 1942), p. 21.

38. *Ibid.*

39. *Ibid.*

40. "Poetry as a Task of the Mind," in *Eranos Jahr-Buch*, 1965 (Zürich: Rhein-Verlag, 1966), p. 214.

ACKNOWLEDGMENTS

In addition to my gratitude to the publishers, institutions, journals or individuals who have graciously permitted the reprinting of essays, or portions thereof, on which they hold the copyright (such permissions being duly noted on the first page of each of the essays reprinted in this volume), I am also grateful to the following:

Farrar, Straus & Giroux, Inc. and Faber & Faber Ltd. for lines from *Memories of West Street and Lepke* by Robert Lowell; reprinted with the permission of Farrar, Straus & Giroux, Inc. and Faber & Faber Ltd. from *Life Studies* by Robert Lowell, © 1958 by Robert Lowell.

Random House, Inc. and Faber & Faber Ltd. for lines from *The Labyrinth* by W. H. Auden; © 1945 by W. H. Auden; reprinted from *Collected Shorter Poems* 1927-1957 by W. H. Auden, by permission of Random House Inc. and Faber & Faber Ltd.

Alfred A. Knopf, Inc. and Faber & Faber Ltd. for *Anecdote of the Jar* by Wallace Stevens; © 1923 and renewed 1951 by Wallace Stevens; reprinted from *The Collected Poems of Wallace Stevens* by permission of Alfred A. Knopf, Inc. and Faber & Faber Ltd.; for lines from *Notes Toward a Supreme Fiction* by Wallace Stevens, © 1942 by Wallace Stevens; reprinted from *The Collected Poems of Wallace Stevens* by permission of Alfred A. Knopf, Inc. and Faber & Faber Ltd.; and for lines from *An Ordinary Evening in New Haven* by Wallace Stevens; © 1950 by Wallace Stevens; reprinted from *The Collected Poems of Wallace Stevens* by permission of Alfred A. Knopf, Inc. and Faber & Faber Ltd.

Holt, Rinehart & Winston, Inc. and Jonathan Cape Ltd. for *Come In* by Robert Frost; from *The Poetry of Robert Frost* edited by Edward Connery Lathem; © 1942 by Robert Frost; and © 1970 by Lesley Frost Ballantine; reprinted by permission of Holt, Rinehart

& Winston, Inc. the Estate of Robert Frost, Edward Connery Lathem and Jonathan Cape Ltd.

W. W. Norton & Company, Inc. and Insel Verlag for lines reprinted from *Sonnets to Orpheus* by Rainer Maria Rilke; translation by M. D. Herter Norton; by permission of W. W. Norton & Company, Inc. and Insel Verlag; © 1942 by W. W. Norton & Company, Inc.; translation copyright renewed 1969 by M. D. Herter Norton.

The Belknap Press of Harvard University Press for *The Auctioneer of Parting* by Emily Dickinson; reprinted by permission of the publishers and the Trustees of Amherst College from Thomas H. Johnson, Editor, *The Poems of Emily Dickinson*, Cambridge, Mass.: the Belknap Press of Harvard University Press, © 1951, 1955, by the President and Fellows of Harvard College.

Harcourt, Brace & World, Inc. and Faber & Faber Ltd. for lines from *An Event* by Richard Wilbur; © 1956 by Richard Wilbur; reprinted from *Things of this World* by Richard Wilbur by permission of Harcourt Brace & World, Inc. and Faber & Faber Ltd.